The Philosophy of Mind

Edited by
V. C. Chappell

Dover Publications, Inc.
New York

Published in Canada by General Publishing Company, Ltd.,
30 Lesmill Road, Don Mills, Toronto, Ontario.
Published in the United Kingdom by Constable and Company, Ltd., 10 Orange Street, London WC2H 7EG.

This Dover edition, first published in 1981, is an unabridged
and unaltered republication of the work originally published in
1962 by Prentice-Hall, Inc., Englewood Cliffs, N. J.

International Standard Book Number: 0-486-24212-9
Library of Congress Catalog Card Number: 81-68488

Manufactured in the United States of America
Dover Publications, Inc.
180 Varick Street
New York, N. Y. 10014

Acknowledgments

"Experience" by B. A. Farrell, copyright 1950 by *Mind*; reprinted by permission of the author and of the editor of *Mind*.

"The Concept of Mind" by John Wisdom, copyright 1950 by The Aristotelian Society; reprinted by permission of Basil Blackwell & Mott, Ltd. (on behalf of the author) and of the editor of The Aristotelian Society.

"Behaviour" by D. W. Hamlyn, copyright 1953 by *Philosophy*; reprinted by permission of the author and of the editor of *Philosophy*.

"Wittgenstein's *Philosophical Investigations*" by Norman Malcolm; reprinted by permission of the author and of the editorial board of *The Philosophical Review*.

"Is Consciousness a Brain Process?" by U. T. Place, copyright 1956 by *The British Journal of Psychology*; reprinted by permission of the editor of *The British Journal of Psychology*.

"Emotions" by Errol Bedford, copyright 1957 by The Aristotelian Society; reprinted by permission of the author and of the editor of The Aristotelian Society.

"Persons" by P. F. Strawson, copyright 1958 by the University of Minnesota; reprinted by permission of the author, of the editors of *Minnesota Studies in the Philosophy of Science*, Vol. II, and of the publisher.

"About Behaviourism" by Paul Ziff, copyright 1958 by *Analysis*; reprinted by permission of the author and of the editor of *Analysis*.

"Knowledge of Other Minds" by Norman Malcolm, copyright 1958 by *The Journal of Philosophy*; reprinted by permission of the author and of the managing editor of *The Journal of Philosophy*.

"Sensations and Brain Processes" by J. J. C. Smart; reprinted by permission of the author and of the editorial board of *The Philosophical Review*.

Preface

The essays in this volume were first published between 1950 and 1960 in British and American journals. They testify to a renewed interest in the philosophy of mind, a subject which stood at the center of the philosophical stage in the eighteenth and early nineteenth centuries, joining metaphysics, epistemology, and morals, and which now bids fair to occupy the same central place again. The contemporary interest in the philosophy of mind—or, as it is sometimes called, philosophical psychology—is due in large part to the work of two men, Ludwig Wittgenstein, Professor at Cambridge until 1947, and Gilbert Ryle, current Waynflete Professor at Oxford. Each is the author of an influential book dealing with philosophical problems about mind: Ryle's *Concept of Mind* was published in 1949 and Wittgenstein's *Philosophical Investigations* appeared in 1953, although its contents were known before that to the many philosophers who either attended or heard about Wittgenstein's Cambridge lectures during the thirties and forties. The present collection contains no selections from these two books, but it does include a long review of the latter and a critical article on the former; some idea of the books can be gained from these.

Wittgenstein and Ryle not only attacked philosophical problems about mind and influenced others to do so; they also developed new methods of attacking philosophical problems generally and a new conception of the philosopher's task. Both thinkers, and especially Wittgenstein, deserve major credit for the recent "revolution in philosophy," as it has been called by some of its more enthusiastic adherents. Just how revolutionary the new methods and conception of philosophy are, and just how great their difference is from those of the past, is arguable; but there is no doubt that substantial changes have occurred in Anglo-American philosophy in the past twenty years or so, and that the new ways have become firmly established and indeed dominant in the philosophical life of Britain, Australia, and the United States, and, to a lesser extent, of Scandinavia as well. And there is also no doubt that, however the soundness and success of the new "analytic" or "linguistic" philosophy may finally be judged, great progress in solving traditional philosophical problems has been made and great gains in philosophical understanding achieved. This progress and these gains are nowhere more evident than in the philosophy of mind.

The philosophy of mind, which is one part of philosophy as a whole, is itself divided into a number of parts; there are distinguishable subfields, topics, and problems within it. The main division is between questions about mind as a whole or in general, and questions about different particular features or departments of mind; further distinctions are then made within each of the two resulting groups. Under the first heading fall, for example, questions about the nature of mind or mental phenomena as things of a distinctive sort—including the question whether there *is* any such thing; questions about the relation of mind to things of other sorts—body, person, machines, nature, animals, the gods; questions about the different sorts of things that make up minds or the mental aspect of persons—powers, dispositions, capacities, actions, states, processes, events, susceptibilities, properties, and so forth; questions about the workings of mind, whether they proceed according to mechanical principles or teleological principles or principles of some special kind or no principles at all; questions about our own minds and the minds of others, our basis for believing that they exist at all as well as for making particular judgments about them—such questions lead naturally into, if indeed they do not belong to, epistemology; and questions about the mental element in human conduct and the relevance of mental factors to our judgments of people's responsibility and worth —such questions are sometimes grouped under the rubric "moral psychology" and form a bridge between philosophy of mind and ethics. Under the second heading distinguished above—questions about the different particular features or departments of mind—fall questions about various mental concepts and families of concepts: cognitive concepts, such as knowledge, understanding, thinking, belief, memory, perception, and imagination; will concepts, such as decision, choice, intention, wish, and will itself; and emotion, feeling, and sensation concepts, such as anger, fear, generosity, boredom, pleasure, desire, and pain; as well as questions about motives, consciousness, attention, the unconscious, dreams, and conscience. Some idea of the range and variety of topics and questions treated by philosophers interested in mind can be gained from the bibliography at the end of this volume. And this represents only a selection from the literature in English of the past fifteen years or so.

The essays in this volume deal mainly with the more general issues concerning mind, those listed under the first of the two headings above. They contain discussions of the so-called "problems" of other minds and of mind and body, investigations of the concept of a person, and inquiries into the nature of a mental phenomenon—in particular its alleged "privacy" and its relation to "public" behavior. These issues, it is generally agreed, are more fundamental than those concerned with particular mental concepts, in the sense that discussions of the latter almost always presuppose some familiarity with the former. Of course the distinction between general and particular questions about mind is anything but sharp, and most of the essays included here contain dis cussions of particular issues as well as of the more general ones. But it is mainly for their treatments of the more general issues that these ten essays were selected.

Several of the essays fall naturally into pairs or groups—some contain comments on others, attack the same problems from the same or different points of view, or continue discussions started elsewhere. Despite these affinities, however, the papers are printed in the chronological order of their first appearance. For each is very rich in material; each can be mined in a number of ways and made to yield a variety of ores; and to arrange them in any but this natural order would be to encourage one way of approaching them to the exclusion of others. A way of approaching and grouping the essays is indeed suggested in the Introduction, but this can be ignored.

The place and date of original publication of the essays are as follows:

I. B. A. Farrell, "Experience," *Mind,* LIX (1950), 170-98.

II. John Wisdom, "The Concept of Mind," *Aristotelian Society Proceedings,* L (1949-50), 189-204; repr. in John Wisdom, *Other Minds* (Oxford: Basil Blackwell & Mott, Ltd., 1952), pp. 220-35.

III. D. W. Hamlyn, "Behaviour," *Philosophy,* XXVIII (1953), 132-45.

IV. Norman Malcolm, "Wittgenstein's *Philosophical Investigations,*" *Philosophical Review,* LXIII (1954), 530-59.

V. U. T. Place, "Is Consciousness a Brain Process?" *British Journal of Psychology,* XLVII (1956), 44-50.

VI. Errol Bedford, "Emotions," *Aristotelian Society Proceedings,* LVII (1956-57), 281-304.

VII. P. F. Strawson, "Persons," in *Minnesota Studies in the Philosophy of Science,* Vol. II, *Concepts, Theories, and the Mind-Body Problem,* ed. Herbert Feigl, Michael Scriven, and Grover Maxwell (Minneapolis: University of Minnesota Press, 1958), pp. 330-53.

VIII. Paul Ziff, "About Behaviourism," *Analysis,* XVIII (1957-58), 132-36.

IX. Norman Malcolm, "Knowledge of Other Minds," *Journal of Philosophy,* LV (1958), 969-78.

X. J. J. C. Smart, "Sensations and Brain Processes," *Philosophical Review,* LXVIII (1959), 141-56.

I wish to thank the authors for their kind permission to reprint their essays, and the editors of the journals in which the essays first appeared for their permission also. Essays IV, VI, and X have been slightly revised by their authors for their republication here. The remainder appear as originally published, except that misprints have been corrected, and spelling and punctuation have been revised to accord with American usage.

V. C. Chappell

Table of Contents

Introduction

The essays in this volume all have to do in some way with a group of fundamental problems in the philosophy of mind. My purpose in this Introduction is to make clear what these problems are, indicate the connections among them, and give some idea of how they arise and of what makes them problems worthy of philosophical interest. In doing this I shall, in effect, be suggesting one way of reading the essays that follow, and calling attention to one pattern of relationships among them. But I wish to emphasize that this is only one line of approach and that, although this line is in my view especially helpful for an understanding of these essays, there are other lines that might be taken as well.

My method is as follows. I shall first present an argument for *solipsism*, interpreted as the doctrine that only my experiences exist or are real and hence that minds other than my own do not exist or are not real. This argument is, I think, plausible, but since the conclusion is unacceptable at best, the argument must be faulty. It is not obvious, however, where the fault lies, and since the solipsistic conclusion can be avoided by taking exception to any of a number of the argument's steps, locating the fault would seem to be a matter of considerable choice. The refusal or denial of each of several steps leads, indeed, to a view of mind and mental phenomena that has actually been held in recent times, and the avoidance of solipsism has in fact been a motive for the construction and adoption of many of these views. So, in presenting some of the possible responses to my argument for solipsism, that is, some of the possible means of attacking it so as to avoid its conclusion, I shall at the same time be sketching certain recent views of mind and indicating at least one of the reasons for holding them.

An Argument for Solipsism

I shall state the argument as it applies to one specific sort of mental phenomenon, pain. The general conclusion, respecting experiences or mental phenomena as a whole, is then warranted by the fact that the same form of argument applies also to, and can be stated for, mental phenomena of other sorts. The argument has three stages, which I label *A*, *B*, and *C*; separate steps within each stage are labeled "1," "2," "3," etc.

A

1. People have pains; I have them and so do other people.

2. I can often tell that another person has a pain or that he does **not**, although I cannot always do so. When I tell, it is by what the person says and does that I do so, i.e., it is by his behavior, including his verbal behavior, that I tell.

3. People pretend to have pains and not to have them, and sometimes their pretence is successful, in which case others think that the pretenders have pains when they don't and that they don't have pains when they do.

4. In a case of successful pretence, what the pretender says and does is indistinguishable (to whomever is successfully pretended to) from what he would say and do if he were not pretending. That is, the pretender's behavior is indistinguishable from the behavior he would exhibit if he did (or did not) have the pain he is feigning (or hiding). For if the behavior were not indistinguishable the pretence would not be successful.

5. Any case in which I think that another person has (or doesn't have) a pain because of what he says and does could be a case of successful pretence, i.e., could be a case in which he doesn't (or does) have a pain and I am mistaken in thinking that he does (or doesn't). For he could say and do just what he does say and do in either case, whether he has (or doesn't have) the pain or not, i.e., his behavior could be just the same as far as I can tell.

6. Hence to have a pain cannot *be* to say and do things; a pain *is* not a piece of behavior. Hence behaving and having a pain, or behavior and pain, must be different things.

7. Further, although pains and behavior may be related in certain ways (e.g., causally), they are at best contingently related. They cannot be necessarily or logically related, for if they were, successful pretence would be logically impossible. Hence behavior and pains must be logically independent, no matter how connected or associated in other ways.

8. Hence in order to be absolutely certain, to know, in a particular case that another person does (or does not) have a pain, I must not confine myself to what he says and does, but must either apprehend his sensations or experience directly, or else infer what they are by some method that I know to be perfectly reliable.

9. But I cannot apprehend another person's sensations directly. The notion of a direct apprehension of sensations must get its sense from my own case, for I do not tell that I have a pain, when I do, by anything other than the pain itself. The pain itself is available to me, and it is so because I feel it. But to feel a pain is just to have it; *esse* is *percipi* for sensations. And I cannot, of logical necessity, have another person's pain. Even if someone else and I both had a single pain, what he had would be his pain and what I had would be my pain; we still could not, logically,

have one another's pains, even though in this case his pain was also mine and mine was also his. Hence for me to apprehend another person's sensations directly is logically impossible.

10. Nor is there any method of inferring what another person's sensations are that I can know to be perfectly reliable. For to know that a method of inferring x from y is perfectly reliable is to know that x occurs whenever y occurs. This means that it must be possible to know that x occurs in some other way than by the method of inference in question. Either, then, it must be possible to apprehend x directly, or else it must be possible to infer the occurrence of x by some other method, from something other than the occurrence of y. But this further method will itself have to be known to be perfectly reliable if its use is to yield knowledge that x occurs. And the same holds for any further method of inference that might be employed to provide knowledge that x occurs and hence knowledge that a given method is perfectly reliable. Hence it must be possible to apprehend x directly at some point, or else no method of inferring that x occurs can be known to be perfectly reliable. And since it is not possible to apprehend another person's sensations directly, it follows that no method of inferring what they are, or even that they occur, can be known to be perfectly reliable.

11. Hence in no case can I be absolutely certain, can I know, that another person has a pain.

B

1. Even though I cannot know that another person has a pain, it would seem that I could, on occasion, be warranted in believing that he does. If I cannot be absolutely certain that a person who is behaving in the way that someone who had a pain would behave really does have a pain and is not merely pretending to, I surely can be reasonably certain that he does; I can judge that he does with a fair chance or with some likelihood of being right; I can be justified in claiming, on occasion, that probably another person has a pain.

2. But in order to be warranted in believing that something, p, is the case, in order to be reasonably certain that p, or to judge that p with a fair chance or indeed with any likelihood of being right, or to be justified in claiming that probably p, there must be something, e, that I can know to be evidence for the truth of p.

3. It is natural to think that a person's behavior, what he says and does, is evidence for the truth of the proposition that he has a pain. But in fact neither behavior nor anything else can be known to be evidence for the truth of this proposition.

4. For I can only know that something, e, is evidence for the truth of a proposition, p, if I can know that p is true, always or often, when e is present. But since I can never know that another person has a pain, I can

never know that the proposition that he does is true. Hence I cannot know that behavior, or anything else, is evidence for the truth of this proposition. And this means that I cannot be warranted in believing that another person has a pain.

5. It might be thought that I need not *know* that a proposition, *p,* is true, always or ever, in order to know that something, *e,* is evidence for its truth. For all that is necessary—it might be claimed—is that I have good reason or perhaps even some reason for thinking that *p* is true on occasion. But even so, the conclusion is the same: I cannot know that anything is evidence for the truth of the proposition that another person has a pain. For if I can have good reason or indeed any reason for thinking that a proposition, *p,* is true, it follows that I can have evidence that *p* is true, evidence other than the evidence in question, *e.* And this means that I can know that *p* is true, always or sometimes, when this further evidence is present. But if I cannot know that *p* is true, ever, then I cannot know that this supposed further evidence is evidence for its truth, from which it follows that I cannot have good or indeed any reason for thinking that *p* is true. And I cannot know that another person has a pain. Hence, again, I cannot know that anything is evidence for the truth of the proposition that he does, and hence can have no warrant for believing that he does.

6. It might be thought that I need not *know* that something, *e,* is evidence for the truth of a proposition, *p,* in order to be warranted in believing that *p,* but that it is enough that I should have good reason or perhaps even some reason for thinking that *e* is evidence for the truth of *p.* But even if so, again, the conclusion is the same: I cannot be warranted in believing that another person has a pain. For in order to have good or indeed any reason for thinking that something, *e,* is evidence for the truth of a proposition, *p,* I must at least have good or some reason for thinking that *p* is true, at least sometimes, when *e* is present. But again, if I cannot know, ever, that *p* is true, then I cannot have any reason, ever, for thinking that *p* is true, from which it follows that I cannot have any reason for thinking that *e* is evidence for the truth of *p.* And I cannot know, ever, that another person has a pain. Hence there is nothing that I can, with any reason, think to be evidence for the truth of the proposition that he does. And so again, I cannot be warranted in believing that another person has a pain.

7. Hence in no case can I be warranted in believing that another person has a pain; in no case can I judge with any likelihood of being right that another person has a pain, or be justified in claiming that probably he does.

C

1. Even though I cannot know that another person has a pain, and even though I cannot be warranted in believing that he does, it would seem that I could at least suppose that he does on occasion, that I could at least imagine or conceive another person's having a pain. If I cannot be absolutely or even reasonably certain that another person has a pain, surely I can at least entertain the hypothesis that he does; if I cannot be justified in claiming that probably another person has a pain, surely I can be justified in claiming that possibly he does.

2. But in order to suppose that something, *p*, is the case, in order to be justified in claiming that possibly *p*, I must be able to specify conditions under which I could know, or at any rate be warranted in believing, that *p*. For if I could not do this the proposition *p* would have no sense for me, and I cannot suppose what I cannot understand; I cannot be justified in claiming that something is possible if I do not know what that something is, if I do not know what it means to claim that that thing is possible.

3. And since I cannot know that another person has a pain, or even be warranted in believing that he does, I cannot specify conditions under which I could know or be warranted in believing that he does. Hence the proposition that another person has a pain is without sense for me; I cannot understand what it would be for another person to have a pain. And this means that I cannot suppose that another person has a pain, that I am never justified in claiming that possibly he does.

4. It might be thought that I *could* specify a condition under which I could know that another person has a pain. For it is granted that I can know that a person has a pain if I can apprehend that pain directly. I do apprehend my own pains directly and hence do know, on occasion, that I have a pain. I do not apprehend other people's pains directly, and hence do not know that they have pains. But all that I would have to do in order to know that another person has a pain is apprehend his pain directly. Hence there is a condition—it might be claimed—under which I could know that another person has a pain, viz., that I apprehend his pain directly.

5. It is, however, logically impossible that this supposed condition should be fulfilled. For I am barred from directly apprehending another person's pain by logical necessity; I can directly apprehend only the pains that I have, and I can have only my own pains. To apprehend another's pains I would have to *be* him, which is logically impossible; or, if I *could* be him, it would then be, not another's pain that I was directly apprehending, but my own.

6. Not only does the supposition that another person has a pain have no sense for me, there is no way in which the thought that someone be-

sides myself has a pain could have occurred to me. For if there is nothing that I can know or even with any reason think to be evidence for another person's having a pain, the very idea of a pain that is not my pain could not have arisen. And even if this idea had arisen, I should have rejected it as a logical absurdity. The very phrase "his pain" must be without sense for me; my use of the word "pain" must always carry an implicit reference to myself, such that the phrase "my pain" is a pleonasm.

7. But then it follows that all pains necessarily are my pains; that only I have pains is a logical truth. Also, that other people have pains must be logically false; to say that someone other than myself has a pain is a logical absurdity, in the same way that it is a logical absurdity to say that some bachelor has a wife. Hence solipsism with respect to pains is true, of logical necessity. That only I have pains and that other people do not, that no pains other than my own exist or are real, is true in just the same way that "No bachelors have wives" is true.

8. Since the above form of argument can be applied to all other sorts of mental phenomena besides pains—e.g., to thoughts, perceptions, decisions, and feelings—it follows that solipsism in general is true, of logical necessity. That is, it follows that only I have experiences or a mind and that other "people" do not, that mental phenomena or minds other than my own do not exist or are not real. It does not follow that there are no other things besides myself, nor that some of these other things are not "people"—just that if there are any "people" they are necessarily mindless (and the quotation marks show the oddness of the notion of a mindless "person").

Some Comments on the Argument

Many of the particular moves as well as the over-all strategy of the foregoing argument will be familiar to readers versed in recent British and American philosophical literature. Much in the argument is based on suggestions made by Wittgenstein and his followers; some of these suggestions are found or described in the papers by Wisdom, Malcolm, and Strawson that are included in this volume (Essays II, IV and IX, and VII, respectively). None of these thinkers, of course, accepts the conclusion of the argument. All use it (or parts of it) rather, as I propose to do, to establish other conclusions and to discredit certain assumptions which naturally arise in philosophical thinking about mind.

As I have stated it the argument is, I think, plausible. It begins from obvious truths and contains no obvious mistakes of fact or logic. But its conclusion is, nonetheless, quite unacceptable. Solipsism is at least false; it may be necessarily false or even unintelligible. In any case, it follows that something in the argument is illegitimate. Something has been stated or assumed as a premise that is false, or a step has been taken that is logically fallacious, or both. The argument has, indeed, the form of a *reductio ad absurdum,* and what it really shows is not that solipsism is true but that something is wrong with the premises and/or with the reasoning that leads to the solipsistic conclusion. But here as in every *reductio ad absurdum* argument of any complexity, the absurdity of the conclusion does not show what precisely in the argument is wrong; it leaves it open which premise or which step is at fault.

As it happens, there are several things in the argument about which questions can be raised. A plausible case can be made for rejecting any of a number of premises or steps so as to destroy the argument; hence a number of different ways of avoiding the solipsistic conclusion seem to be possible. Several of these ways amount or lead, furthermore, to philosophical positions, to logical doctrines or theories of mind, which have actually been held in recent times. Hence a survey of these ways, of these possible responses to my argument for solipsism, can at the same time serve as a survey of some recent views about mind.

In the first place, exception might be taken to stages *B* and *C* of the argument. One might, that is, grant the soundness of stage *A* and accept its conclusion, that I can never know that another person has a pain. One might then go on to claim that I could nonetheless believe that another person has a pain and support my belief by appealing to the so-called *argument from analogy.* On the other hand, exception might be taken to stage *A* of the argument, with or without rejecting *B* and *C* as well; it might be claimed that the conclusion of *A*, that I cannot know that another person has a pain, is already unacceptable and hence that the mistake, or a mistake, must lie somewhere in *A*. The step most likely to be rejected in this case is 6, but this can be done in different ways. One way leads to *behaviorism,* in any of a number of its forms. Others lead to certain half- or qualified-behavioristic views, in particular to the *two-meanings view* and to the *expression theory.* Another step to which exception might be taken is 7, and one way of doing this leads to the *criteriological view* of Malcolm and Strawson. On this view step 6 is not denied, although its statement is somewhat altered. Again, the step rejected may be 10; a way of rejecting it is provided by the *identity theory* of Place and Smart. Acceptance of this theory does not commit one to the denial of any step of the argument before 10.

I shall now say a few words about each of these alternatives in turn.

The Argument from Analogy

Many philosophers would accept stage *A* of my argument for solipsism, or at any rate would accept its conclusion, but would seek to forestall the ultimate, solipsistic conclusion by refusing to accept stages *B* and *C*. They would grant that one cannot know that any person other than oneself has a pain, but would deny that this commits them to solipsism. For they would claim that it is possible to justify beliefs in other people's experiences by inductive, or more particularly, analogical reasoning. Not only can I believe, in their view, that someone else has a pain; I can support my belief, provide a warrant for it, by appealing to an argument, the so-called argument from analogy.

This argument has been presented in a number of different forms; some of these are noted by Malcolm in Essay IX below. In general, however, the argument runs as follows. I can know that I have a pain, when I do, and I can notice the sort of behavior that I exhibit when I have a pain. I can then establish, after a while, a correlation in myself between pain and a certain sort of behavior; I observe that a certain sort of behavior is always or often associated with pain in my own case. But then I notice that other people behave, on occasion, in ways similar to that in which I behave when I have a pain. I observe that others exhibit behavior that is similar to the behavior that is associated in myself with pain. I then infer that something similar to my pain is going on in them when they exhibit such behavior. The principle of this inference is something like: similar phenomena have similar associates; and this principle has been found to hold in a wide variety of cases and hence has a solid inductive warrant—experience amply illustrates and supports it. Hence my inference is itself warranted; the conclusion, that other people have pains like mine, is justified by the analogy which exists between their behavior and mine, or rather by the inference which proceeds from this analogy.

This reasoning has an initial plausibility, but it has been roundly criticized and is now rejected by most contemporary philosophers, in whatever form. Malcolm, in Essay IX, mounts what is probably the most severe and sustained attack on the argument from analogy in the recent literature. (Strawson sketches a similar attack in Essay VII, but does not develop it at any length.) Malcolm's main argument, it will be noted, parallels stages *B* and *C* of my argument for solipsism; my argument in fact spells out what Malcolm evidently assumes but does not make explicit. He would, then, regard this part of my argument as sound. Indeed he claims that acceptance of the conclusion of *A* makes the final solipsistic conclusion inevitable, a result which amounts, in his eyes, to the reduction of the conclusion of *A* to absurdity.

Objections can, however, be raised against Malcolm's argument and so against stages *B* and *C* of my argument for solipsism—subtle objections having to do with the notions of evidence, justification, verification, and sense. If sound, these objections destroy Malcolm's case against the argument for analogy and also my case for solipsism. But even so it does not follow that stage *A* of my argument is sound and that its conclusion is true; at the very least this remains open. And neither does it follow that the argument from analogy is legitimate and that it provides the proper or even a possible means of certifying our claims to know or have warranted beliefs about the minds of others. Despite some recent attempts to revive the argument from analogy and to defend it against Malcolm's type of criticism (see, e.g., A. J. Ayer, *The Problem of Knowledge,* chap. v[1]), most philosophers now agree in rejecting it. As Malcolm points out, there is no need for the argument from analogy if the conclusion of my stage *A*—that I can never know that another person has a pain—is rejected, and most contemporary philosophers agree also in rejecting that. Hence the major fault in my argument, most would say, is to be sought somewhere within stage *A,* however *B* and *C* be regarded.

Behaviorism

In its crudest form behaviorism is the view that mental phenomena, experiences, sensations, just *are* pieces of behavior, that having a pain, for example, *consists* in doing and saying things. The behaviorist, therefore, rejects step 6 of stage *A* of my argument for solipsism; he denies that pain and behavior are different things. This denial has a good deal to recommend it—even though behaviorism is not the only basis for making it and behaviorism itself has many forms, different from and more sophisticated than the crude view just stated. For step 6 comes close to expressing, or anyhow suggests, Cartesian dualism, a traditional and still common theory of mind which nearly all contemporary philosophers oppose. (That step 6 does not quite express Cartesian dualism is shown by the fact that holders of the criteriological view and the identity theory do or need not reject it while they do reject Cartesian dualism—see below.) According to the dualist, mental phenomena such as pains and behavior are irreducibly different sorts of things. Behavior, being physical, is public and can be observed by all. Pains, on the other hand, are private to the person whose pains they are; they can only be "observed" by him and cannot be known about, except indirectly, by anybody else. There are, of course, further aspects of this contrast between pains and behavior, or generally between the mental and the physical, as the dualist conceives them; but it is the necessary privacy of mental phenomena, as opposed to the public observability of physical behavior, that is most important in the present context.

Cartesian dualism has been attacked on many grounds; arguments against it are presented and/or discussed in several of the essays included in this volume, notably by Farrell, Malcolm, Place, Strawson, and Smart in Essays I, IV and IX, V, VII, and X, respectively. One common argument is that sketched by Smart: mental phenomena, as the Cartesian conceives them, are "queer" entities, the existence and operations of which violate the principles of science, both the principles discovered and established by science and the principles which specify the nature of legitimate

---

[1] Bibliographical information about this and most of the works cited subsequently in this Introduction is given in the Bibliography at the end of the volume; information about cited works not listed in the Bibliography is given in footnotes.

scientific inquiry itself, principles of evidence and of intelligibility, for example. A more radical sort of argument is employed by Ryle in the *Concept of Mind*: the truth of the "two-worlds story" (as Ryle calls it) is inconsistent with all sorts of plain facts, such as the fact that other people are very often able to determine what a person's mind is—his thoughts, mental powers, and emotions at least—and sometimes, indeed, are in a better position to do so than he himself is. (Bedford, in Essay VI, has a good discussion of this point.) More radical still is the argument proposed by Malcolm and Strawson, among others: the notion of a necessarily private phenomenon which lies at the heart of the Cartesian view is at bottom unintelligible. We may continue, according to those who press this sort of argument, to recognize a distinct class of mental phenomena, and to distinguish pains, for example, from behavior. But we cannot think of mental phenomena, in the way that the Cartesian dualist does, as necessarily private, and hence we must conceive the basis of the distinction and the relation between the distinguished elements in a way different from his.

The desire to avoid Cartesian dualism has perhaps been the main thing that has led philosophers to adopt behaviorism in recent times. But of course the denial of dualism is not equivalent to behaviorism, and behaviorism itself, at least in the crude form whereby having a pain simply consists in doing and saying certain things, is open to a number of objections. Indeed there are almost as many attacks upon behaviorism in the essays in this volume as upon Cartesian dualism; Wisdom, Hamlyn, Bedford, Strawson, and Malcolm (in Essays II, III, VI, VII, and IX, respectively) all say things against it, in effect if not by name. There is the obvious point that when I say of someone that he has a pain I do not *mean* that he is behaving in a certain way, as is shown by the fact that there is no contradiction in my saying that he has a pain and is not behaving in that or indeed in any way—from which it follows that behaviorism cannot be true as a philosophical doctrine, i.e., on logical grounds. More sophisticated are the two arguments cited (and rejected) by Ziff in Essay VIII: (a) if behaviorism were true, I could find out that I myself had a pain by observing my behavior, but since I do not find out that I have a pain, when I do, by observing my behavior, since, indeed, I do not observe my own behavior or, in general, find out that I have a pain at all, it follows that behaviorism is not true; and (b) if behaviorism were true, I could always in principle find out when you had a pain by observing your behavior, but since I cannot always find out, even in principle, that you have a pain, when you do, whereas I can always observe your behavior, it follows that behaviorism is not true. (It will be noted that this second argument parallels part of stage *A* of my own argument for solipsism.)

Now there is no doubt, I think, that the foregoing objections are successful against the crude behaviorism that we have been discussing. But it is also clear that behaviorism need not be held in nearly so crude a form as this—indeed it is possible that no philosopher ever has held the view that a pain just is a piece of behavior and nothing else. More sophisticated views that are still recognizably behavioristic are certainly defensible and some such view may well prove invincible. Such would seem, at any rate, to be the conviction of Farrell and Ziff, who, in Essays I and VIII below, respectively, either propound or indicate sympathy with behavioristic views but would certainly reject the crude view stated earlier.

There are four ways at least in which the crude view may be refined. First, mental phenomena may be identified not just with actual behavior but with actual behavior plus certain dispositions to behave. A pain is not simply what a man says and does but what he says and does together with what he would say and do but for certain inhibiting factors or were the circumstances different or some such. It is clearly this dispositional form of behaviorism that is defended by Farrell in Essay I, and his defense of it is impressive. Even so, objections have been raised against his sort of view as well as against the cruder view which it in part replaces. Bedford in Essay VI notes various difficulties in the dispositional analysis of certain mental concepts. And Place and Smart, in Essays V and X respectively, although they admit the soundness of the dispositional analysis for some sorts of mental phenomena, reject it for others—sensations, experiences, images—though without giving any developed arguments for this rejection.

A second refinement of behaviorism concerns the notion of behavior itself. There is a tendency, on the crude view, to regard behavior as an observable sequence of happenings in the same sense that the movements of a machine constitute an observable sequence of happenings. That this is a mistake is argued both by Hamlyn in Essay III and by Ziff in Essay VIII below; a piece of human behavior is not a series of movements. (Indeed the failure to make this point constitutes a further fault in the crude view.) The view that results when mental phenomena are identified with human behavior, properly so-called (together with dispositions to behave, in the requisite sense), and not with human movements, is a form of behaviorism, but an obviously more defensible form than is provided by the crude view. (It is interesting to note that, although both Hamlyn and Ziff accept and indeed insist upon this refinement, the one rejects whereas the other accepts the resulting behavioristic view.)

A third way in which crude behaviorism can be refined is by placing behavior, so to speak, in its natural home, and so regarding a pain, for example, as a piece of behavior and/or set of dispositions to behave, not just by itself, but in a certain context, in certain surrounding circumstances, including social circumstances—the existence of social institutions, customs, practices, and rules. A pain is a response or readiness to respond to a certain stimulus, which occurs in a wider situation and against a background of learned habits and usages. Hamlyn makes this point explicitly in Essay III, and Ziff suggests it in Essay VIII; Bedford, in Essay VI, also has some things to say about it.

A fourth improvement that may be made in the crude view first stated, so as to produce a more defensible behaviorism, is noted by Ziff in Essay VIII. This consists in distinguishing what a man says from his behavior generally, in recognizing that his verbal behavior or his avowals occupy a special place with respect to his mental states and acts. The point is not that one's avowals—first person utterances ascribing mental phenomena to oneself—are not behavior but that they have a privileged status; they count for more in other people's judgments about his mind than do his bodily activities. What a man says may be opposed to what he does, in the sense that the two together may lead us in opposite directions in ascribing a pain, for example, to him: he may say that he has a pain and act (bodily) as if he did not. Furthermore, what he says or would say in certain circumstances constitutes a final and conclusive authority in questions concerning his mental phenomena. These facts, if they are facts, enable us to draw the sting from the objections made to the crude view, and so maintain behaviorism, albeit in a new, sophisticated form—or so it is claimed.

Is, then, behaviorism true? The answer is by no means clear at the present time, when "behaviorism" means a view embodying the refinements just discussed (as well as others). But it is plain that behaviorism of this sort is a leading contender in the current contest among theories of mind, and that the considerations relating to it which are cited in this Introduction and in the following essays constitute an important part of the basis on which this contest will eventually be decided.

The Two-Meanings View

A way of responding to my argument for solipsism that is somewhat different from behaviorism, in any of its forms, is provided by the so-called two-meanings view. This has not been an important view historically; it was defended by Ayer in *Language, Truth and Logic*[2] but has hardly been heard of since. It is, however, useful to consider it, for the mistakes it makes are instructive.

According to this view, the word "pain," for example, has a different meaning when it occurs in first-person utterances from what it has when it occurs in second- and third-person utterances. When I say "I have a pain" I mean something different from what I mean when I say that you or he has a pain—and different not only in that in the one case I talk about myself whereas in the others I talk about another person. When I say that he has a pain I mean that he is behaving, or is disposed to behave, in some certain way. But when I say that I have a pain

---

[2] A. J. Ayer, *Language, Truth and Logic*, 2nd ed. (London: Gollancz, 1946), pp. 128 ff.

I mean that a certain private sensation is occurring in me, that I have or feel this sensation. It is clear, therefore, that this view represents a kind of combination of behaviorism and Cartesian dualism, although it *is* neither; it is behavioristic with respect to other people and dualistic with respect to oneself. As such it can be looked upon as a rejection of step 6 of stage *A* of my argument for solipsism, just as behaviorism can, for it implies the denial of the claim that pains and behavior are in general different; they are different, on this view, only in my own case.

At first glance it might seem that the two-meanings view avoids the difficulties of both dualism and behaviorism. For behaviorism is most paradoxical when applied to oneself, and one main fault of dualism— its incompatibility with my knowledge of the minds of other people— only shows up when it is applied to others. But this appearance is delusive. Not only does behaviorism retain some paradoxicality when it is applied to others, but the most radical of the objections, noted earlier, to dualism—that the notion of a necessarily private (mental) phenomenon is unintelligible—tells even more clearly against the two-meanings view. It is just possible that the dualist might deny that, on his view, mental phenomena are necessarily private, in which case the objection here does not apply; but it is impossible for the proponent of the two-meanings view to save himself in this way. The pain which a man has, that to which the word "pain" refers when he uses it of himself, must be private on this view; it is logically impossible for someone else to know that any such thing exists.

The argument of those who object to the notion of a necessarily private "pain" is this. Private or not, a "pain" (in this sense) is supposed to be one definite sort of thing, and a sort of thing which a man who has one can himself identify. For if he did not know what a pain was he would not know when to say he had a pain, he would not know how to use the word "pain" in this sense, i.e., as the name of a private sensation. But how, if pains are necessarily private, could he know what a pain is; how could he have learned this? He could not have been taught by someone else to identify pains, to say (correctly) "Now I have a pain," for no one else could know when indeed he had a pain and hence tell him when it was correct to say he had one. Suppose he just happened to say "I have a pain" when in fact he had one. But this would not help. For since he would not know that what he had was a pain (and no one else could tell him that it was) he would have no reason to connect these words with his pain; he would have no way of knowing that "pain" was the word for what he was now having. Perhaps then he could decide to use the word "pain" for a certain sort of sensation that he noticed in himself and just happen to get it right, i.e., to use the word for the right sensation. But no, for he could not know that he was using the word consistently, that he was using the same word for the same sensation each time it occurred. For he could not know that, in any given instance, the sensation was the same as that which occurred on some earlier occasion. It might seem to him to be the same but that is not enough; his use of the word would not be consistent unless it really was the same. And he would have no way of determining that it was the same and did not merely seem to be so; in fact the distinction between being and seeming so could not be made. It follows that no such use of the word "pain" could exist, viz., as the name of a necessarily private sensation; the word "pain" could not have the meaning which, according to the two-meanings view, it has, in its first-person use. And it follows also that no such thing as a pain in this sense, a necessarily private phenomenon known only to the person who has it, could possibly exist.

The foregoing argument is suggested by Wittgenstein in the *Philosophical Investigations*; versions of it are presented by Malcolm in Essay IV and Strawson in Essay VII below. (A somewhat similar argument is sketched by Farrell in Essay I.) Most recent thinkers, though not quite all, regard it as conclusive; Ayer, in his paper "Can There Be a Private Language?" is one who does not. But there are other difficulties in the two-meanings view in any case. In the first place, it is a fact that words such as "pain" do *not* have two meanings, as Strawson points out in Essay VII. And second, the view becomes self-contradictory as soon as it is stated in general form, as soon as it is offered as a view that one might hold and not simply as a view that the person stating it might hold. (Ayer himself notes both of these difficulties in chap. v of *The Problem of Knowledge*.) These difficulties surely do destroy the two-meanings view, even if the argument sketched above does not.

The Expression Theory

Another way of responding to my argument for solipsism is provided by what may be called the expression theory. This too entails the rejection of step 6 of stage *A* of the argument; pains and behavior are not, on this view, to be regarded as separate sorts of things. The theory is behavioristic with respect to people other than oneself but is not fully behavioristic in that it singles out one's own case for special, non-behavioristic treatment. In this it resembles the two-meanings view, but it differs from that view in being non-dualistic with respect to oneself. On the expression theory pains are never to be distinguished, as a distinct sort of thing, from behavior, no more in one's own case than in the case of others. The difference between one's own case and that of others shows up rather in this way. When I say of someone else that he has a pain I am referring to his behavior, actual or potential; "has a pain" in third- (and second-) person utterances means "is behaving and/or is disposed to behave in a certain way." But when I say "I have a pain" I am not referring to my behavior, nor, as on the two-meanings view, am I referring to a private sensation. I am not referring to anything at all; in saying that I have a pain I am not saying that there is some x such that I have x, x being my pain; I am not reporting the existence or occurrence of anything, or describing it, or naming it, since there is no such thing to be reported or described or named—although it is misleading to say that there is no such thing. For it is not that I am trying, in saying that I have a pain, to refer to or describe something and somehow failing to do so. Rather, I am not even purporting to refer or describe; my utterance does not even purport to be a report or a descriptive statement, although it does have the grammatical form of one. My utterance is an *expression* of my state or condition; it *shows* pain and does not convey the proposition that I have one. Saying that I have a pain is like grimacing or crying out; my utterance is itself a piece of pain-behavior. To say that *he* has a pain is to refer to or describe behavior, his behavior, but to say that *I* have a pain is just to behave in a certain way; it is not to describe at all and certainly not to describe my behavior.

The expression theory has probably not been held in the pure form just indicated, whereby all first-person utterances in which the word "pain" occurs are counted as expressions (and all second- and third-person utterances as reports or descriptions). There is some evidence that Wittgenstein was sympathetic to it (see the discussions in Essays VII and X by Strawson and Smart, respectively); and some philosophers (notably Malcolm in Essays IV and IX) seem to accept it in part and in combination with other views. The main argument in favor of the expression theory, or more particularly of the analysis of first-person sensation utterances as expressions, is given by Malcolm in Essay IV. This runs as follows. When I say of someone that he has a pain I may be mistaken. No matter how good my evidence, it is always possible that I am wrong in thinking that another person has a pain (cf. step 5 of stage A of my argument for solipsism). But I cannot be wrong in thinking that I myself have a pain. It does not even make sense for anyone to say, when I say I have a pain, "No, you are mistaken," nor indeed to ask, "Are you sure?" What basis could another person have for denying or questioning my statement? Indeed what basis could I myself have for doing so— since I do not say that I have a pain on any basis? I do not tell that I have a pain *by* anything; I do not establish or ascertain that I do so, or come to the conclusion that I do. The very notion of thinking that I have a pain proves, on examination, to be without sense. I cannot think that anything is the case unless it is at least possible for me to be mistaken in thinking it, and mistake is impossible here. It follows that I cannot know that I have a pain either, for the same reason; any proposition that I know to be true must be one that I could be wrong about, and what is stated by "I have a pain" is not such a proposition. The utterance "I have a pain" is *incorrigible;* the very notion of being wrong does not apply to it—and neither, therefore, does the notion of being right. "I have a pain" is not the sort of utterance to which right and wrong apply, and hence we must conclude that it is not the sort of utterance which even states a proposition. These words are not used to state anything at all, nor, *a fortiori,* to report, refer to, or describe anything. What then is their use? It does not follow from what has been said that their use is expressive, in the way that a wince or a cry is expressive. But this is a natural conclusion to draw. First-person sensation utterances then cannot be mistaken in the way and for the reason that a grimace or a sigh cannot be mistaken—they assert nothing and make no claim.

This reasoning is weakest in its final step, to the conclusion that first-person sensation utterances, because incorrigible, are expressive. There is a weakness also in the penultimate step, where it is inferred that such utterances do not (cannot be used to) state, refer, or describe. Malcolm himself points out this latter weakness in Essay IV and argues that the step in question need not be taken, although Strawson had argued (in his review of Wittgenstein's *Investigations*) that it must, given the steps and premises which precede it. Malcolm also claims, against Strawson, that Wittgenstein himself did not take this step, and hence did not deny that "I have a pain," though incorrigible, might nonetheless refer to or describe something in oneself—though not a necessarily private something—and might therefore be a report and not or not merely an expression. The points in dispute here are fine, but they are also important, for they raise the questions of how mental phenomena or sensations can be referred to, how identified, and how known or known about, if at all, and hence, ultimately, the question of what such things are. Certain answers to these questions are assumed in stage *A* of my argument for solipsism, especially in steps 8, 9, and 10. The dispute between Malcolm and Strawson shows, if nothing else, that these steps and these assumptions bear examination.

Fine points aside, it is fairly obvious that the conclusion of the above argument will not do, at least as a general account of first-person sensation utterances and their relation to third-person utterances. As Strawson points out in Essay VII, the expression theory both "obscures the facts, and is needless" (cf. Smart's discussion in Essay X). Among other things, it makes no place for first-person utterances in the past tense: there seems to be no reason why "I had a pain" should not be an expression, if "I have a pain" is, but to say that it is, is to go against the plain fact that we can be mistaken about what we ourselves felt yesterday. Furthermore, the main premise of the argument may be questioned; it may be doubted whether first-person pain utterances are in fact incorrigible (see Strawson's review of the *Investigations* and J. L. Austin's "Other Minds"). And in any case, the expression theory fails as a theory of all mental phenomena, for there are many first-person "mental" utterances which are plainly not incorrigible. That I am intelligent, am generous, am in love, and have a strong will are all things about which I may well be mistaken, and for these the expression theory is obviously false.

The Criteriological View

So far I have considered possible responses to stage A of my argument for solipsism which imply the denial, in one way or another, of step 6, in which it is asserted that pains and behavior are different things. I come now to a view, which I shall call the criteriological view, in which what is denied is not that pains and behavior are different things but that the relation between them is merely contingent. This view implies the denial, not of step 6, but of step 7 of stage A of my argument—although the denial of step 7 has an effect upon the meaning of step 6. According to the criteriological view, the relation between a person's behavior when he has a pain and his pain itself is the relation between a criterion and that of which it is the (or a) criterion. This relation is a logical relation; it is not just a fact that certain things are said and done by a man who has a pain. The relation is logical because, as Malcolm puts it in Essay IV, "the satisfaction of the criterion of y establishes the existence of y beyond question," or because, to use Strawson's phrase in Essay VII, the presence or satisfaction of a criterion constitutes a "logically adequate basis" for asserting the existence of the thing of which it is the criterion, or for ascribing that thing (if that is the sort of thing it is) to something. Behavior is a criterion of pain, according to those who hold this view, because an appeal to a man's behavior does establish beyond question that he has a pain, because if he is behaving in a certain way he must have a pain.

This view of the relation between behavior and pain can be found in Wittgenstein's *Investigations*, but it is Malcolm and Strawson, in Essays IV and VII below, respectively, who have developed and defended it most explicitly—though not, to be sure, in just the same way. The view does destroy my argument for solipsism since it provides a means of forestalling the conclusion of stage A, even though step 6 be accepted. For if a man's behavior constitutes a logically sufficient basis for ascribing a pain to him, if his behaving in a certain way means that he must have a pain, then I can know, at least in principle, that he does or does not have a pain, since I can know what his behavior is. But what reason is there to suppose that behavior is a criterion of pain in the way that Malcolm and Strawson claim it is? Part of the answer is provided by the argument, outlined above, designed to show the impossibility of a necessarily private phenomenon, and the impossibility, therefore, of pain's being such a phenomenon. For this argument shows, according to Malcolm at any rate, that there must be criteria of pain—unless, of course, we accept behaviorism, and this Malcolm is unwilling to do.

If the notion of a necessarily private thing is unintelligible then private things such as pain (to anyone but a behaviorist) cannot be private of necessity; and this is just to say that some publicly observable phenomena are criteria of things such as pain, i.e., are logically linked to them, such that the presence of the public phenomenon guarantees the presence of the private one. But why suppose that behavior is a criterion of pain, in this sense? There is nothing, I think, which makes this necessary; but on the other hand it seems an obvious fact that, if there are criteria of pain at all, behavior is one such criterion. For it is on the basis of people's behavior that we do decide whether they have pains or not, it is by what they do and say that we do tell, or think we tell, what their sensations and feelings are, whatever else there might be by which we tell or on the basis of which we ascribe mental phenomena to people.

In fairness to Malcolm it must be noted that it is not simply behavior, in his view, which is the criterion of someone's being in pain, but behavior in certain circumstances. Or perhaps his view is that behavior is a criterion of pain in certain circumstances. In either case, the view he actually holds is more subtle than that which I have been presenting. Furthermore, Malcolm often distinguishes behavioral criteria, strictly so-called, from testimony or avowals, which also provide criteria of a man's mental states. The recognition of this distinction strengthens his view in the same way, noted above, that it strengthens behaviorism. For if behavior and testimony are genuinely different and independent criteria of people's feelings, then it is possible to confirm judgments about feelings made on the strength of the one by appealing to the other. Malcolm does not, as Ziff does, rank testimony above behavior as a criterion, or treat avowals as the final court of appeal in determining a man's mental state; hence this distinction, as he makes it, provides no basis for decisive disconfirming judgments in cases of conflict—which may or may not be a weakness in his view. Indeed, Malcolm's suggestion that some avowals be regarded as expressions—and Malcolm does seem, to this extent, to accept the expression theory—would seem to rule out any such basis.

The main critical question to be raised about the criteriological view concerns the nature of the relation which it supposes to hold between behavior and sensations, and in general between a criterion and that of which is the (or a) criterion. For it is not altogether clear what this relation is. It is a logical relation; behavior and pains are not merely found together; they are not associated as a matter of fact or connected by any merely contingent relation, such as causation. On the other hand, Malcolm at least denies that the relation is that of logical entailment or that the existence of a thing can be deduced from the satisfaction or presence of its criterion. (Even the use of the term "criterion" seems not to be altogether fixed, for criteria are sometimes things which are "present" or which "exist," and sometimes things which are "satisfied.") There is no statement describing Jones's behavior which entails that Jones has a pain, nor which entails that, in certain circumstances (or failing certain circumstances) Jones has a pain; there is not even any statement describing Jones's behavior and circumstances from which the statement that he has a pain can be deduced. And this is surely right, for there surely is no contradiction in saying that a man has a pain and yet is not behaving in any way or saying anything at all, no matter what the circumstances. But then the question arises as to what the relation here is if it is not that of entailment. It is not that there are no logical relations apart from entailment, for it seems fairly clear that there are such relations. But what they are, their various features and properties, has yet to be explained in any very detailed or precise way. Some illuminating questions have been raised about this criteriological relation, notably by Rogers Albritton and Alvin Plantinga in the papers listed in the Bibliography at the end of this volume. And some helpful suggestions as to how to answer these questions have been provided by Albritton in the same paper and by Malcolm in his book on *Dreaming*. But the questions have not been answered in a final or conclusive way, and until they are, final judgment as to the truth of the criteriological view must be reserved. On the other hand, it seems safe to say that this view, like the sophisticated behaviorism described above, is a leading contender in the present competition among theories of mind.

The Identity Theory

A different sort of response to my argument for solipsism from any so far considered is provided by the identity theory, proposed by Feigl in his paper, "The 'Mental' and the 'Physical,' " and by Place and Smart in Essays V and X, respectively, below. According to proponents of this theory, pains and behavior are different things, and furthermore the relation between them is merely contingent. Hence steps 6 and 7 of stage *A* of my argument are retained. The step whose rejection is implied by the identity theory is rather 10, in which it is claimed that there is no method of inferring what another person's sensations are that can be known to be perfectly reliable. There is such a method according to the identity theorist, and hence I can know what another person's sensations are, which means that the conclusion of stage *A* cannot be drawn. There is such a method because a person's sensations are processes in his brain, no more and no less, and the occurrence of brain processes can be inferred by certifiable methods—the regular methods of scientific, or more particularly of physiological, inquiry.

It is important to be clear as to what precisely the identity theorist is claiming. He says that sensations, pains for example, *are* brain processes, and this is the "are" of strict, numerical identity. But sensations and brain processes are identical as a matter of fact, and not in virtue of the meanings of the terms "sensation" and "brain process." In this respect the identity theory differs from older attempts to identify experiences with physical or physiological phenomena, i.e., it differs from classical reductive materialism. For in these attempts the identity claimed was held to be logical and not merely factual, and the resulting doctrines were plainly vulnerable to the objections, among others, that are listed by Smart in Essay X—objections which, Smart claims, do not tell against his view.

The identity theory is dualistic but not Cartesian; sensations are neither necessarily private entities nor entities of a special "mental" sort. Sensations are irreducible to behavior, and the relations between the two are merely contingent, but sensations, being physiological phenomena, are of the same general nature as behavior. Pains and behavior, despite their specific difference, are both physical phenomena; both are subject to physical laws and can be described in physical terms.

Proponents of the identity theory, it should be noted, do not claim that all mental phenomena are to be identified with processes in the brain. Both Place and Smart accept the dispositional analysis of many sorts of mental concepts, which is to say an analysis in terms of behavior; hence their total view of mind is in part behavioristic. The identity theory is applied only to sensations and experiences—things such as pains. (The same is evidently true for many of the other views that we have been considering, for the dispositional or behavioristic analysis is widely accepted as an account of certain sorts of mental phenomena, and it is mainly over sensations and the like that the disagreements noted above have arisen.) It should also be noted that the holders of this theory do not put their view quite so strongly as I have represented them as doing—or at least that Place and Smart do not. They stop short of saying that sensations *are* (now known to be) brain processes, and say instead that they *may* be, that there is no reason to deny that they are and some reason to affirm it, if not perhaps sufficient reason at the present time. Granting that nothing prevents the identification of pains with brain states (and of course this may not be granted; see below), what more is needed to make this identification plausible, if not mandatory? Part of the answer is: a vast number of detailed correlations between the occurrence of specific brain processes and the presence of specific sensations (in one's own case) or the utterance of sensation statements (in the case of other people), many more such correlations than are now known to hold. But this is only part of the answer, since even a perfect correlation between two items does not establish that they really are one thing and hence are to be identified. Certain criteria of identity, certain conditions under which it is correct or reasonable to say that two correlated items are parts or aspects of one single thing, must also be satisfied. What are these criteria? Place suggests one plausible answer in Essay V, but what he says is not developed very fully, nor is it, I think, definitively established.

Hence the truth of the identity theory has by no means been demonstrated. More work of both an empirical and a philosophical sort needs to be done before the claim that it is true can be made out. Furthermore, it is not altogether clear that the theory even could be true. Smart devotes his main efforts in Essay X to proving this, that there is nothing to be said against the theory—nothing, that is, of a logical or philosophical sort. But it may be questioned whether he has considered all the objections that might be made to his thesis, even supposing that he has adequately met those that he does consider. Has he an answer, for example, to the following argument, and could he have one? If *x* and *y* are to be identified with one another it must be possible to identify (specify) each of them by itself; it must be possible to pick out *x* without in any way referring to or making use of *y*. But now is this possible when *x* is a sensation? Can sensations be identified (picked out) independently of the brain processes with which they are held to be identical? The sensations to be thus identified cannot be tied logically to behavior, for then the connection between behavior and certain brain processes, viz., those which are identical with the sensations in question, would no longer be contingent; whereas it surely always is a contingent matter that a certain brain process accompanies a certain sort of behavior. And if sensations are not tied logically to behavior, how can we avoid the conclusion that they are necessarily private objects, with all the difficulties that that entails, including the difficulty that no such object can be identified in the first place?

Perhaps this argument could be countered by the identity theorist. But it is plain, I think, that the identity theory needs to be developed further and examined more fully before any sure judgment of its success can be delivered. It too, like sophisticated behaviorism and the criteriological view, deserves serious consideration as a solution to the various problems about mind that we have been discussing. But whether it, or one of them, or some entirely different view, in fact is the solution to these problems remains to be seen.

Concluding Remarks

I have presented a series of views of mind as different responses to a single argument, my argument for solipsism, in order to bring out their various connections and to indicate something of the reasons for holding them, and some of the problems which they are designed to solve. In doing this I have been able to present a kind of survey of much recent work in the philosophy of mind and also indicate a way of approaching the essays chosen for inclusion in this collection, each of which offers an important sample of this recent work. But I wish again to note that this is but one way of approaching these essays, and that they may be profitably studied for things quite different from those that I have singled out. I also wish to note that I have not by any means said all that could or should be said about my argument for solipsism. Other difficulties than those I have suggested might be pressed, and it might turn out that no general theory of mental phenomena, of the sort that I have considered, is necessary to destroy the argument. I have already noted that various objections to points I make or assume about the concepts of evidence, justification, verification, and sense (or nonsense) in stages *B* and *C* of the argument might be made. Other objections might be made to the claims I make about knowledge, and in particular to my implicit claim, in stage *A*, that one can know what one's own sensations are. Finally, exception might be taken to what I say or take for granted about pretence and the detection of pretence; it might well turn out that a more accurate account of these concepts would stall my argument at its start. These at any rate are the points that now seem to me most obviously to require examination, and doubtless there are many others.

I ❧ Experience
B. A. Farrell

I want to deal with a question that bothers physiologists and psychologists. It is a familiar question for philosophers, but I want to deal with it as it appears to *them*, not to us. Consequently, I shall begin by explaining at some length how the problem does arise for them.

Adrian, in *The Basis of Sensation* (New York: Norton, 1928), said many years ago that "whatever our views about the relation between mind and body, we cannot escape the fact that there is an unsatisfactory gap between two such events as the sticking of a pin into my finger and the appearance of a sensation of pain in my consciousness. Part of the gap is obviously made up of events in my sensory nerves and brain." In his Waynflete lectures, *The Physical Background of Perception* (Oxford: Clarendon Press, 1947), he purports to fill the gap even further by telling us about the structure and activity of the brain. He discusses the nature of the mechanism which would be needed to copy the activity of the brain—in particular, the activity of recognizing significant relations and of learning skilled movements. After suggesting the sort of material events and changes that must occur in the brain to account for this sort of activity, he says "Yet there remains the formidable problem of the intervening events. The human mind comes in somewhere in the chain of causation between the physical events in the sensory and the motor pathways." Mental events, he goes on, must be closely connected with the material process going on in the cortex, and we must try to make such a connection seem plausible. In an endeavor to make this connection seem plausible, he discusses the suggestions of Kenneth Craik and says that "Craik could only suggest that consciousness comes in at certain points in the process of neural transmission where the physiological patterns have a particular kind of definiteness. . . . On this hypothesis, we could tell what someone was thinking if we could watch his brain at work, for we should see how one pattern after another acquired the necessary brilliance and definition."

This attitude of Adrian's seems fairly representative among physiologists working in this field. They suffer severely from the occupational disease of traditional dualism.[1] Adrian's talk is also illuminating because

---

[1] See also, for example, C. T. Morgan (of Johns Hopkins), *Physiological Psychology* (New York: McGraw-Hill, 1943).

it brings out the acute difficulty these neurologists are in. They would be only too thankful if they could ignore the intervening mental events altogether. What they would like to have is the assurance that they—as physiologists and neurologists—can in principle give a *complete* account of what happens when we think, recognize things, remember, and see things; and that they are safe in ignoring the mind and all intervening mental events whatever. But the road to their professional heart's desire is blocked by what seem to them overwhelming objections. In particular, there is the old objection. To assert that a complete account of thinking, of having a sensation, and so on, can be given in physiological terms alone appears to entail that mental events are either reducible to physiological and neural ones (which is absurd), or else do not exist (which is false). So physiologists are reluctantly also ready to agree that *any* physiological and neural account of what happens when we think, etc., even if it is a definitive one for the time being, will leave out certain essential parts or aspects of the total process—the parts or aspects "where the mind comes in." They might be inclined to express their dissatisfaction with their own accounts like this: "When a person sees things, thinks, and so on, it is obviously not true that *all* that is going on are the material processes that we physiologists describe. Certain mental processes are also going on. He is having certain sensations and feelings. In general, he is having certain experiences. And it is this that we have to leave out and cannot cope with."

But at this point the physiologists, like the plain man, are apt to get an idea, and to turn with relief, if not with hope, to psychology. "It is the business of psychology," they may say, "to deal with our sensations and feelings. And if it would only hurry up, then, with the physiological account of the neural basis of experience, the two sciences jointly might be able to offer a presentable account of what happens when we see and feel," etc. This is a very reasonable and obvious appeal for assistance, since the psychologists do almost invariably and expressly accept "experience" as falling within the subject matter of the science. Almost invariably, they describe the subject matter as covering both "behavior and experience." [2] Presumably therefore they do claim to give a scientific account of both.

Let us remind ourselves how psychologists do set to work to deal with "experience"—with our sensations, our feelings, and so on; and what sorts of discoveries they make about them.

Consider sensation. What a psychologist does is to take a Mr. X and use him as a subject in a laboratory. He might use Mr. X as a subject by, for example, subjecting him to the important classes of stimuli that are

---

[2] This conjunction soon becomes familiar to anyone perusing the textbooks, e.g., R. H. Thouless, *General and Social Psychology* (London: University Tutorial Press, 1951), Ch. I. In E. G. Boring, H. S. Langfeld and H. P. Weld, eds., *Foundations of Psychology* (New York: Wiley, 1948), the conjunction appears as "behavior and consciousness."

likely to affect X's sense organs—viz., mechanical, thermal, acoustic, chemical, and photic stimuli. In this way he will discover from X's responses and discriminations whether X's sensitivity is normal or not—whether, for instance, X is color blind or not, or has abnormally acute acoustic sensitivity, and so on. Or he might vary the stimuli in respect of their quality, intensity, extension, or duration in order to discover whether X's responses show corresponding variations. The sort of generalization the psychologist produces is exemplified in the Weber Law about differential thresholds, and later modifications of this; or in a generalization about the primary qualities of the stimuli in question from which all other qualities are obtained (e.g., "in vision, the primaries are red, yellow, green, blue, white, and black").

In experimenting on X as subject, it is not necessary for the psychologist to make X talk to him. *In principle,* everything he wants to know can be discovered by making X behave like a dog and depress keys or open lids or perform some such motor response that shows the psychologist he has made the discrimination in question. Just as we can discover that a dog can distinguish between red and green colors by successfully training the dog to distinguish that the red light over a door means it is open, whereas the green light means it is shut, so the psychologist can in principle discover that X is or is not color blind, can or cannot react to this or that variation in the stimulus, and so on. But of course, it is ever so much more convenient, and indeed very often necessary at present with our limited experimental techniques, to ask X to report what he does see. Provided that these reports are of the very simple Yes-No variety, and the psychologist has good reason to believe that X is cooperating with him, there is no methodological objection whatever for not also using X's verbal reports.

One further thing a psychologist also does. Quite often he places himself in the role of subject. For laboratory purposes it is often convenient for him to play the role of X. Now it may or may not be the case that, when he does so, he makes observations of quite a different sort to those he makes when he merely observes X reacting to the same stimulus—e.g., a red disc. I will come to this later. What is important to note is that by playing the role of observer-subject, he does not add anything to the discoveries of psychological science that he could not in principle obtain from the observation of X alone; and no new concepts are required to deal with what his own subject-observation reveals which are not also required by what was, or can be, revealed by his observation of X.

This, then, though very roughly, is how contemporary psychologists go to work. They investigate remembering, learning and thinking, feelings, attitudes and traits, temperament and personality in the same sort of way as they investigate sensations.

But this seems to psychologists an awkward and ridiculous situation. For it means that the science of psychology does not deal with "experience" either. Thus, in describing how subject X reacted to different types of stimuli, it is clear that we were not dealing with X's sensations at all, but with his behavior; and the discoveries that psychology claims to have made about "sensation" have not been about "sensation" at all, but about the sensitivity of organisms to physical stimuli. To describe all this work as being about "sensation" is just false. This situation is awkward because it means that we are no nearer dealing with the facts of experience, which brain-physiology leaves out; and so no nearer providing a scientific account of it, which could supplement the account given by physiology, and thereby provide a reasonably complete picture of what happens when we have a sensation, or feel, etc. This situation is ridiculous because, while psychology purports to be the scientific study of experience, and lip-service is paid to this attempt in the usual definitions of its subject matter, the science, in effect, does not include experience within its purview. What psychologists feel the science should *somehow* also include is, for example, the sensation-quality that X undoubtedly experiences when, rat-like, he discriminates a red disc; and the mental state he is in when he thinks, and not merely his behavior; and (to quote Stout[3]) the "unique kind of feeling-attitude towards an object" which we experience when we are in some emotional state, not merely the readiness and dispositions we exhibit towards the object of our emotion. Moreover, psychology should also aim at giving us the laws governing these sensation qualities, emotional states, and so forth. But all this is just what contemporary psychology does not include and do. The fact that the subject X and the psychologist himself both have sensations, and so forth, is simply ignored.

No doubt all this sounds stale and naïve to puzzle-wise professional philosophers. But to date we cannot flatter ourselves that we have done much to help the psychologists, poor animals, out of their maze. Like the physiologists, the ordinary working psychologist would be quite pleased in a way to get rid of sensations, feelings, etc., as items of experience, and deal solely with reactions, discriminations, behavior-readinesses, and so on. But he cannot bring himself to do so. For he sees himself faced by the old unpalatable alternative. To get rid of "experience" can only be done by denying that we have sensations, etc., or by refusing to bother with them. But to assert that we do not have sensations, or that no experiences occur, is to assert what is palpably false; and to refuse to bother with them is to leave out certain phenomena, or aspects of phenomena, that psychologists are supposed to investigate.

Some psychologists, chiefly American I think, have paraded their embarrassments (being less inhibited than their British colleagues), and have tried to deal with them. For example, Tolman (of California), in his *Purposive Behavior in Animals and Men* (New York: Appleton-Cen-

---

[3] G. F. Stout, *A Manual of Psychology*, 5th ed. (London: W. B. Clive, 1938), Bk. III, Ch. IV.

tury-Crofts, 1932), distinguishes between discriminations, discriminatory readinesses, and so forth, on the one hand, and what a psychology of discriminations leaves out on the other. What it leaves out he calls "raw feels." These raw feels, he says, are not capable of scientific treatment, and he admits at the end of the book that he does not know what on earth to do with them. He suggests three scrap heaps on to which they may be thrown. They may be ignored as scientific will of the wisps. They may be assumed to correlate consistently with our responses and response readinesses, so that in so far as X and Y behave alike they have the same sort of experience. Thirdly, "Raw feels may be the way physical realities are intrinsically" so that, e.g., experienced qualities may be "the intrinsic nature of a nervous process." By contrast, Boring (of Harvard) will stand no such metaphysical nonsense. In *The Physical Dimensions of Consciousness* (New York: Century, 1933) (note the word "physical"), and again in a more recent article,[4] he has argued like this. In the early stages of our physiology and psychology, interaction seems the obvious answer, because we find stimulus causing sensation and sensation causing movement. But as our knowledge advances, psycho-physical parallelism is suggested, because sensation then seems to parallel some middle part of the series of material events, between, say, the prick of the pin and the jerking away of my arm. But were our knowledge to be complete, so that we had a perfect correlation between sensation and neural process, we should *then* identify the two. We are not inclined to do so now, but we will, when the time comes. And he proposes to hurry up the transition a bit by doing some propaganda himself and saying "Neural process and sensation *are* identical."

First Steps: "Behavior" and "Experience"

Well, what can be done about this? Let me simplify the question by talking for the most part about that form of experience we call sensation.

Suppose subject X is asked in a laboratory: "Please tell me what you are seeing now"; and suppose he answers: "I see a red patch." Now take the sentence: "If we merely consider all the differential responses and readinesses, and such like, that X exhibits towards the stimulus of a red shape, we are leaving out the experience he has when he looks at it." I shall call this sentence "A" for short. It is, no doubt, only a sentence that someone doing psychology would ever utter. But, when we appreciate this, it seems quite a straightforward sort of remark, with nothing odd about it. It has this appearance because it seems to resemble quite ordinary remarks like the following.

Sentence 1. "If you merely consider what Y says and does, you leave out what he really feels behind that inscrutable face of his."

[4] E. G. Boring, "Mind and Mechanism," *American Journal of Psychology*, LIX (1946), 173-92.

Sentence A resembles sentence 1 in that both are apparently saying that if you rely only on the publicly observable behavior of the person, you will be ignoring his private experience; and you may be wrong in the guesses you make about it. It is quite sensible and often true to utter sentence 1, or something like it. Why not also sentence A?

Sentence 2. "If you only consider the obvious overt behavior of an ape when solving one of Köhler's problems (e.g., getting the banana from the roof by piling up boxes on each other and climbing up), you leave out that when it sat still once or twice, it was obviously doing something like 'cogitating' about the problem." And

Sentence 3. "If we just treat a small child as a bundle of reflexes gradually being conditioned à la Watson, we are in danger of forgetting that the child also has feelings and vague wants of its own, and is not just a performing rat."

The resemblances between sentence A and sentences 2 and 3 are similar to those between sentences A and 1. I deliberately chose two technical examples that have cropped up in the history of the subject, because it is these that are apt to influence psychologists more immediately than those from ordinary discourse.

But of course sentence A is also *quite different* from sentences 1, 2, and 3. Take sentence 1. What we leave out here is something that Y can tell us about. We might say of him: "Can't he be persuaded to be a bit more open and tell us what he really feels about our proposal?" Or "If Y goes on being so secretive and withdrawn, I shall persuade him to go for psychological advice. Perhaps the chance to talk to a sympathetic person may help him to get things off his chest." Contrast this with X in sentence A. What is left out here is something that X cannot in principle tell us about. He has already given us a lengthy verbal report, but we say that this is not enough. We want to include something over and above this, viz., X's experience. It is useless to ask X to give us further reports and to make further discriminations if possible, because these reports and discriminations are mere behavior and leave out what we want. It is obviously pointless, therefore, to recommend X to go to an analyst, so that he can then tell us about the experience he has when he looks at a red shape and that we have so far ignored.

The same sort of differences hold for sentences 2 and 3 as well. This can be seen by imagining that the ape and the child were suddenly given the gift of human adult speech and the discriminatory capacity that goes with it. They would then give us the *same* sorts of reports that X gives us in the laboratory, and thereby enable us to include what we might have been in *real* danger of leaving out of our account of how they (ape and child) solve problems—viz., that they too cogitate, have wants, and so on. Again, therefore, it is quite obvious that what we were in danger of leaving out in the cases of the ape and the child is quite different from what we feel we are leaving out in the case of X.

At this point the commonsensical objection is useful (that we *must* be leaving out X's experience if we only consider his behavior) because it emphasizes that we do not normally use "experience" and "behavior" as synonyms, but more often than not as contrasts. Thus, e.g., you might say: "I did nothing but felt a shiver down my spine"; or we might say: "Those factory hands who do a routine job usually have a rich day dream life"; or "He plays tennis quite well but he still does not enjoy it." In these examples, it would be quite wrong, or odd, English to describe your shiver, the day dream life of the factory hands, or the joyless experience of the tennis player as "behavior." This contrasting use of "behavior" and "experience" reinforces our tendency to say that behavior sentences inevitably "leave out" the person's experience. But, of course, when we look more closely at the sentences where we do use "experience" in a way that contrasts with behavior, we notice at once that these sentences, like numbers 1, 2, and 3 already mentioned, also differ from sentence A in the same sort of way. The experiences of the factory hands and the tennis player are describable, the "left out" experience of X is not.

This normal use of "behavior" and "experience" draws attention to the odd and stretched use of "behavior" we are now employing. For, in order to show that what we are alleged to be leaving out is something very odd, we stretch the word "behavior" to cover, at least, the covert verbal and other responses of the person, his response readinesses, all his relevant bodily states, and all the possible discriminations he can make to the presented red shape. But, in spite of this stretching, we are *still* dissatisfied. We *still* want to draw a line between X's behavior in this sense and his experience. We want to do so because this distinction still seems to have a point here. For example, we still want to pose the schoolboy question: "When X and Y both look at a red patch, and show no discoverable differences of response, how do we know that what X sees is like what Y sees?—that their experience is qualitatively identical?" We still want to say that when a congenitally blind person has his sight restored, it is not simply the case that he now does and can respond differentially to a new range of stimuli. We want to say that his experience is now qualitatively different. We still want to distinguish between robots and men by saying that the former have no sensations. We also want to use this distinction between "behavior" and "experience" whenever we think of the Martians, or of the "men whose heads do grow beneath their shoulders" and wonder what it would be like to be one of them. To stick to this distinction seems to be the only way of satisfying our wants here and of talking like this. So even if it be true (as Mace alleges it is[5]) that "statements about mind or consciousness just turn out to be, on analysis, statements about the behavior of material things," we still feel like retorting

[5] C. A. Mace, "Some Implications of Analytical Behaviourism," *Aristotelian Society Proceedings*, XLIX (1948-49), 1-16.

that this is at best only true for psychological purposes, and in any case, so much the worse for the psychology that demands such a result.

Now I could go through these queer and difficult cases at once in order to discover whether we *do* need the distinction between "behavior" and "experience" to talk about them. But this may be a little premature and produce unnecessary resistance. So I shall try another tack first.

Why This Experience Is So Odd

I shall say that the experience of X, which we are alleged to be leaving out, is featureless. This is in contrast with the experiences referred to in sentences 1, 2, and 3 above. The experience of X is featureless because there is nothing about it that X can discriminate. If he does discriminate something that appears to be a feature of the experience, this something at once becomes, roughly, either a feature of the stimulus in the sort of way that the saturation of the red in the red shape is a feature of the red shape, or a feature of his own responses to the shape. X merely provides us with further information about the behavior that he does and can perform.

But surely this is mistaken? Surely it is wrong to say that it has no features? For even if it is always false to say of the experience we are leaving out that, e.g., "It is red," or "It is extended," what of the so-called "formal" predicates or properties? No doubt we cannot say of it that it stands in spatial or causal relations to anything else. But surely we can say, e.g., "At least X's experience happens." Surely, that is, we can say that it stands in "temporal relations" to other events or processes? No —this will not do. For to say that "something or other happens quite frequently" is to say that the something occurs at different times. To say this is to say that this something is in principle datable. How now do we set about dating the occurrence that is X's experience at any time? All *we* can do is to date X's responses. But suppose X, as subject-observer, sets himself the task of dating the onset of a certain raw feel experience, for example, the one that is supposed to happen when he sees two changing shapes as equally elliptical. When X times himself here, say by stopping a stop watch, all that he *can* time is his "seeing"—e.g., his subvocal "Ah! that's it," his accompanying release of breath and muscular tension, and so forth. What, therefore, he dates is the onset of his seeing the shapes as equally elliptical. Difficulties only multiply if we now retreat and say "But we time the experience indirectly by timing the behavior that it accompanies?" E.g., What sort of "accompanying" does this ghost do?

But surely we *can* say: "X's experience (in the raw feel sense, of course) is not identical with Y's?" The answer seems to be "No" again. Obviously we cannot be saying here that X's experience differs qualitatively from Y's, because admittedly neither have the sort of features that permits them to differ qualitatively. If we are saying that X's experience is not numerically identical with Y's, then presumably we are saying something like: "Oh no! Mr. Shaw is our grocer—not G.B.S.!" "It's the same cheering you heard a minute or so ago"; "It was the same explosion we both heard." I.e., we are presumably talking about things, or processes, or events. But X's and Y's experiences are not things, processes, or events. We notice the difference if we ask: "As they have no properties like 'red,' 'long,' 'loud,' etc., how, in the first place, do we distinguish these two processes (or events), viz., X's and Y's experiences, so that we can *then* assert that they are not the same?" In the case of the cheering, or explosions, it is possible to do so. Here it does not seem to be.

But I *have* been saying quite a lot of things about experience in the course of this paper—if not positive, then at least negative, things. Thus, for example, I have said: "X's experience is such that there is nothing about it that X can discriminate." If this is to be true, then presumably I am saying something about experience, if only in the indirect way that negative assertions do say things. But observe that, when I do come out with this assertion, and others like it, what I say is easy to follow and seems plausible because we are comparing it unconsciously with an assertion like "Ultra violet radiation cannot be discriminated visually," or "When I play a chord on a piano, X just experiences a blur—he cannot discriminate a note." Yet my assertion about experience is quite unlike these examples—obviously. Because of this, it is a confusion-producing assertion. It gives us the impression that we have been told something about the raw feel experience, just as we really are told something about ultra violet radiation, or X's experience on hearing a chord.

Yet I have suggested that we say "X's (raw feel) experience is featureless." Should I have said this? No! It is equally muddling. For it looks like saying: "The landscape in a desert is featureless," or "The faces in his paintings are quite featureless," or "*The Times* is almost featureless." But to say this sort of thing is compatible with the something talked about having all sorts of other properties; to say "X's experience is featureless" is not. If it is suggested again at this point that what we can do is simply to reject it as non-existent, we are in trouble too. For to say that X's experience does not exist, or is unreal, or that "There is no such thing as X's experience," etc., is quite *unlike* saying:

1. Unicorns are unreal, Johnny.
2. There is no such process as perpetual motion.
3. Dodos don't exist any more.
4. There are no round squares.
5. No prime number exists between 19 and 23.

Unicorns are unreal because they are the creations of legend and heraldry. Perpetual motion is a physical impossibility. Dodos are extinct. There are no round squares because the concept is self-contradictory; and there is no prime number between 19 and 23 for logical reasons, since it can be proved quite simply that there is not one. "X's experience" is quite unlike these cases. For one thing, we know what it is we are denying in these cases; with X's experience we do not. The snag is that we cannot discuss the question without using a substantive, like "experience," and the pronoun "it" (as in "It is featureless"). But this at once traps us into supposing that we are talking about some thing, process or event or state of affairs (or what not), to which this noun and pronoun, like other nouns and pronouns, are being used to refer. Obviously they are not being used in this way here, however difficult it is to get clear just how they are being used.

The upshot so far, then, is that to talk about X's experience as a process, or an event, etc. is just confusion-producing. It is foolish to say that it has, or has not any, features. It is foolish to label it as a shadow or ghostly process on the model of Ayer (in *Thinking and Meaning* [London: H. K. Lewis, 1947]), and then deny that it occurs. In particular, it is foolish to say that physiology and psychology ignore it and leave it out. There is no need whatever for Adrian to imagine that he is in danger of leaving anything out; and it is folly for Tolman to invent a special term, "raw feels," to refer to this unreferable something. For X's experience is not the sort of thing that can be ignored or noticed, left out or included. It is not the sort of thing of which one can fruitfully say "it is a sort of thing," and for which it is appropriate to use nouns and pronouns at all.

The Objection of the Indescribable Experience

"But is the man crazy? The argument so far has simply not shown that experience is featureless. All that it has shown, if that, is that our experience has no features that can be described, or discriminated, or reported in a laboratory. But the fact that it lacks *such* features does not entail that it lacks *all* features. For it may still possess features with which we can only be acquainted. And this, of course, is the case. When, for example, we look at a red patch, we all just *know* what it is like to have the corresponding experience, and we all just *know* how it differs from the experience we have when looking at a green patch. We cannot describe this difference. But what of that? The fact that we cannot describe it should not be used to suggest the absurdity that nothing of the sort exists. We only land in this absurdity by restricting the sort of observations psychology can make to the observations of a third party (or subject), and by restricting acceptable observation-sentences to those in the third person. If we do this, it is no wonder that we are restricted to the observation and recording of behavior and that we feel we are leaving out experience."

What makes this plausible? The fact that this situation appears to resemble stacks of cases where we do say or believe that some experience can only be appreciated at first hand, and cannot be described at all. "Oh! I cannot possibly begin to tell you what it was like—you must experience it for yourself." And the "it" here may be anything from the beauty of the Alps or the thrill of skiing, to the prophetic character of the Epilogue of R. Vaughan Williams's Sixth Symphony and the esoteric pleasures of the professional philosopher. This sort of remark, moreover, is a well-established response with all of us, since it goes back to childhood. The child is continually being put *into* situations in order to appreciate them and learn about them; and he is continually being told: "Oh, you must wait until you are old enough to go to a pantomime yourself, and then you will know what it is like." Clearly, descriptions are pitifully poor conveyors of the qualities of an experience, especially to a child, because, to say no more, descriptions invariably do an injustice to the discriminations actually made and to the excitement with which they are made.

But is the indescribable experience of seeing a red patch like any of these? No—it differs in the relevant respect. When we say "We can't describe the experience of seeing a red patch" (in the raw feel sense) the "can't" is logical. When we say "We can't describe the prophetic character of the Epilogue of R. V. W.'s Sixth Symphony, you have to hear it for yourself," the "can't" is the "hopeless" "can't." No matter how carefully and intelligently the critics talk about it, they cannot work me up in the way the Epilogue itself can. If, however, X's seeing red patches in the past had occurred in unpleasant circumstances, and X had acquired a horror of the things, then I might say: "I can't describe the unpleasant character that a red patch has for X." And then I would be using the "hopeless" "can't." The "hopeless" "can't" seems appropriate where our discriminatory repertoire is poor, and where, from whatever causes, the stimulus (or object in question) produces emotional responses that a description cannot do, no matter how imaginative the listener may be. This points out where the distinction between "We can/We can't describe the experience" is useful. It is useful to say we can't describe the R. V. W. Epilogue, in order to distinguish it from relatively simple and humdrum experiences like going for a ride on a bus or having pins and needles. It is useless to say we can't describe the R. V. W. Epilogue, if we wish thereby to stress the likeness between the raw feel experience of seeing a red patch and the experience of hearing the Epilogue.

Let me try to deal briefly with this in a different way. Suppose we still feel like saying (Moore-wise, perhaps): "But we just do *know* what it is like to have the experience of looking at a red disc, and we just do *know* how this differs from looking at a green one." Presumably we would say that a rat, once trained to discriminate between a red and a green disc, had the experience (in some primitive way) of seeing a red disc. But we would hesitate to say that it knew that it had this experience—or knew what it was like to have this sort of experience. Well, then, what is true of us that is not true of the rat? Looking at it psychologically, we can react to our own responses to the disc by means of substitute, or symbolic, behavior, and the rat cannot do so. When I, or you, claim to know what our experience of looking at a red disc is like, we imply, in part, that we are able to react symbolically to our response of "looking at a red disc." What we react to in this way is the pattern of stimulation produced by this response of "looking." Again, I may react symbolically to a pattern of stimulation that is called "a behavioral readiness" to respond to this red disc as I have responded to others in the past; and I may then say: "Oh, there's something very familiar about this red disc," or something of the sort. When, therefore, I say: "I just know what it is like to have the experience of looking at a red disc," I am saying, for psychological purposes, that I have the capacity to discriminate my own responses in the *same* sort of way as I discriminate the features of the red disc when I say of it, for example: "Oh, it's bright, uniformly red," and so on. If we overlook this capacity to react symbolically to one's own reactions, or if we say we are doing "introspection" and do not inquire what actually happens when we do so, then we are liable to assert, with a flourish and an air of importance, that "we just know how looking at a red disc differs from looking at a green one." In other words, we are then liable to mistake features of our responses to the disc for some indescribable and ineffable property of the experience.

One consequence of all this. It makes no difference if a psychology allows or emphasizes observation-sentences in the first person. "Experience" still remains featureless, and our observation and our recording cannot include it no matter how hard we try.

It is appropriate at this point to return to the difficult cases where it still seems to be essential to keep the distinction between "behavior" and "experience." I only have space to consider two of these cases—the Martians and the robots.

A Difficult Case: The Man from Mars. (a) "What It Would Be Like to Be a Martian"

Suppose we had obtained from our Martian visitor all the information that we, as psychologists and physiologists, could obtain about his sensory capacities. We should probably *still* want to say: "I wonder what it would be like to be a Martian—with his pseudo-radio sense, able, for example, to listen to whatever wave length he chooses. Extraordinary!" This seems to be a perfectly sensible remark. But if there was nothing more to be discovered about the Martian than his actual and possible responses, then this would *not* be a sensible remark. We would know what it would be like to be a Martian and there would be no point in wondering about it. So there *is* something more to be learned about the Martian, and that is what his experience is like. Similarly for our wonderings about babies, mice, and lice.

Now we treat this remark ("I wonder what it would be like to be a Martian") as perfectly sensible because it resembles remarks like:

1. "I wonder what it would be like to be an opium smoker."
2. "I wonder what it would be like to be, and hear like, a bat."

In 1 and 2 the only sort of answer that will satisfy me is the sort of answer I will get if I became an opium smoker or a bat myself. That is to say, I am imagining myself in the role of observer-subject, i.e., the role of the privileged observer, and I will be satisfied only with the sort of answer that I can then obtain. The demand for this sort of answer here is quite reasonable, because it is a contingent fact that I am not an opium smoker or a bat (after all, a witch could easily change me into a bat for a day or so). Hence there is nothing absurd in the supposition that I should become a privileged observer here. Similarly, my wonder about the Martian seems to be the sort that can be satisfied only by a privileged observer's answer. What makes this answer seem so imperative is that the Martian's experience differs, *ex hypothesi,* from mine so much more than the opium smoker's, or even the bat's. It is this vast difference that inclines us to reject any attempted description of the Martian's experience as feeble and inadequate. Moreover, as with the opium smoker and the bat, it is perfectly sensible to suppose that I should become a privileged observer here also; and it is this wonder what it would be like to be a privileged observer that leads us to say there is something *more* to be learned about the Martian, namely, "What his experience is like."

But our wonder about the Martian is quite different from our wonder about the opium smoker. For what we want to know about the Martian is something that no privileged observer can give himself or us. Suppose I become an opium smoker and I then say: "I now know what it is like to be one." What do I know here? In part, I know the sort of thing I could embody in "Confessions of an Opium Smoker"; the sort of dreams the smoker has; how habit forming goes on so that ultimately his whole life becomes dominated by the drug. If I am confronted by another alleged opium smoker, my knowledge is such that I may be able to use it to help determine whether the other man really is an opium addict, or whether he is just lying or putting over an act. In part, also, what I know here is something that can be discussed in a court of law or by medical psychologists. My claim to have this knowledge may be rejected by them, wrongly, as bogus, or it may be accepted as veridical, when in fact it is bogus. In short, when I take up opium smoking and learn what it is like to be an opium smoker, what I learn is a lot about the expandable and describable experience of the smoker. Or, to put it differently and paradoxically, I do not learn anything more about it except what the scientific methods of the nonprivileged observer are still too clumsy to discover for themselves. All, therefore, that happens when I become a privileged observer is that I give myself the opportunity of making certain observations for myself. I give myself the opportunity of making the same discriminations, etc., as the opium smoker, of learning to react to these as he does, and so of coming to "know what it is like to be an opium smoker."

What, however, we want to know about the Martian is quite other than this. It *must* be, because if it were not, there would be no point in distinguishing between "behavior" and "experience" in our talk about him. The "experience" of the Martian would then be assimilable under "behavior" in the way we have just suggested for the opium smoker. It is perfectly sensible to wonder what it would be like to be a Martian *if* we are thinking of one of us becoming a privileged observer. But clearly we cannot *only* be thinking of this because this supposition is not enough. In fact, it is not what we want at all. For, as we have seen, if I *were* to become a privileged observer, I could still only come to learn what it was like to be a Martian as I come to learn what it is like to be an opium smoker. I would still not have learned what the Martian's "experience" was like in the sense in which we purport to be interested. The *same* puzzle, of course, can be raised about the opium smoker also. We can wonder what it would be like to be an opium smoker, in the *sort* of way in which we would remain dissatisfied with the knowledge that a privileged observer comes to possess. But it is easier to spot the sources of the puzzle here than in the case of the Martian. So when we feel the urge to say that "there is something more to be learned about the Martian than his actual and possible responses" (viz., "what his experience is like"), we feel this urge partly because we have overlooked the difference between saying: "I wonder what it would be like to be a Martian," and "I wonder what it would be like to be an opium smoker"—a difference that makes the former wonder pointless and the latter sensible.

(b) "Knowing at First Hand"

But this still leaves us dissatisfied for various reasons. Consider one of them. "When I take up opium smoking, I do not only get the chance of making certain discriminations, etc., that otherwise would not be open to me. I also come to know at first hand, or become aware at first hand, of an experience that I could not otherwise have known. When, therefore, I wonder what it would be like to be a Martian, I am wondering what it would be like to have first hand knowledge of the experience of a Martian. What I am aware of here is not the sort of thing that can be talked about at all. If it were, there would be no difference between hearing a description of it, and knowing it at first hand for oneself. But obviously there is a world of difference between the two—a difference that we recognize if we are not suffering from Left Wing perversity. And it is this immediate experience that I am interested in when I wonder what it is like to be a Martian."

This objection is puzzling because it is so very compelling and yet hardly bears looking at. What is it "to know something at first hand?" When we say, for example, "I know at first hand what it is like to smoke opium," we are normally saying that other people need not tell me what it is like, because I know this already; that I could, if pressed, produce a lengthy description of it; that, if deliberately given some other drug, I could tell the difference unaided, and, if asked how I told the difference, say: "This stuff hasn't the kick of opium" or something of the sort. And so on. But this is *not* the use of "know at first hand" in this objection. For here "to know at first hand" of the experience of the opium smoker and the Martian is to know something that other people *cannot* tell me about, that is not describable at all, and that is such as to make nonsense of the question: "How do you tell the difference between opium and the stuff you are smoking now?" Again, when we normally talk about "knowing at first hand," we are contrasting this with "knowing at second hand," i.e., learning from someone else. But with what is "knowing at first hand of the experience of the Martian" to be contrasted? Not with "knowing at second hand," because this is logically impossible. Not with "knowing it from my own description," because this is also impossible. However, we now see that it is not contrastable with anything, because "to know the Martian's experience at first hand" is the only way in which I can know it at all. But then this objection simply has not given a use to the expression "to know at first hand." We think it has because we are mistakenly supposing that this expression is being used in the normal way in this objection. Similar difficulties break out when we look at *what* it is that we are supposed to know at first hand, and ask whether we can be mistaken about it, and so forth. Similar difficulties also break out for the other favorite expressions used, such as "immediate experience," "immediate awareness," "direct experience," and "direct apprehension." These expressions are given no use either, and because of this they have disfigured discussions about Behaviorism and the subject matter of psychology.[6] Then, because these terms do not contrast with anything, some of us fall into the trap and say: "Ah! we are obviously dealing with a unique and fundamental mode of cognition. Terms like 'immediate experience' are confusing because we continually suppose them to function here as they do in ordinary speech. We had better, therefore, invent a special technical term to do the job—say 'enjoyment.' " And then we *are* sunk in the traditional philosophical bog!

[6] For such a discussion see Carroll C. Pratt, *The Logic of Modern Psychology* (New York: Macmillan, 1939).

(c) *"The Experience of the Martian" and "the Red Shape"*

But what impels us to produce this objection about knowing at first hand? What is its point? What impels us is the likeness between "the red shape" and "my experience" or "the experience of the Martian," and the point of the objection is to draw attention to this. A red shape presents a stimulus pattern that I react to immediately, in contrast with the surrogate reaction by means of symbols. My experience is like a structured series of such stimulus patterns, including those produced by my own responses, to which patterns I seem to react in the same sort of immediate way. We now identify the properties of the whole with the properties of a part, and suppose that "my experience" is just like "a red shape." We are assisted in this by the parallel talk we use about "a (the) red shape" and "an (the, my) experience." We talk about "noting a red shape" and "noting an experience at the time"; "attending to the red shape" and "attending to the experience"; "very conscious of a red shape" and "very conscious of my own experience at the time"; "laughing at the red shape" and "laughing at the experience." And so on. That is, both expressions function as objects of "awareness" verbs. Naturally, therefore, we are tempted to say: "I can know my experience at first hand." The usefulness of this is that it brings out how, for psychological purposes, "my experience" is like a series of non-surrogate reactions to a series of stimulus patterns; and how it is like the reactions of an organism that is only capable of reacting in a non-surrogate fashion to a series of stimulus patterns consisting of red shapes. This comparison of "my experience" with "a red shape" also helps us to understand why we resist the psychological move to talk about "experience" as reactions to stimuli. For if "my experience" is to function like "a red shape," then this move is like saying: "When you see a red shape, what you are doing is to see a mass of almost invisible red dots." To this the objection is that you are then not aware of a red shape at all. So we object to this move on the ground that it leaves out our experience altogether.

However, we do not *really* want to compare "an (my) experience" to "a red shape" at all. We do not really want it to function like a stimulus word. For if it were to function like this, it would be sensible to ask the embarrassing question: "What receptors do you use to observe it?" Moreover, we can see the point of saying: "I know at first hand the experience I have when I know a red shape at first hand." But what is the point of saying: "I know at first hand the experience I have when I know my experience at first hand?" This is an odd statement in that the main clause is redundant, precisely because we are using "my experience" here to embrace everything that I know at first hand, *including* "my experience of my experience." Yet, when we are aware of a stimulus, we may or may not also be aware of our reaction to it, and hence of our experience when we react to it. Further, if "my experience" were like "a red shape" here, we should be able to talk about it in the same sort of way as we can talk about a red shape. But then the whole point of saying that "I know my experience at first hand" is lost, since "my experience" is now something describable and not just a "raw feel." Finally, this comparison with a red shape suggests that, when I say "I know my experience at first hand," all I am saying is: "I am reacting, or can react, in a non-surrogate fashion to a certain stimulus pattern, viz., my experience." But, as we saw, this suggestion is the very one we resist as "leaving out my experience." Hence to treat "my experience" as a stimulus word or expression, like "a red shape," as the sort of thing that I can know at first hand, is to destroy the whole point of the distinction we want to draw between "experience" and "behavior" when we wonder what it is like to be a Martian.

Incidentally, this should help to make it clear that we cannot use introspection to observe "experience," since this is not an observable something. It is not the case, therefore, that when an experimenter studies a subject he is observing the latter's behavior, but that when he studies himself in the role of subject-observer, he is observing his "experience." In both cases the experimenter is responding to organizations of stimuli, with the difference that in the case of the subject they are produced by another person, but in the case of the subject-observer they are self-produced and the observation-response to them can only be made from a privileged position. Consequently, what an experimenter observes when he takes note of a subject X reacting is not nearly as different as we are apt to think from what he observes when he plays the role of the subject-observer himself.[7]

The conclusion, then, is that our wonder about the experience of the Martian does not require us to draw this distinction between "experience" and "behavior." Our difficulty about his experience is very like our difficulty about that of babies and animals. The diagnosis we have outlined for the former applies, I think, *mutatis mutandis* to the latter also. But while there is yet no such subject as the psychology of Martians, there is of babies and animals. These branches of psychology are closely beset by the philosophical difficulty about experience that I have been dealing with. The advantage of considering the Martian is that this is a much more difficult case, and one on which we are apt to fall back if we start off with infants and mice.

[7] In Ch. I of *Foundations of Psychology, op. cit.*, Professor Boring says that "consciousness is what you experience *immediately.*" This comical and pathogenic remark is the result of overlooking the differences between "consciousness" and stimulus words and expressions like "red shape." "Consciousness" does not seem to be the sort of thing that we experience, or know immediately or directly.

A Difficult Case: The Robot

Now what about robots? Is there any point in keeping the distinction between "experience" and "behavior" in order to distinguish between robots and ourselves? It looks like it because we are inclined to say: "If a robot were to behave just like a person, it would still not have any sensations, or feelings." And this seems to entail saying that we have experience (in the raw feel sense), and that the robot does not have it. But this will not do. For we mean, in part, by "a robot" that the thing in question has no sensations, etc., in the ordinary sense. That is, we normally use the word "robot" in such a way that while it can duplicate our *overt* behavior, it cannot duplicate our internal or *covert* behavior when, e.g., you say "I'm having a funny sensation in my tummy." But we are not aware of this when we are inclined to say: "If a robot were to behave just like a person, it would still not have any sensations." When we say this, we seem to be talking simply about the overt behavior of the robot. But we *want* to talk about its covert behavior as well. It is only if we do this that the objection has any force. Yet, if we do so, we depart from the ordinary use of "robot." The first thing to note, therefore, is this. All that is entailed, on the ordinary use of "robot," is that while *we* can make the internal discriminations etc. required for us "to have a sensation," the robot cannot. Obviously, it is not necessary to use the notion of "raw feel" to describe this difference. We are only tempted now to use this notion if we say "Ah, but 'to make a discrimination,' etc., is not identical with 'having a sensation'—it leaves out something." But this is an old objection by now, which we have already dealt with in principle, and which is, in any case, quite independent of puzzles about robots.

The second thing to note is how the unobserved departure from the ordinary usage of "robot" is apt to muddle us and to make us overlook how we *do* use the word. If we found an alleged robot that behaved, overtly and covertly, just like a person as far as adjusting to stimuli like red shapes and loud noises was concerned, we would be in some doubt, and might say at least two different things. We might say (*a*): "This thing obviously has sensations, and is not really a robot at all, but some new sort of thing altogether—some new type of organism." That is, we might keep to the present use of "robot" ("machine," etc.), stretch the use of "organism" to cover it, and stick to our usual criterion of "having a sensation," viz., manifesting the appropriate behavior-readinesses, and covert and overt behavior. However, we might say (*b*): "This thing can't really have sensations because we know it is a machine and not a living thing." That is, we might stretch the use of "robot" (or "machine") to cover this different case, and thereby, by implication, introduce a new criterion for "having a sensation." For a thing "to have a sensation" it must *now* not only exhibit the appropriate internal and external behavior, but also be, and hence in other situations behave like, a living thing. If we say (*a*), then clearly robots give us no reason for retaining the distinction between "behavior" and "experience." Likewise, if we say (*b*). Suppose we are asked: "If the robot hasn't any sensations at all, and yet behaves in respect of a red shape just as X does, what is the difference between them? Surely you have to say that Mr. X has a certain experience in addition to merely behaving?" Then the answer is: "No, we are not obliged to say this, since the criterion of 'having a sensation' has altered." To say "X has certain sensations when looking at a red shape" is not now *only* to say: "X exhibits appropriate internal and external behavior in respect of it." It is also to say that X exhibits *other* behavior characteristic of an organism. And *this* is the difference to which we point to distinguish between X and the robot. X's behavior towards the red shape is part of the stream of behavior of a living thing; the robot's is not. If we now construct a slide and start supposing the robot to be more and more like a living thing (e.g., eating food, not oil, showing affective disturbances, and so on), then at various points on the slide different individuals will switch to saying (*a*) and so giving it "sensations." General agreement to say (*a*) would perhaps be obtained when we reach a machine that exhibited the robot-like analogue of reproduction, development, and death.

If we overlook semantic points of this sort, we are apt to be confused and taken in by arguments like the one of Broad's so often quoted.[8] "However completely the behavior of an external body answers to the behavioristic tests for intelligence, it always remains a perfectly sensible question to ask: Has it really got a mind, or is it merely an automaton? . . . Since the question can be raised, and is evidently not tautologous or self-contradictory, it is clear that when we ascribe a mind or a mental process to an external body, we do not mean simply that it behaves in certain characteristic ways." This argument is persuasive because (i) Broad is using "external body" (and, by implication, also "robot" and "machine") in the ordinary sense which entails that it has no mind; and (ii) he makes us concentrate unwittingly on the overt behavior of the external body or robot. But if a robot were produced whose covert behavior was also like ours, then the question: "Has it a mind?" will cease to be sensible for those of us who take line (*a*) above and say: "This thing is a new sort of organism." For to say that something is a sort of organism entails saying that it exhibits certain mental functions of some order, low or high. On the other hand, for those who take line (*b*) above, and say the thing is just a new sort of robot, the question: "Has it a mind?" remains sensible but Broad's argument becomes irrelevant. For to these people the criterion of "having a sensation" or "mind" is not merely that

---

[8] See C. D. Broad, *The Mind and Its Place in Nature* (London: Routledge & Kegan Paul, 1925), Ch. XIV.

the thing should satisfy certain behavioristic tests, but that it should also be, and hence behave like, an organism. Consequently, the question: "Has it a mind?" remains sensible, and has a negative answer. But now this argument is of no use to Broad. All it establishes is that by "mind" we do not mean "external bodies behaving in certain characteristic ways." It does not help him to establish that by "mind" we do not mean "organisms behaving in certain characteristic ways." But it is *this* question in which behavioristic psychologists are interested; it is to them that Broad specifically addressed himself and for whom his argument is irrelevant.[9]

Some Other Sources of the Problem

So far I have pointed to some of the causes of the philosophical difficulty we are in about "behavior" and "experience." There are *many* others. Here are a few of the many.

1. "If, when I see a red shape, I am supposed to be behaving only and not experiencing anything, what is this stimulus to which I am reacting? If you say it is the physical energy or the light waves, then I don't react to these at all—I may know nothing about them. If, on the other hand, you say it is the red shape, then this red shape is not a physical stimulus, but a 'seen' or 'experienced' something. So I am not just behaving. I am experiencing something."

2. There are all the sentences where we use predicates of sensations, e.g., "The sensation was intense," "It was a painful sensation." These sentences are used for all the sensory modalities and for all the respects in which "sensations" vary in quality, intensity, extensity, and duration. These sentences lead us to want to say that there are such things as mental states, processes, and events with properties, and so lead us to resist noting how the experience we want to talk about has no properties at all.

3. There are all the sentences where we use "feeling" and "emotion" words and expressions in ways comparable to the ways we use "sensation" words and expressions.

4. There is the array of sentences where we use "conscious of," "aware of," and their variants.

5. There are the sentences where we say, e.g., "I was ashamed of myself," or "I was acutely self-conscious at the time," or "That child is still charmingly unself-conscious."

All these sentences in 2 to 5 can be used to frame an indefinite number

[9] Confusing talk on this topic, however, is not the monopoly of the philosophers. Boring and Hull have both argued that psychological subjects should be regarded as robots, and Boring has suggested substituting "robotology" for "psychology." See Boring, *American Journal of Psychology, op. cit.;* and C. L. Hull, *Principles of Behavior* (New York: Appleton-Century-Crofts, 1943), Ch. I.

of specific objections of various sorts to the diagnosis offered—as I have done in 1. I shall not consider any more objections here. What I have said, therefore, is inevitably something of a hit or miss affair. If the sources which I have discussed are also the chief sources for any given individual, then what I have said may help him to become aware of, and acquire control over, the sources of the difficulty in the special form it takes with him. I shall venture the hypothesis that when an objection is raised, it will be obtained from some sources that I have not noted. Hence I suggest that when one is raised, it should not be looked on as an objection to a philosophical thesis, because I have not produced one—although misleading language in places, adopted for brevity, may convey this idea. I suggest, rather, that an objection be looked on and treated in the *sort* of way I have tried to do above. In the course of doing this, the gaps in my diagnosis of this philosophical problem will be amply revealed.

The Relevance of This Account

Let me summarize the bearing of all this on the problem that faces the physiologists and psychologists.

We noted the crucial difficulty that faces the physiologists. If their science is to give a complete account of what happens when a person, for example, sees something, this mental event or process of "seeing" is either reducible to, and so identical with, some neural events, or else it does not exist. Neither alternative is acceptable. Hence it cannot give a complete account. Now, if it is said that a simple reflex reaction, like the knee jerk, is just a matter of certain neural events or processes, and can be completely accounted for in neural terms, neither plain man nor physiologist resists this suggestion. But if it is said that "seeing" is just a set of neural events, no matter how complex, we all protest because we want to say that "seeing" is not just a matter of reacting, as the knee jerk was, but something else as well, which is now being left out. I have tried to point to some of the sources of this protest. If we appreciate them, we may then be readier to appreciate the futility (a) of saying: "But when I see something, all that is happening is that certain neural events (or processes) are taking place"; and (b) of adding: "This is false" (or "absurd" or some similar remark). It is futile to say (a) because the ordinary discourse of plain men and physiologists makes it patently false. This leaves them very uneasy about the proposed identification with nervous processes, and vulnerable to the usual objections against it. Their uneasiness becomes intolerable when they are trapped into discussing the question by means of the antithesis of "mental" and "material," or "mental" and "neural." For this use of "mental" is itself a product of the dualistic tradition in philosophy. Hence to argue for identity by means of the words "mental" and "material" is to use self-destructive weapons. But it is equally futile to say (*b*) "It is false (absurd) to identify 'seeing' with any neural events." For this suggests that it is quite all right to presuppose there are two sorts of events here anyway. But, if pressed, we *can* only defend this presupposition by falling back on "seeing" as a raw feel experience. I hope this is clear from what has already been said. When we do appreciate this, we also see the point of saying that mental events *are* identical with neural ones. But if the "mental events" are the queer "raw feels" that we have discussed, then we also see that it is absurd to *try* to identify them with neural ones, because they are not the sorts of things that can be identified with anything else. They are not like the transmission of an electric current that can be identified with the passage of a nervous impulse. So even to *talk* about "seeing" etc., and "neural events" in the way that this traditional Adrian-cum-Ewing line[10] does talk about them will just produce intellectual confusion.

Similar remarks apply to the parallel difficulty that confronts psychologists. (i) If all that goes on, when X looks at a red shape, is that X is just discriminating, is in a state of behavioral readiness, etc., then he is not experiencing anything at all. But (ii) if he does experience something, then it is false to say that this experience is identical with his behavior, etc. The first alternative is compelling because if *all* that happens is that Mr. X behaves, etc., then by our *ordinary* use of "behavior" and "experience," it is true to say: "X is not experiencing anything." But this alternative is silly, because if we *were* to discover an X who was producing all the usual behavior, internal and external, we would hesitate and want to say: "X is also experiencing something." The objection to this ("But to say this is to go beyond our evidence") can only be supported by *now* using "experience" in the unusual raw feel way. Alternative (ii) moves us because we normally use "experience" and "behavior" as contrasts. But this alternative is also silly because we can only give it the force we want it to have by unwittingly restricting the use of the word "experience" to "raw feels." Only by doing this can we go on defending the view that "experience" and "behavior" are not identical; and this line of defense is hopeless. It is futile to try to rescue ourselves by admitting that "When, e.g., I see something, all that is happening is that I am reacting, etc."; and it is equally futile for anyone to retort: "But this is absurd (or false)." These moves are futile for reasons similar to those that make the parallel moves futile for the physiologist.

It should be apparent by now that "experience" is a nonobservable something to a physiologist or psychologist; and that, unlike concepts such as "homeostasis" or "the unconscious," he has no need to use or postulate it. Contemporary science, in short, does not seem to require the notion of "experience," and is getting to the brink of rejecting it, in effect, as "unreal" or "non-existent." If the relevant sciences go on developing in this direction, and if Western societies assimilate their work,

[10] For Dr. Ewing again, see "Mental Acts," *Mind*, LVIII (1949), 78.

then it is quite possible that the notion of "experience" will be generally discarded as delusive. If and when this happens, our present philosophical difficulties about it will disappear. But it is just because we are in conflict, and perhaps transition, about the notion that we cannot either accept or reject it at present without absurdity or falsehood. In these respects, the notion of "experience" can be shown to resemble an occult notion like "witchcraft" in a primitive community that is in the process of being acculturated to the West. Philosophical difficulties about "witchcraft" in such a community can be found and constructed that parallel in an uncanny way the difficulties confronting us about "experience." So if we are puzzled by the question, "What does this notion of experience resemble?" we may find it useful to notice the likeness between the capacity of men to have experience, which we still accept, and the capacity of men to exhibit witchcraft, in which primitives still believe.[11]

Some Recommendations about Language

If the confusion we are in at present about this whole question leads us to talk in foolish ways about some concepts in physiology and psychology, how should we talk instead? Now *merely* to recommend that we talk in *this* way rather than *that* is not much use. Merely to recommend, for example, that we talk a Behaviorist jargon will only arouse opposition and do little, if anything, to treat the intellectual confusion we are all in. It is partly for this reason that the recommendations of Physicalists and the American Behaviorists have been of such little help. The place where recommendations are appropriate (when they are appropriate at all) is at the end of a diagnosis of a philosophical difficulty. For we can then better appreciate their value and their limitations. The few recommendations I shall offer briefly must be placed and read in this context.

The negative ones first. Do not contrast mental and material (or physical) events, or mental and neural (or physiological) events. Do not therefore talk about "gaps" between them, e.g., the gap between the sticking of a pin into my finger and the appearance of a sensation of pain in my consciousness. Do not talk about intervening mental events in the chain of causation between the physical events in the sensory and in the motor pathways. Do not speak about consciousness coming in at certain points in the process of neural transmission. Do not use the double terminology that is so common, e.g., "visual sensitivity" and "visual experience," "intensity of response" and "intensity of experience." For psychologists in particular, I suggest the following. Do not succumb

[11] Reference to a work like E. E. Evans-Pritchard's *Witchcraft, Oracles and Magic among the Azande* (Oxford: Clarendon Press, 1937) makes this parallel easy to see and to work out.

to the current physiological talk about "sensations" and "feelings" because of the prestige of physiology as the science that is foundational to psychology. Accept physiological discoveries gratefully, but do not feel committed to using the terminology in which physiologists express them or talk about them. Do not, e.g., take over Adrian-like talk, as S. Smith Stevens does, and speak of the sense organs as "windows" that "start the messages along the nerves, the highways to the brain," which "bare messages themselves . . . we call sensations." [12] Do not use the double terminology indiscriminately—"responses" and "sensations," "sensitivity" and "experience," and so on—under the pretence that psychologists can safely ignore the question, or in the hope of impressing readers with your open-mindedness. Indiscriminate talk will just confuse, and open-mindedness just be exposed for the muddle that it is.

Some positive recommendations. Talk about neural events (or processes) and behavior or conduct, or responses of an organism or person. Or, if you like, talk of physiological and psychological events (or processes). In this case the distinction is one of present convention and convenience only—between those events that are dealt with by people called neurologists or physiologists and those dealt with by psychologists. Get rid of the nuisance words like "sensation," "experience," and so on, by defining them provisionally by means of concepts like: stimulus patterns, a discrimination by an organism, a readiness to discriminate, a discrimination of a discrimination. If we must talk "causally," talk of one causal nexus that assists in providing "the basis" of the capacities and dispositions of the organism. When a neural impulse reaches the cortex, certain other neural events are produced, and these in turn contribute to produce the organism's total response that is its "seeing" or "recognizing" or "having a pain." Talk about the gap in our knowledge as lying between the neural discharge in the cortex and the organism's total response—for this is an empirical gap. Say that when we can fill this gap, we will be able to give the physiological basis of the capacity of the organism, e.g., to recognize something, and of the correlate of his recognition of it on any occasion. Say that when we can do this, we may be able to offer generally acceptable definitions of psychological concepts in physiological terms. Say that when we possess a definitive psychology and physiology, the relation between the two sciences is likely to be this: psychology will use "conduct" or "behavior" notions and no "experience" ones; and these will be definable in physiological terms, so that psychology will be a sub-theory inside physiology.[13] Instead of including "expe-

---

[12] This ghastly quotation comes from Boring, Langfeld and Weld, *op. cit.* To those who know the work of Professor Stevens (of Harvard) and who appreciate his sensitivity to questions of method, it is all the more astonishing and unfortunate that this remark should be in a chapter that he prepared.

[13] It should be obvious that when I speak of "psychology" here I am speaking of "foundational" psychology alone. My remarks at this point, therefore, do not apply to social psychology and to subjects like the psychology of personality.

rience" and "behavior" within the subject matter of psychology, regard the subject matter as including "behavior" only. But add the proviso that this view will cease to have any point as it becomes generally accepted and successfully eliminates the notion that contrasts at present with "behavior."

Final Remarks

The conclusion, therefore, for Adrian and Tolman and Co. is that their worry that they have left out, or are in danger of leaving out, something is needless. Their fears are groundless that their sciences cannot in principle provide accounts that are complete. They *can* get rid of mental events and experience. But they get rid of them in a queer way—by realizing it is just foolish to suppose that there are, or are not, any such things. When they have given us a definitive psychology and physiology, what they will have done is not an impossible and absurd correlation between physiological and mental events. What they will have done is to have given the physiological correlates of behavior. This is quite a feasible thing to attempt; and there is nothing else to do.

This conclusion has a bearing on various philosophical questions. It makes obvious the foolishness of the traditional questions and answers about the relation between mind and matter, and mind and body. So the variants of Materialism, Epiphenomenalism, Interactionism, and so forth are left behind as inadequate treatments of the problem involved. It shows, for example, in a new way just *what* an extraordinary doctrine is Reductive Materialism, and how equally extraordinary is the usual refutation of it. This conclusion also reveals the queerness in a question like: "How do I know I am conscious?" and suggests, as we have noted, that "my consciousness" is not the sort of thing I am immediately aware of. It also has a bearing on the "other minds" puzzle. For the question: "Do you feel pain when you squeak?" is bogus in so far as it is a question about a "raw feel"; but it is empirical and difficult in so far as it is a request for further information about your covert responses.

A point about method. I have already mentioned one respect in which my remarks in this paper may not be of help. There is another, even more obvious respect. I said at the outset that this paper would be an attempt to deal with a problem felt by physiologists and psychologists. But what I have done (in fact) is to treat the difficulty as *I* felt it by doing some "self-analysis" (to borrow Karen Horney's term). The paper represents a summarized record of some of that self-analysis. This will only be of service to physiologists and psychologists in so far as I have appreciated the problem as it confronts them. To obtain this appreciation I have tried to observe their behavior in respect of it. But this is a very difficult thing to do well; and my effort at what social anthropologists would call "field work" was quite certainly not careful enough. So my appreciation of the psycho-physiologists' problem is likely to be defective. Consequently, my self-analysis may not be nearly as helpful to them as I should like it to be.

II 〜 The Concept of Mind

John Wisdom

.This paper is not a review of Professor Ryle's book *The Concept of Mind* but it is an attempt to criticize and at the same time to continue it. Before coming to the criticism, may I say how much I admire the power, the simplicity, and the grace of Ryle's work. It is an achievement and a part of the progress of philosophy.

Wittgenstein said that we have the idea that the soul is a little man within, and also that we have the idea that within us is a mental mechanism. Ryle says (p. 22) that he will be concerned with the dogma of the ghost in the machine. He has assembled a thousand instances to illustrate the influence and demonstrate the menace of the myth, the myths, of the hidden stream, the concealed mirrors, the private pictures, the invisible incidents, the flames of passion fanned by the winds of fancy.

I am not suggesting that Wittgenstein's treatment of the metaphysics of mind is not very different from Ryle's. He did not neglect what Ryle never adequately recognizes, the difference between the method of verification of statements about thoughts and feelings and the method of verification of statements about the movements of wheels, levers, limbs, electricity, and the wind that bloweth where it listeth, visible to none though we hear the sound of it.

To come to the ghost, Stuart Hampshire, in his excellent review in *Mind* of Ryle's book, says that Ryle has given the impression that philosophers have foisted this myth, these myths, on the masses, and that this impression is a false one. He is right, surely? Philosophers have made us aware of the myth and in such a way as to increase its power, not free us from it. But it wasn't they who impregnated our talk and thought with this myth. And this is important to the explanation of its merits and demerits.

Hampshire points out that Ryle often draws attention to the evils of the myth in a misleading way. He says: "On what grounds does Professor Ryle decide that there are no acts 'answering to such verbs as "see," "hear," "deduce," and "recall" '?" Ryle here has put his point in the old form: "There are no such things as so-and-so's"—compare "There is no such thing as matter," "Belief in the causal connection is superstition," "There are no such things as infinite numbers," "There are no such things as numbers," "Universals do not exist," "We have the idea that the meaning of a word is an object" (Wittgenstein). Russell began to put part of Ryle's point when he wrote "Empirically I cannot discover anything corresponding to the supposed act" (*Analysis of Mind*, p. 17). No sea serpents in the depths of the ocean, no acts behind the "presentational continuum" (an old phrase from Ward's *Principles of Psychology*).

The old form for putting a metaphysical point, namely, "There are no such things as so-and-so's," tempts people to object in the old inappropriate but powerful way in which Moore objected to "There are no material things." Moore said: "I have two thumbs. Thumbs are material things." It also tempts people to reply in the newer inappropriate way: "The question 'Are there any so-and-so's?' asked metaphysically is meaningless." [1]

Moore forces those who say "There are no so-and-so's" to hasten to explain that they mean "There are no so-and-so's over and above such-and-such's, that so-and-so's are nothing but such-and-such's, that so-and-so's are logical fictions though not fictions, that they are logical myths not myths." (This is still not what they mean but it is a great improvement.) And Ryle has explained that this is what he means to say. He writes (p. 22): "I am not, for example, denying that there are mental processes. Doing long division is a mental process and so is making a joke. But I am saying that the phrase 'there occur mental processes' does not mean the same sort of thing as 'there occur physical processes,' and therefore that it makes no sense to conjoin or disjoin the two."

To conjoin or disjoin the two is to make what Ryle would call a "category mistake" comparable to that made by a child who, having observed the passing of men and guns, asks "And has the division passed, too?"

He says (p. 22): "The 'reduction' of the material world to mental states and processes, as well as the reduction of mental states and processes to physical states and processes, presupposes the legitimacy of the disjunction 'Either there exist minds or there exist bodies (but not both).'" This shows that he does not mean by the reduction of X's to Y's the claim that there are no X's, over and above Y's, but the claim that there are no X's, only Y's. Thus the average man is not reducible, in Ryle's sense, to individual men. He does, however, often use words which suggest that he does wish to say that in the sense in which the average man is reducible to individual men the mind is reducible to the body, that in the sense in which the passing of a division is reducible to the passing of men and guns, mental processes are reducible to bodily processes, that consciousness is to its manifestations as electricity to its manifestations.

[1] For example Carnap, "Empiricism, Semantics, and Ontology," *Revue Internationale de Philosophie*, IV (1950), 25.

And now two things emerge—one is, I submit, a confusion and the second an inadequacy in Ryle's work—a serious inadequacy.

The confusion is one which has lasted since James's exposition of his theory of emotions and of thought. He didn't make clear whether what he was concerned with was the connection between (1) statements about emotions and (2) statements purely about the bodily changes associated with emotions or with the connection between (1) statements about emotions and (2¹) statements about the feelings and sensations of the bodily manifestations associated with emotions. It is true that statements only about the bodily changes associated with an emotion are not sharply separated from those which are also about the sensations of those changes. "He is shivering," even "His breathing is harsh," usually tell not only of bodily changes but also of how he feels—though not when he is plainly under an anaesthetic. "He is walking very fast" many philosophers would call a description of bodily performance and "He is thinking about the trade cycle" a description of a mental performance. And yet both are both—like the novelist's "He turned away, his eyes filled with tears." Ryle sets this fact in the light. But though many statements which philosophers would call descriptions of bodily performance are not merely that, and there are no statements about sensations to which nothing about bodily symptoms is relevant, it remains true that a philosopher who is concerned with "How do I know I am wishing for this, fearing that, thinking of so-and-so, since all I know is that my heart is fluttering or feels as if it is, that I have a sinking feeling, that I hear as it were a voice? How can I from these presentations that float on the stream of mental activity know the condition of the currents in it?" is concerned with a very different problem from that which concerns the philosopher who asks "How do I know from the fluttering of Bill's heart that he has a feeling as of his heart fluttering?"

There are two myths: the myth of the stream of pure spiritual activity on which or in which float patches of oil, sensations and images, and the myth of the inner, mental, spiritual, sensual, stream which drives the bodily machine and is in its turn affected by that machine. The reduction of the spiritual to the sensual is Sensationism about mental events. It corresponds to Sensationism about material events. The two combined give Neutral Monism. The reduction of the sensual and, with it, the spiritual to the material is Materialism. In both cases only when categorical statements about that which is to be reduced are presented as involving hypothetical statements about that to which it is reduced are the doctrines not obviously utterly absurd.

This brings us to the second point—Ryle's insufficient explanation of the purpose of his demonstration of the omnipresence in our minds of the model of the hidden stream, his insufficient explanation of the purpose and merits of that model, and the consequent insufficiency of his explanation of the defects of that model.

All this begins to emerge if we ask "What is the dispute between Ryle and Hampshire? One of them says 'Our language is riddled with the myth of the ghost in the machine,' the other says 'Certainly, certainly our language is riddled with the myth of the ghost in the machine.' " Only the tone of voice is different.

Plain men and philosophers have continually presented the peculiarities in the way classes of statements are known as a peculiarity in their subject matters, as a peculiarity in the sorts of things to which they refer, that is, they have presented the peculiarities of the ultimate logical characters of statements in the form of myths of other worlds—the world of legend, the universe of fiction, the womb of Time, the realms of logical space. But what's the harm? What's the harm of a myth impregnating our language? And what is the harm of developing and rendering explicit that myth?

To plain men, by and large, no harm. It is true, perhaps, that for every class of statements there are outlying areas on the manifold of discussions in which they appear where the myth in them bedevils discussion. And with some classes of statements these areas are more important to us and larger than with other classes. This is true, I think, of ethical statements and also more than we realize of statements about minds. But exactly how it is that misleading models of statements about minds mislead discussion carried on *in* these statements it is not easy to bring out, any more than it is easy for a psychoanalyst to assemble in a moment the evidence to prove that a person is dominated and harmed by a model from the past, by the idea, for example, that "They are all against me."

It is easier to bring out how a myth harms discussion *about* a class of statements, that is, it is easier to bring out how the myth suggested by a language in which a class of discussions is conducted befuddles those who step back and consider the discussions themselves—in short, metaphysicians. For the befuddlement shows in curious skepticism, in talking of a class of statements as myths without realizing that speaking in this way one is misleadingly employing a myth—that of proving a myth a myth, that of proving harpies fictions.

Ryle, of course, realizes that minds aren't myths like harpies or sea serpents—that it is to use a myth to call them myths. And he says so. And his proof of the prevalence of the myth or myths he speaks of is not invalidated by his sometimes expressing himself in terms of that myth. The proofs a philosopher offers of "There are no integers" are not invalidated by the fact that he puts his point in terms of the very myth he purposes to extinguish. Ryle's point is that statements about minds are not related to what in the end gives a man a right to make them, as statements about a temporarily hidden mechanism to that which makes us guess it is present.

Nevertheless, it seems to me that Hampshire is not being merely doctrinaire when he claims that Ryle's exposition is in places obscured by being put in terms of the logical model the fascination of which it is designed to destroy and does destroy. Had Ryle put his point more often in terms of a misleading pattern for the ultimate logic of a class of statements he would have said more of the purpose of exposing the inadequacy of that pattern.

He may reply "The purpose of saying that our language is riddled with this myth is to say that our language is riddled with this myth; the purpose of saying that we continually talk as if the logic of statements about thoughts and feelings were what it is not is to say just that." He may say that he doesn't wish to put his point in the form "Philosophers, metaphysicians, have got into difficulties about how we know what we claim to know about minds. These difficulties are removed by noticing how we are dominated by the idea that a mind is a hidden stream."

Again Ryle may reply that my accusation is false and that he has made it clear that he aims to give such an apprehension of the logic of the soul that one will not be troubled by such questions as "How does a man know from the images and feelings which float on the surface of the stream of spiritual activity the currents in that stream or whether it exists at all? How does a man know from the behavior and surroundings of another the feelings of the other?" "How does a mental state explain a bodily act?"

But I submit that he has not. The peculiarity of the soul is not that it is visible to none but that it is visible only to one. Unless we understand this we cannot understand why people have so persistently clung to the model for the logic of the soul which gives rise to skepticism not only about the mental acts of others but also about their aches and pains, feelings of quickened heart beats, sensations as of voices, daggers, snakes.

Ryle rightly stresses the fact that pictures in the mind are not like pictures in a gallery, that statements about what is in or on the mirror of the mind have a different logic from those about what is in the mirror on the mantelpiece and that sensation, or the "observation of the presentational continuum," has a different logic from the observation of a film, and that knowledge that one is observing the presentational continuum or this or that in it, for example knowledge that one is seeing as it were snakes, has a different logic from knowledge that one is observing a film or this or that in it. He rightly insists that if we talk of sensations as observations and then of these observations as reasons, everything falls into confusion if we expect the same of these reasons as we expect of the reasons garnered from the observation of the scenes of a show.

I don't think he explains clearly *how* things fall into confusion and how solipsism and subjectivism are born, but that is not my point. My point is that, though the sources of solipsism are also sources of doubt about the minds of others, there is also a source of this doubt other than those sources of it which also lead to solipsism. And this source lies in the facts covered by the words "The soul is visible only to one."

What are these facts? They are the facts which lead people to say that a person has a way of knowing how he feels which no one else has, has a right to say what he does about how he feels which no one else has ever had or ever will have.

But what are the facts which have led them to say this? And do these facts justify the skeptic in saying "No one but Bill really knows how Bill feels. No one but Bill has any real reason for saying anything about how Bill feels"?

First, what are the facts which have led people to say that a man can know himself in a way others can't? They are the same as those which have led people to say that other people have a peculiar difficulty in knowing how a man feels.

One might think that the special facility and the special difficulty lie in the fact that while Bill, if he is in pain, has every right to say that Bill is in pain, Arabella has not because she is in pain the right to say Bill is in pain. Bill, when he feels a choking in his throat, has a reason for saying he is angry, while Arabella has not because she has a choking in her throat a reason for saying that Bill is angry.

But isn't this an accident? Suppose Arabella, having a pain or a choking feeling, says with confidence "Bill is in pain" or "Bill is angry" and suppose that she is again and again right. We should say "Extraordinary thing, she knows from her own feelings that Bill is in pain or angry—as if she were Bill himself." Were she never to learn of the success of her telepathy we should not say that her confidence was reasoned and hardly that it was reasonable, any more than we say this of the young antelope who instinctively knows that lions are dangerous. But we should say that she had every reason for her confidence once she had learned of the unvaried correctness of her claims, like the antelope that has been repeatedly clawed. Again, from a sensation of snakes in blue or in a monogram B, I, L, Arabella might know that Bill was having a sensation as of snakes or was in for the horrors.

Under such circumstances we would say that Arabella has an extraordinary knowledge of Bill's mind, that she can see into his mind, that while the rest of us have to guess from external signs at what is in his mind, she can know what is in his mind as well as he can himself and in the way he does himself. Like Bill, because she has a sensation as of snakes, she has a right to say "Bill sees as it were snakes"; a choking feeling in her throat, angry words coming to her mind, give her the right to say "Bill is angry" as they do Bill himself; other pictures, other feelings, give her the right to say "Bill's in love."

But the philosophical skeptic says "Do they *as* they do Bill himself?" No doubt some people do, much more than others, know how another person is feeling by "feeling themselves into" the other person, and the connection between this and telepathy deserves attention. But the question at the moment is "Does the philosophical skeptic when he says that a person, A, never really knows how another, B, feels refer to the fact that it seldom or never happens that one person knows the mind of another as we have imagined Arabella to know Bill's mind, that is altogether from feeling as she feels Bill feels?"

And the answer is No. For in so far as a person is referring to this fact, whether or no he is right is to be settled by investigation and experiment, not by philosophical reflection. If someone says philosophically "One can never really know the mind of another, only the way he lays back his ears and frowns" and we say to him "That is upon the whole true but it is said that sometimes a person knows the mind of another without at all relying upon external signs and for good or ill this sort of thing may become more common," then the philosopher will reply "I don't think you quite understand. I am not denying that there occur the most striking instances of telepathy, of a person knowing from his or her own feelings the mind of another. But such a person wouldn't be really and directly knowing the mind of another. Even one with such insight as Arabella's would not because she saw as it were snakes have that right to say that Bill sees as it were snakes which Bill has because he sees as it were snakes."

It might now be thought that what the philosopher refers to is the fact that while what gives Bill the right to say that he sees as it were snakes or is in for the horrors is *his* sensation of as it were snakes, what gives a telepathic person the right to say that Bill sees as it were snakes or is in for the horrors is *her* sensation of as it were snakes. I am sure that some skeptics about the minds of others would seek to prove their point this way. But this proof proves that no one really knows there's a snake in the grass just as much as it proves that no one really knows that there's a snake in Bill's mind. And therefore let us now ignore this proof; for we are concerned with a skeptic who finds in some feature of our knowledge of the mind of others a reason for saying that we never know the minds of others, which reason does not plunge him into solipsism and make him say we can never know whether or no there's a snake in the grass.

We must now again try to say what that feature is. It is this: while one can from one's own sensation as of a snake have a right to say that there is a snake in the grass *in the way anyone* can, one cannot from one's own sensation as of a snake have a right to say that there is a snake in someone else's mind *in the way he* can because of his sensation as of a snake. And the familiar but complicated facts to which this refers are the following: suppose that a certain person, Arabella, upon seeing as it were snakes, says "Bill sees as it were snakes." Upon being asked, Bill says he sees no such thing. Arabella is impressed by this but doesn't regard it as proving her wrong; instead she asks the rest of us whether we can see snakes, and when we say "Yes, we can," she says "There you are, Bill sees them." "But," we say, "look, he has blundered into them." "Ah," she says, "he saw them all right. I can see them, you can see them, the camera can see them. That settles it." In this story we have indeed arranged that Arabella shall know as well as Bill what Bill sees and that the rest of us can do so too. And with this we have arranged too much. For if Arabella uses the words "Bill sees as it were snakes" in the way described, then with them she makes a statement of a well-known sort, a statement whose familiar features now begin to show through its disguise, the statement "Snakes, real, live, snakes."

We must tell a different story if we are to tell one of how Arabella knows as well as Bill the snakes in his mind. We must tell a story in which it doesn't turn out that what she is talking about are real snakes. And we can easily do this. Suppose that Arabella, elated by many proofs of her telepathic powers, now on a new occasion says "Bill sees snakes." We ask Bill and he says he does not see snakes. We may, because of Arabella's past successes as a telepathist, suspect that Bill is lying and that later he will say he did see snakes. But if he does not and this happens again and again and Arabella pays no more attention to the evidence we offer against her statements than she would have done had she made them of herself, then we say "When Arabella says 'Bill sees snakes,' although she uses Bill's name, what she says amounts to 'I see snakes' or 'I see snakes and have a feeling about Bill.' She has lost her power of insight into Bill's mind and conceals this from us and from herself by using still the words 'Bill sees snakes' while using them in such a way that all that counts in a dispute as to whether he does is just the same as what counts in a dispute as to whether she does."

If we talk about Bill as Arabella does and ignore or treat lightly Bill's protests, then, of course, we may say, as she, perhaps, does, that she knows better than Bill how he feels or what he fancies.

"Exactly so," says the skeptic, "when Arabella's statement becomes really one about herself she knows better than anyone else whether it is right, but while it is still about Bill she doesn't know it to be right like she would were it about herself, that is, like Bill does."

It is true that the circumstances which make us say of a statement, S, made by A that A has a right to make it just like B has a right to make a statement about how things seem to him, are also the circumstances which make us say that S is not about how things seem to B but about how things seem to A. It thus appears that it is perfectly true that A cannot make a statement about how things seem to B and have a right to say it just like B has.

Now it is not unnatural to express this by saying that A never has that reason for a statement about how things seem to B which B has. And it is not unnatural to express this by saying that when one person makes a statement about the mind of another then he never has all the reason one could have for such a statement.

And this leads to "No one ever knows anything about the mind of another." For though we often speak of a person knowing something even when he hasn't all the reason he could have for what he says—for example, we say that a man knows that a stream is flowing because he sees the mill wheel turning—in these cases we speak of knowledge only because, though on the particular occasion in question the person of whom we speak hasn't all those reasons one could have for what he says, on other occasions he has been better placed and has had, not only the reasons he has on this occasion, but also those which one better placed would have—seen beneath the wheel the water. Further, it is only because one who sees a mill wheel turning has on other occasions had other reason to say that the water is high today that we allow that now seeing the mill wheel turning, he has a right to say "The water's high today."

Now we have said that no one who makes a statement about the mind of another *ever* has the right to make it which that other has, that therefore he never has had all the reason one could have for the statement he makes.

It is tempting to infer that no one ever knows anything about the mind of another and even that no one ever has any right to assert anything about the mind of another, since it is not true of him that on some other occasion he has been better placed and had then the reason, the ground, the data, the premise, he now lacks.

But we must notice that if we express the facts referred to by the soul is visible only to one by saying that a person, A, never has all the right, all the reason, one could have for a statement about the mind of B, then we are using these words here very differently from the way we use them when we say of one who sees only a mill wheel that he hasn't on this occasion all the reason one could have for what he says about the mill stream. One who sees only the mill wheel could have all the reason one could have for what he says about the stream and could have all the reason he could have for what he says about the stream. One, A, who has all the reason one ever has for a statement about the mind of another, B, couldn't have all the reason one could have for what he says —not in the sense of "has all the reason one could have" which requires that he should have the reason B has, in the sense which requires that, like B, he need not look to the face of another for confirmation of what he says. For such a requirement guarantees that what he says is not about another but about himself. When we say of one who sees only the mill wheel that he hasn't all the reason one could have for what he says about the stream one contrasts him with someone better placed. But if because of the facts about statements about the minds of others of which the skeptic reminds us we say that no one ever has all the right one could have, all the reason one could have, for a statement about the mind of another, then we contrast ourselves with no one, in earth or heaven. If we use "has all the right he could have" in the way the skeptic does, then "A has all the right he could have for a statement about the mind of B" becomes self-contradictory. And if we wed in the usual way "has all the reason he could have" to "has all the right he could have" then "A has all the reason he could have for a statement about the mind of B" becomes self-contradictory. And if we then wed in the usual way "knowledge" to "sometimes has all the reason he could have," then "A has knowledge of the mind of B" becomes self-contradictory and the paradox that no one ever knows the mind of another a necessary truth.

It is not unnatural to describe the facts about the usage of statements about people, particularly about what is in their minds as opposed to what is in their stomachs, by saying that the person the statement is about can have a right to·make it which no one else has. It is tempting then to say that the person the statement is about can have reason to make it which no one else can have. It is tempting then to say that he can know the statement to be true in a way no one else can and then to say that no one else can really know it to be true. But we do not in fact in connection with statements about thoughts and feelings use the expression "has all the right *a* person could have" like we use "has just the sort of right some person could have, including the person it is about"; still less do we use "has all the right *one* could have" in this way; still less do we use "has all the right *he* could have" in this sense in which no one could have all the right he could have. Nor do we use "has all the reason one could have" in this way. Still less do we use "one knows how he feels" in this way, that is, in such a way that one could not, because one could not without having reason for saying it in that sense in which it is senseless to say that one could. That is, we do not use these expressions in such a way that "No one has real right, real reason, to make, real knowledge of, statements about the minds of others" is a necessary truth. In other words, when in the course of life we say "Arabella knows how Bill feels, Clarissa does not" we do not mean to deny that, were Arabella to make a statement about how Bill feels according to how *she* feels just as Bill does according to how *he* feels, then she would be making a statement not about Bill but about herself. So if we express the fact that it is ridiculous to speak of her doing this by saying that Arabella must always lack reason Bill could have, and therefore reason one could have, for statements about the mind of Bill, we must remember that this form of words means the facts it refers to and no more, and that these are not facts from which it follows that she never knows the thoughts and feelings in Bill's mind. When we claim that someone knows the thoughts and feelings of another we do not deny any of those facts about what ultimately gives a right to make statements about thoughts and feelings to which the skeptic draws our attention. And therefore what the skeptic says does not show that what we claim could not be true nor that what we claim is false.

This does not show that what we claim is true, it does not settle the question whether sometimes we do know what is in the mind of another. This is a question of fact and not of philosophy. But the fact is we do.

III ❧ Behavior

D. W. Hamlyn

One of the distinctions which Aristotle makes is that between ἐνέργεια (activity) and κίνησις (movement). κίνησις itself is sometimes said to be an ἐνέργεια, but one which is ἀτελής (incomplete), while ἐνέργεια in the proper sense is ἐνέργεια τοῦ τετελέσενου (activity of the complete).[1] The sense of "complete" here may be given by saying that an activity is something which contains its end in itself, which is carried out for its own sake, and not, as in the case of movement, for the sake of something else.[2] κίνησις, Aristotle says, arises out of a δύναμις (a potentiality) and may lead to a ἕξις (a state or disposition). The ἐνέργεια itself is the realization of that ἕξις. Perfect activity would be quite independent of any potentiality (ἄνευ δυνάμεως) but human activities only approximate to this state of affairs which is characteristic of the divine. The πρᾶξις (conduct) with which ethics is concerned is one form of ἐνέργεια.

This seems to be an important distinction, which has consequences for any form of study which is concerned with human affairs—for example, for psychology and ethics. (It has, indeed, importance for any form of study which is concerned with anything which is capable of forming a ἕξις, in Aristotle's sense.) Certain things can be said of activities which cannot be said of movements, and one such is reflected in the way in which Aristotle defines the distinction. To say that a movement is incomplete is to say that it is made for the sake of something outside itself. Its final cause is not in itself. But to talk of final causes is one way, and perhaps a misleading way, of referring to the reasons for which the movement is made. No movement is in itself and by itself intelligible. It is always possible to ask why it was made (if it can be said to be made rather than merely to occur, if it can be said to be an ἐνέργεια of any sort, even ἀτελής), and one form of answer is that in terms of "in order to . . . ," or in terms of "because" where there is a sentence beginning with this which is equivalent to one beginning with "in order to." Thus if someone moves his hand towards a pillar-box, and is asked why he made the movement, he can say, "In order to post a letter," or "Because I

---

[1] Cf. De An. 417a, 16; 431a, 6; Phys. 201b, 31; 257b, 8.
[2] Cf. Eth. Nic. 1174a, 13 ff., where Aristotle says that movement could be complete, if at all, only ἔν ἅπαντι τῷ χρόνῳ.

wanted to post a letter." At the same time it may be possible for someone, say a scientist, to give the efficient cause or causes of that movement,
and in doing so he will be treating the movement as something which
can be said to occur rather than to be made; he may say what produced
the particular muscle-movements in the arm. In the case of an activity it
may, in the same way, be possible for the man to give the same sort of
answer—"I posted the letter in order to fulfil my promise." But it is
intelligible that no answer of that sort should be given. He might refer to
the ἕξις from which the activity is derived—"I posted the letter because
I wanted to," but to do this would be to imply that no further explanation is or need be forthcoming. The action of posting a letter is quite
intelligible in itself; we understand what is going on and at any time
during an appropriate series of movements it is still possible to use intel-
ligibly the phrase "posting a letter." At the same time it would be absurd
to ask for the efficient cause of the activity, as was possible in the case of
a movement. One answer to such a question as "What caused you to post
the letter?" would be, "Nothing *caused* me to post it; I just wanted to."
This is not to say that the causes of activity can never be given in any
sense, for, clearly, if someone posted a letter after having expressed his
intention not to do so, we should be quite justified in asking, "What
made you post it?" and in expecting an answer. Yet this answer would
not give the cause of his posting the letter in the same sense as that in
which a scientist might be said to give the cause of his arm-movement if
he could give an account of its mechanism. Rather it would afford an
explanation of his deviation from expectation, and to refer to the cause
here is an elliptical way of accounting for such a deviation by showing
that it could be subsumed under some law. When someone expresses his
intention of not posting a letter we are justified in expecting him not to
do so. If something occurred to make him alter his decision, then we
should feel that this accounted for his posting the letter—was the cause
of it—if such an occurrence could be said to lead to a change of decision
for the most part. That one occurrence leads to another does not mean
that the first is the efficient cause of the second, though we might use
the word "cause" here in another Humean sense. The fact that we can
use the word both in this case and in the case where a mechanism is
provided in the strict sense reveals the ambiguity of the word. The
mechanism case could be brought within the deviation from expectation
case by saying that it accounts for a movement which is a deviation from
what we would expect if the series of movements were random. But all
the uses of the word "cause" do not imply the possibility of providing a
mechanism. No mechanism can be given of activities, as opposed to
movements. (This, incidentally, shows what is wrong with Freud's
characterization of neurotic symptoms as "mechanisms of defense"; in
some sense the symptoms do provide defense, but they are the means
adopted by the person to secure this, not mechanisms. Freud's hope for

a biology of the mind cannot be fulfilled along these lines, for his explanation of the neurosis is really in terms of what the person does, not in terms of what produces a reaction by that person.)

I take it, then, that the point of Aristotle's distinction, or one of them, is to show that an activity is intelligible in itself—that is, does not necessarily require an explanation in terms of anything else—whilst a movement is not. A movement could not occur unless there was already a possibility of it before it actually occurred. Continual occurrence of a movement in certain situations may, on the other hand, lead to the setting-up of a ἕξις. An activity always arises out of such a ἕξις, and it is a sufficient explanation of it to point to this, though not perhaps an explanation which is always satisfying, however adequate logically. It is a similar point, I take it, which is often made by moralists when they say that an act which is free is one which is derived from the personality of him who exhibits it. Activity which is perfectly free would be activity entirely so derived, the explanation of which could be given entirely in terms of ἕξεις, and none of which is independent of such ἕξεις. In Aristotle's terms, activity which is independent of ἕξεις would be ἀτελής, and thus mere κίνησις, not ἄνευ δυνάμεως.

One of the troubles about the distinction as Aristotle made it is that it sounds as if it is a material distinction, one between different kinds of entity. Are we being presented merely with an account of how activity develops? It may indeed be the case that, with regard to certain features exhibited by a person, to talk of activity is inappropriate, and to talk of movement is not. But where activity is exhibited, it is not necessarily inappropriate to talk of movements, but it will be so to do so in the same context, in the same universe of discourse. To represent the distinction as one between two kinds of entity is misleading, for sometimes the distinction might better be put as one between terms belonging to different modes of talk. Now the term "ἐνέργεια," which is usually translated "activity," is equivalent, where people (or organisms in general) are being talked about, to the term "behavior." The qualification is necessary because Aristotle does not make it concerning "ἐνέργεια"; the term is used for a variety of purposes. However, as my interest is in the study of human affairs, I propose to use the term "behavior" in the following as opposed to "movement" or equivalent terms which I may specify. I am, in general, less concerned with what Aristotle actually says than with the relevance of what I interpret him as saying. In any context, then, in which it is possible to describe a person's behavior, it seems possible also to describe the movements exhibited by him. Such descriptions will not serve the same purpose, and do not belong to the same level of generality. Indeed, it is fair to call descriptions of behavior "interpretative." With movements we are concerned with physical phenomena, the laws concerning which are in principle derivable from the laws of physics. But the behavior which we call "posting a letter" or "kicking a ball" involves a very complex series of movements, and the same movements will not be exhibited on all occasions on which we should describe the behavior in the same way. No fixed criteria can be laid down which will enable us to decide what series of movements shall constitute "posting a letter." Rather we have learned to interpret a varying range of movements as coming up to the rough standard which we observe in acknowledging a correct description of such behavior as posting a letter. Any form of interpretation implies the adoption of some standard; in this case the standard can be only loosely defined. This, too, is implied by the statement that behavior is derived from a ἕξις—a disposition or capacity (Aristotle makes no distinction here; "δύναμις" should sometimes mean "capacity," but "ἕξις" is often used in its place without distinction). To refer to a person's possessing a capacity is not to say what will happen on a certain occasion; it is to indicate only roughly what may perhaps happen, although some restriction is put upon what is capable of happening.

At the same time as we can describe a form of behavior, we can describe the movements which constitute the behavior on this particular occasion. Are there any occasions on which this is not possible? We have seen that there are occasions on which we can describe the movements, but on which there is nothing that can be described as behavior, though where the dividing line comes may well be a moot point. A reflex is clearly not a piece of behavior. Aristotle implies that there are occasions on which we can describe the behavior but not the movements, for he maintains that sometimes the ἕξις and the δύναμις are coincident. Sense-perception is an example.[3] It is odd to call perception and the like "behavior" unless what is meant is the sort of interpretation which is carried out in seeing patterns *as* something. To see something is not to behave in any normal sense; it is, among other things, to come up to the standard implied in our ability to identify that something correctly. "To see" is what Professor Ryle calls an "achievement verb" as opposed to a "task verb." It is significant that in *Metaphysics* 1048*b*, 18 ff. Aristotle hints at such a distinction and uses it to make his familiar distinction between ἐνέργεια and κίνησις.[4] He points out, in effect, that the present and perfect tenses of such verbs as "see" may be used at the same time of any person; and the force of the perfect tense is to point out the achievement. What is odd about the point as made in this passage is that learning is classed as a movement. The fact is, I think, that Aristotle has made one distinction where we should make two. We can distinguish between movements and behavior, and between the latter and achievement. To describe behavior requires interpretation of movements according to certain stand-

---

[3] Cf. *De An.* 417*b*, 18 and *Eth. Nic.* 1174*a*, 14.

[4] Especially *Met.* 1048*b*, 23 ff. ὁρᾷ ἅμα ⟨καὶ ἑώρακε⟩, καὶ φρονεῖ ⟨καὶ πεφρόνηκε⟩, καὶ νοεῖ καὶ νενόηκεν. ἀλλ' οὐ μανθάνει καὶ μεμάθηκεν οὐδ' ὑγιάζεται καὶ ὑγίασται. . . . τούτων δὴ ⟨δεῖ⟩ τὰς μὲν κινήσεις λέγειν, τὰς δ'ἐνεργείας.

ards; to indicate achievement requires interpretation of behavior according to the standard by which we recognize success. Both the terms "behavior" and "achievement" are interpretative though at different levels and in terms of different kinds of standard. Aristotle realizes that there is a distinction to be made, corresponding, in material terms, to that between interpretation and description, and often applies this to behavior and movement, counting perception as a form of behavior. In this passage of the *Metaphysics* he realized that there was another distinction to be made, but instead of making it, he merely shifted the original distinction up a stage, so that what might otherwise be called "behavior" is now called "movement." It might be said in justification that the distinction between ἐνέργεια and κίνησις is really meant to point to the completeness of the former, and that what counts as complete must be relative to the context. Here only success is to count as completeness. But the reason why Aristotle suggests that on some occasions we can describe the behavior but not the movements (where these terms are being used in the ordinary sense and not that as shifted in the passage of the *Metaphysics*), is that he does not see clearly that on these occasions we are not concerned with behavior in the ordinary sense but with achievements. We are concerned with "seeing" and not "seeing-as." "ἐνέργεια" should not be used to cover both.

Students of human affairs may concern themselves with movements only. Physiologists do so and they might have a claim to be members of this class. In doing so they will be able to investigate, among other things, the causal mechanism of these movements; such a mechanism may be very complicated and unlike that involved in classical machines such as clocks. The seventeenth-century view of machines as exemplified by the clock will have to be modified if the movements of animals are to be explained in terms of mechanism. Even if it is too bold to assert that we already know what type of machine is required, we at least know far more than did Descartes. Human movements are not all reflex-like, by any means, and there is some justice in the claim that the simple reflex is, in any case, an abstraction. Granted, however, that it is in principle possible to give an account of some mechanism—perhaps of the self-adjusting type which is now becoming familiar, the study of which has been dignified by the title of "cybernetics"—this mechanism will account for movements only. While physiologists knew little about the structure of the nervous system they were content to deal with such things as reflex action, which is essentially a movement in my sense, though not one which is made by a person; a reflex merely occurs, and we cannot ask for the reason for it, except, perhaps, in terms of a theory of evolution. Any reaction which is more or less mechanical can be classified as of this sort. The increase in our knowledge about the nervous system should not tempt us to suppose that we can do more. No mechanism of any sort can do more than account for movements, reactions, and the like. It may, of course, be the case that a particular movement or series of movements may exemplify a kind of behavior; it may be classifiable as such, and capable of such an interpretation. It is this possibility which permits us on any particular occasion to describe both the movements and the behavior, though to do these things will by no means be to do the same thing. Thus, no mechanism can be given which will account for behavior per se however much we may feel that the behavior will have been accounted for incidentally in providing a mechanism for the movements which constitute behavior on a particular occasion. At other times, however, the movements involved may be different, though we may still describe the behavior in the same way. This is the case because, as Aristotle saw, behavior is derivable from a ἕξις and is explicable either in terms of this or in terms of what is akin to this—the final cause of the behavior. Talk of final causes is akin to talk of ἕξεις because, as I mentioned earlier, both really provide reasons for the behavior and not causes, in our sense. I take it that the ἕξις is, in fact, the formal cause of the behavior. (A certain amount of qualification is needed in attributing these views to Aristotle with consistency. For example, in *Eth. Nic.* 1139a, 31, he says that choice is the efficient cause of action or conduct.[5] It is to be noted that he is forced, in consequence, to consider conduct in this case as a κίνησις. I take it, however, that this is a surrender to common modes of talk, as when we might say, "His hurry is due to (caused by) his decision to catch the next train." The act of choice, the decision, leads to the behavior, it is true, but it does not cause it in any mechanical sense.)

As I have said, Aristotle uses the term "ἕξις" both where the term "disposition" and where the term "capacity" would be appropriate. To attribute a capacity to something implies that it has at least a prima facie claim to be considered intelligent. (Instinctive behavior is prima facie intelligent, but it fails to pass all the tests; e.g., it is too rigid and insufficiently flexible.) Thus if it is said that behavior is derivable from a capacity or capacities, it is implied that such behavior is at least likely to be intelligent. To say that it is derivable from a disposition may or may not imply this. The term "disposition" (in this sense a philosopher's term) is akin to the term "habit," and whereas we often use the latter in order to point a contrast with intelligent or skilful behavior, we may do this in a relative as well as in an absolute sense. That is to say that, sometimes, in saying that something is a matter of habit, we mean to imply that there is nothing intelligent about it, that it was purely mechanical and unthinking. At other times, we may use the term "habit" to point to the relative inflexibility of a mode of behavior, and in this sense it belongs to the same family of terms as "custom" and "usual." In the former sense it belongs to the same family as "reflex" and "automatic."

---

[5] πράξεως μὲν οὖν ἀρχὴ προαίρεσις—ὅθεν ἡ κίνησις ἀλλ' οὐχ οὗ ἕνεκα.

In the latter case it is likely that the habit will not have been instituted without prior behavior which is both intelligent and spontaneous, to some degree or other. If we called such habitual behavior unintelligent, it would be in the relative sense—i.e., in that implied by the epithet "stupid." On the other hand, it would be entirely inappropriate to call a reflex either stupid or intelligent. Behavior can be relatively automatic but never absolutely so. Behavior can always be called intelligent in the sense of that word which is opposed to "mechanical" or "automatic," though not always in that opposed to "stupid." It is sufficient to say that anything which is capable of behavior is capable of being intelligent in this former sense. It is not necessary to attribute to human beings any spontaneity other than this, in which the behavior is explicable by reference to a ἕξις, to the personality of the person concerned. Aristotle is not so clear on this point. Apart from suggestions that positive spontaneity may be attributed to human beings on occasions, he tends to identify reason with the divine; and the divine is said to have ἐνέργεια ἄνευ δυνάμεως. In ordinary beings the forms in which intelligence may be exhibited are limited by the movements which they are capable of making. Aristotle seems to imply that no such limitation exists in the case of the divine. But surely it would be a mistake to identify intelligence with the exercise of pure reason alone.

I think that it will be clear what implications this has for psychology as the science of behavior. The ways in which we may account for behavior will not be the same as those in which we may account for movements. Causes of behavior cannot be given as causes of movements can. It is this very fact that allows us to talk sometimes of behavior as spontaneous. But the proviso must always be added that in the case of any particular case of behavior which is exhibited by a particular series of movements, it may always be possible to give the causes of members of that series, to show that they can be subsumed under specific causal laws. But the laws which deal with behavior will be generalizations of a non-causal sort, if laws are to be formulated in this context. We may say that in certain circumstances people behave in certain ways without implying that the one is the cause of the other. We might, of course, content ourselves with the program of accounting for behavior in terms of the capacities or dispositions from which it is derivable. This, however, is not a scientific program, but one which may be carried out by anyone with sufficient experience of human affairs.[6]

The distinction which, following Aristotle, I have been anxious to make has consequences, also, for two, perhaps connected issues—that of behaviorism, and that of free will together with the implications which any standpoint on the latter issue may have for the question of the function of moral judgments. The thesis of behaviorism was first intro-

[6] Cf. some of the things said by E. Gellner, "Maxims," *Mind*, LX (1951).

duced by John B. Watson as a methodological postulate, and only later did it attain the dignity of a metaphysical theory. As a piece of methodology it is clear that it would be a useful move against those psychologists who confined themselves to the frustrating program of investigating and classifying mental states. It would be useful to point out that often, and perhaps generally, mental states, ideas, and the like occur in the context of particular forms of behavior, and should be looked at in this context. But Watson and his successors were impressed by the conditioned reflex and sought to analyze all human activities in terms of this, even thinking. For reasons which I have given this is a mistake, though there might have been some profit in investigating the mechanisms of movements which constitute behavior on particular occasions. That this mechanism would consist solely of reflexes, conditioned or otherwise, is most unlikely, for reflex movements are not by themselves the sorts of movement which could constitute behavior on particular occasions; reflex movements occur and are not made by the subject, they are not self-adjusting or purposive, in the sense that we could ask the subject why he made the movement. The point which I wish to make is that the thesis that organisms are entities which behave does not *ipso facto* imply that they are machines of the sort presupposed by behaviorists; conversely the thesis that they are machines would not, *ipso facto,* imply that they are not capable of intelligent behavior, as long as a sufficiently liberal view of machines were taken. The main mistake of behaviorism, as it has developed, is that of taking the machinery for the behavior and oversimplifying this. If this mistake is not made there is no bogey to be feared in behaviorism, unless it is the very idea that man may be a machine, albeit a very special one, that is feared. (It must be admitted that the facts of consciousness and all that is implied by that vague expression have to be reckoned with, and to deny this would be foolish, however much it requires analysis.) At any rate as a piece of methodology, behaviorism would be a sound thesis in the modified form which I suggest, in which the distinction between behavior and movements or reactions is made. It is the tragedy of much modern psychology that this distinction has not been made, and much time, labor, and expense has been devoted to the vain task of making impossible identifications. That is to say that attempts have been made to identify behavior in general with mechanical movement of one form or another. Pavlov was right in refusing to call reflexology "psychology," whatever his reasons for this were. Intelligent behavior of any sort is by definition not mechanical, and it is with behavior that psychologists are concerned. Human behavior can be said to be mechanical in a relative sense only. Our ways of accounting for intelligent behavior must be very different from the ways in which we would account for the movements of machines. Nevertheless, it may be the case that the movements in which behavior is exhibited on any particular occasion are explicable in terms of some machine, albeit of a peculiarly subtle sort.[7]

As a metaphysical theory, on the other hand, behaviorism must be wrong, as must all metaphysical theories which, as distinct from speculative theories, depend upon the misuse of language by the failure to make relevant distinctions. It is important to distinguish between the pursuit of metaphysics and speculation, for whereas many metaphysical theories are incidentally speculative, the reverse does not always hold good. When carried on in the appropriate sphere and at the appropriate time, speculation may lead to important discoveries; metaphysical theories of the traditional sort may even prevent discoveries, for it may be thought that conclusions concerning matters of fact may be reached a priori. Part of the seductiveness of many metaphysical theories is due to the fact that they contain statements whose status is uncertain; apparently empirical propositions may be given a character of logical necessity (e.g., statements about sense-data), or partial truths may be generalized. As a form of materialism, behaviorism denies dualism in its Cartesian form and in this, perhaps, it is right. But this does not mean that it is right as a positive thesis any more than idealism. Behaviorists may have been right in pointing out that we do not need to assume a pure ego as a cause of activity, but this does not mean that behavior is merely mechanical. For to assume this would be to deny what is obvious—that there is a sense in which we may be said to have a mental life; and in whatever sense this is true, it is true in the one which is implied in saying that we have some degree of intelligence. Enough has been said by Ryle to make it unnecessary to labor that point. As it is, by its very negativeness, behaviorism has been a hindrance to the progress of the science of behavior in the true sense. As was the case with sensationalism before it, it has been based upon an atomism (in the one case that of sensations, and in the other that of reflexes), and has consequently presented the problem of how an intelligent animal can be built up out of such atoms. Both the Gestalt Psychologists and those who, like Dilthey and others, have espoused an "understanding psychology" as a cultural science, have been justified in their protests against it. But such protests should not themselves be couched in metaphysical terms. In pointing out that organisms capable of intelligent behavior are not merely mechanical, the mistake should not be made of making the term "organic" or similar terms such as "gestalt" a source of mystery. Again, because behaviorism of itself cannot help us to understand intelligent behavior, it should not be assumed that no psychology, as a natural science, can deal with behavior. It is true that we can always talk of behavior in an interpretative fashion,

---

[7] This amounts to a modification, perhaps an important one for some purposes, of what Ryle says on mechanism (*Concept of Mind* [London: Hutchinson's University Library, 1949], pp. 75 ff.), though in other ways it will be obvious that this account is in line with his.

referring to an organism's achievements, reasons, capacities, and the like, but this does not mean that no laws or generalizations can be formulated concerning behavior. Clearly the more we know of the conditions under which people behave as they do, the better shall we be able to apply our interpretations also. If Freud had not told us of the correlation between certain childhood occurrences and behavior in later life, we should understand neurotic symptoms far less. Only the methods of natural science can enable us to establish such correlations. A cultural science could not exist without such matters of fact being known first.

Behaviorism is, then, a bogey. By making a false identification of behavior with movements it has suggested that human and animal behavior may be mechanical. This is clearly to go against common sense, for there are clearly occasions on which behavior might be said to be spontaneous. If, then, it is a bogey, it is not one to be feared. At the same time it has perhaps hindered the progress of science by the suggestion of a wrong model. If the exhibition of any form of behavior in a concrete form is to be interpreted in terms of a model, that model will not be the type of machine exemplified in the clock. In any case, psychologists are not likely to wish to concern themselves merely with the exhibition of a form of behavior on a particular occasion in a certain series of movements; nor do they confine themselves to this, but deal with behavior in general, and in this they are justified. For, the ultimate end of a science is surely to enable us to understand its subject-matter. In psychology we are concerned to understand human beings and organisms, in general, not just the movements of their limbs, however much these may, sometimes, constitute behavior. As the subject-matter of psychology, behavior is and must be intelligible in itself. Whereas we may justifiably expect some answer to the question, "For what reason was this movement made?" we will have no justification in always expecting an answer to the question, "For what reason was this done?" For on some occasions it would be considered silly to ask such a question and it is always logically possible that no answer may be given.

The problem of the freedom of the will is a many-sided problem but what I have been saying has this relevance—that we cannot give the efficient causes of behavior, and, in fact, that the notion of cause is inapplicable to it, in the sense of "cause" which implies mechanism. One of the difficulties connected with the problem is that of reconciling the obvious fact that our actions are sometimes spontaneous with our increasing ability to predict human actions. This, however, will present difficulty only if this latter fact implies that our behavior is mechanical in the sense opposed to that of "spontaneous." This cannot be so, for the only sense of "mechanical" which is applicable to behavior is that equivalent to "stupid" or "unthinking" in being opposed to "intelligent." Behavior is mechanical only in a relative sense. Thus even if it be admitted that science gives us increasing ability to predict human behavior, even if it is true that human beings are machines in some sense, this does not preclude some of our actions being spontaneous. Similarly these facts would not preclude our attributing to people responsibility for their actions, for the mode of discourse in which we should talk of their behavior, actions, or conduct is very different from that in which we should talk of them as machines. People are responsible for their actions if it is possible to say that these actions are derivable from a ἕξις, from their character. The only sense in which actions could be said to be determined, when this is not meant, is that in which they can be said to be compelled. The sense in which compulsion causes behavior is again, however, not the mechanical sense of "cause"; rather compulsion provides a motive for behaving in a certain way which is recognized in the context as being unavoidable. What constitutes unavoidability may vary according to the circumstances, but, at any rate, we are likely to hold a person responsible for an action only where it is derivable from his ἕξις, in some sense or other. As Aristotle saw, there are some occasions on which decision as to whether the action is derivable from the person's ἕξις may be difficult,[8] and only knowledge of further details of the case can make decision possible. Normally, however, we are well able to decide. In the case of compulsion it is clear that there are grounds for not attributing responsibility, and, a fortiori, for saying that the action is not free; but there is no reason for refusing to use the word "free" of behavior in general.

I do not wish to pretend that this is all that need be said on this question. It has many sides and many considerations are relevant. I do wish to maintain, however, that the issue of causal determinism versus indeterminism is irrelevant to any consideration about behavior, as long as they are considered as strict theses. Behavior is derivable from a ἕξις, as Aristotle maintained, and this does mean that there must be some regularity about it in order for it to be intelligible. Otherwise it would be reasonable to make the apparently paradoxical statement that strictly spontaneous behavior would be strictly mechanical, in that no reason at all could be given for it. In saying that there must be some regularity, no reference to the notion of "cause" need be made, however much people might suppose that regularity would not be possible unless causal sequences occurred somewhere. But this is quite another matter, and it is not necessary for present purposes to commit oneself either way. Similarly it is not necessary to say with Stevenson[9] that a limited degree of determinism must be taken for granted in order that our moral judgments may influence behavior. The sense in which our moral judgments influence behavior cannot be a strictly causal sense, for, as I have said, the notion of "cause" in the strict sense is inapplicable to behavior. Steven-

---

[8] *Eth. Nic.* 1110a, 4 ff.

[9] C. L. Stevenson, *Ethics and Language* (New Haven: Yale University Press, 1944), p. 314.

son's account of the function of moral judgments is based upon his account of pragmatic aspects of meaning. Moral terms have an emotive meaning which serves to change people's attitudes. Stevenson might say that they have only a disposition to produce such changes, but the same argument applies. It is clearly true that changes of attitude may sometimes be produced by what people say, but it is still necessary to see how this can occur.

What is it to have taken up a certain attitude? Among other things it is to have come to exhibit a certain more or less delimitable range of behavior-patterns on certain occasions. It does not entail that any one form of behavior is involved, let alone any one form of movement, but only that we can roughly specify what sort of behavior is likely to be exhibited on given occasions. Clearly nothing could cause us (in the strict sense) to take up an attitude, if that is what is meant, although a variety of means might be adopted in order to lead someone to take up an attitude, or to bring about a change of attitude. Propaganda may present people with bad but seductive reasons for a change of attitude—seductive in the sense that they appeal to motives which people have. It may, by constant repetition of statements, or the like, deprive people of the opportunity for, or interest in, considering reasons for not accepting them. Suggestion would not have any effect unless people had some reason or motive for being willing to accept suggestions. The motives may not always be conscious or explicitly recognized by the person concerned, but that is another matter. I take it, then, that the difference between argument and propaganda is that between the provision of good reasons for taking up an attitude and the failure to provide such or to allow such to be considered, while at the same time providing bad reasons.

My point is this—Stevenson is sometimes criticized for the view that the function of moral argument is to persuade. Even granted that his account of persuasion and persuasive definition is more subtle than his original account of emotive meaning suggests of itself, if the view attributed to him entails that persuasion is causative or quasi-causative, he is certainly wrong. On the other hand, it is not right to reinforce the criticism by saying that his view cannot account for the difference between moral argument and propaganda, as if this were a distinction between the provision of reasons for the adoption of an attitude and the causing of the adoption of an attitude. Propaganda does not cause the adoption of or change of an attitude, for reasons which I have given. Until and unless we can influence people's behavior by interference with the mechanism of its exhibition, we will not be able to cause people to behave in any way, in the strict sense. Of course we do use the verb "to cause," especially when followed by an infinitive, in a vague sense, in that the assertion that we caused someone to do something implies only that something which we did led that someone to do something. I am concerned only with the literal sense of "cause." I do not wish to suggest that it is in any way improper to use the verb "to cause" in this other way. But in distinguishing between moral argument and propaganda, we should distinguish between the various ways in which we might influence people, none of which will be causation in the strict sense. Verbal utterances are not stimuli which cause mechanical reactions. In talking in order to influence someone, we always provide a reason or something akin to a reason for that someone's doing what we want. The crucial difference between moral argument and propaganda is that in the former it is possible to say what constitutes a good reason for a particular form of conduct. Good propaganda is not propaganda based upon good or valid argument, but effective propaganda; but it is effective in the sense that appealing to people's motives in certain ways leads them to behave in the desired way for the most part, not because the mere utterance of words causes behavior. What constitutes a good reason for a moral judgment or decision is another story, but if moral arguments are persuasive this has no or little connection with their validity. If propaganda is persuasive this is all that need be said. At the risk of being tedious it is important to stress that neither causes the adoption of behavior, in the strict sense. The function of moral judgment is to inculcate certain modes of conduct, but it does this by the provision of reasons for behaving in this way, by appealing to principles (cf. "unprincipled" as a term of moral condemnation), the acceptance of which can be justified by the provision of different sorts of reasons in other ways; what constitutes a good reason depends on the context. Some systematization of these principles might be possible,[10] but in making moral judgments we do not *ipso facto* provide instruction with regard to them;[11] rather we presuppose them in making moral judgments at all, however much we may be led to argue about them directly in the course of argument.

"Behavior," "conduct," "activity," and "action" are words of one particular type, though there are differences of use between them. "Movement," "reaction," "reflex," and the like are of a very different type. "Achievement" must be separated from both of these in turn. So, indeed, must the word "act," as used by moralists such as Ross, in phrases like "act of promise-keeping." An act of promise-keeping is not any one series of movements, or even any one form of behavior. Promises may be kept by behaving in a number of different ways, in most contexts, and one form of behavior may or may not constitute fulfilling one's promise in different circumstances. In fact, we can talk of human beings in many different ways, at various levels of generality, with varying degrees of abstraction, with different points of view, or with the presupposition of different standards. It is important not to confuse or run together these different

---

[10] Cf. R. M. Hare, "Imperative Sentences," *Mind*, LVIII (1949). Also his article, "Freedom of the Will," *Aristotelian Society Supplementary Vol.* XXV (1951).

[11] As seems to be maintained by Hare, "Freedom of the Will."

modes of talk. In sum, I have wished to point out that we cannot give the causes of achievements in any sense, and that we cannot give the causes of behavior in the mechanical sense; but of movements both these things are possible. On the other hand, the notion of a reason is in principle applicable to behavior (though we would not be justified in always expecting one to be provided), and to movements which constitute the exhibition of behavior in particular circumstances; it is not, however, applicable to isolated movements which could not be said to constitute behavior (e.g., a reflex), nor to achievements, although we can give reasons for claiming achievements as such. The form of explanation depends upon the subject-matter and the context. Behavior is not a series of movements.

IV ✍ Wittgenstein's *Philosophical Investigations*[1]
Norman Malcolm

Ein Buch ist ein Spiegel; wenn ein Affe hineinguckt, so kann freilich kein Apostel heraussehen.

LICHTENBERG

An attempt to summarize the *Investigations* would be neither successful nor useful. Wittgenstein compressed his thoughts to the point where further compression is impossible. What is needed is that they should be unfolded and the connections between them traced out. A likely first reaction to the book will be to regard it as a puzzling collection of reflections that are sometimes individually brilliant, but possess no unity, present no system of ideas. In truth the unity is there, but, alas, it cannot be perceived without strenuous exertion. Within the scope of a review the connectedness can best be brought out, I think, by concentrating on some single topic—in spite of the fact that there are no separate topics, for each of the investigations in the book crisscrosses again and again with every other one. In the following I center my attention on Wittgenstein's treatment of the problem of how language is related to inner experiences—to sensations, feelings, and moods. This is one of the main inquiries of the book and perhaps the most difficult to understand. I am sufficiently aware of the fact that my presentation of this subject will certainly fail to portray the subtlety, elegance, and force of Wittgenstein's thinking and will probably, in addition, contain positive mistakes.

References to Part I will be by paragraph numbers, e.g., (207), and to Part II by page numbers, e.g., (p. 207). Quotations will be placed within double quotation marks.

Private Language

Let us see something of how Wittgenstein attacks what he calls "the idea of a private language." By a "private" language is meant one that not merely is not but *cannot* be understood by anyone other than the speaker. The reason for this is that the words of this language are sup-

---

[1] Ludwig Wittgenstein, *Philosophical Investigations;* German and English in facing pages; English translation by G. E. M. Anscombe (New York, 1953).

posed to "refer to what can only be known to the person speaking; to his immediate private sensations" (243). What is supposed is that I *"associate* words with sensations and use these names in descriptions" (256). I fix my attention on a sensation and establish a connection between a word and the sensation (258).

It is worth mentioning that the conception that it is possible and even necessary for one to have a private language is not eccentric. Rather it is the view that comes most naturally to anyone who philosophizes on the subject of the relation of words to experiences. The idea of a private language is presupposed by every program of inferring or constructing the 'external world' and 'other minds.' It is contained in the philosophy of Descartes and in the theory of ideas of classical British empiricism, as well as in recent and contemporary phenomenalism and sense-datum theory. At bottom it is the idea that there is only a contingent and not an *essential* connection between a sensation and its outward expression—an idea that appeals to us all. Such thoughts as these are typical expressions of the idea of a private language: that I know only from my *own* case what the word 'pain' means (293, 295); that I can only *believe* that someone else is in pain, but I *know* it if I am (303); that another person cannot have *my* pains (253); that I can undertake to call *this* (pointing inward) 'pain' in the future (263); that when I say 'I am in pain' I am at any rate justified *before myself* (289).

In order to appreciate the depth and power of Wittgenstein's assault upon it you must partly be its captive. You must feel the strong grip of it. The passionate intensity of Wittgenstein's writing is due to the fact that he lets this idea take possession of him, drawing out of himself the thoughts and imagery by which it is expressed and defended—and then he subjects those thoughts and pictures to fiercest scrutiny. What is written down represents both a logical investigation and a great philosopher's struggle with his own thoughts. The logical investigation will be understood only by those who duplicate the struggle in themselves.

One consequence to be drawn from the view that I know only from my *own* case what, say, 'tickling' means is that "I know only what *I* call that, not what anyone else does" (347). I have not *learned* what 'tickling' means, I have only called something by that name. Perhaps others use the name differently. This is a regrettable difficulty; but, one may think, the word will still work for me as a name, provided that I apply it consistently to a certain sensation. But how about 'sensation'? Don't I know only from my *own* case what *that* word means? Perhaps what I call a 'sensation' others call by another name? It will not help, says Wittgenstein, to say that although it may be that what I have is not what others call a 'sensation,' at least I have *something*. For don't I know only from my own case what 'having something' is? Perhaps my use of *those* words is contrary to common use. In trying to explain how I gave 'tickling' its meaning, I discover that I do not have the right to use any of the relevant words of our common language. "So in the end when one is doing philosophy one gets to the point where one would like just to emit an inarticulate sound" (261).

Let us suppose that I did fix my attention on a pain as I pronounced the word 'pain' to myself. I think that thereby I established a connection between the word and the sensation. But I did not establish a connection if subsequently I applied that word to sensations other than pain or to things other than sensations, e.g., emotions. My private definition was a success only if it led me to use the word correctly in the future. In the present case, 'correctly' would mean '*consistently* with my own definition'; for the question of whether my use agrees with that of others has been given up as a bad job. Now how is it to be decided whether I have used the word consistently? What will be the difference between my having used it consistently and its *seeming* to me that I have? Or has this distinction vanished? "Whatever is going to seem right to me is right. And that only means that here we can't talk about 'right' " (258). If the distinction between 'correct' and 'seems correct' has disappeared, then so has the concept *correct*. It follows that the 'rules' of my private language are only *impressions* of rules (259). My impression that I follow a rule does not confirm that I follow the rule, unless there can be something that will prove my impression correct. And the something cannot be another impression—for this would be "as if someone were to buy several copies of the morning paper to assure himself that what it said was true" (265). The proof that I am following a rule must appeal to something *independent* of my impression that I am. If in the nature of the case there cannot be such an appeal, then my private language does not have *rules,* for the concept of a rule requires that there be a difference between 'He is following a rule' and 'He is under the impression that he is following a rule'—just as the concept of understanding a word requires that there be a difference between 'He understands this word' and 'He thinks that he understands this word' (cf. 269).

'Even if I cannot prove and cannot know that I am correctly following the rules of my private language,' it might be said, 'still it *may* be that I am. It has *meaning* to say that I am. The supposition makes sense: you and I *understand* it.' Wittgenstein has a reply to this (348-353). We are inclined to think that we know what it means to say 'It is five o'clock on the sun' or 'This congenital deaf-mute talks to himself inwardly in a vocal language' or 'The stove is in pain.' These sentences produce pictures in our minds, and it *seems* to us that the pictures tell us how to *apply* them—that is, tell us what we have to look for, what we have to do, in order to determine whether what is pictured is the case. But we make a mistake in thinking that the picture contains in itself the instructions as to how we are to apply it. Think of the picture of blindness as a darkness in the soul or in the head of the blind man (424). There is nothing wrong with it *as a picture.* "But *what* is its application?" What shall count for or against its being said that this or that man is blind, that the picture applies to him? The *picture* doesn't say. If you think that you understand the sentence 'I follow the rule that *this* is to be called "pain" ' (a rule of your private language), what you have perhaps is a picture of yourself checking off various feelings of yours as either being *this* or not. The picture appears to solve the problem of how you determine whether you have done the 'checking' right. Actually it doesn't give you even a hint in that direction; no more than the picture of blindness provides so much as a hint of *how* it is to be determined that this or that man is blind (348-353, 422-426, p. 184).

One will be inclined to say here that one can simply *remember* this sensation and by remembering it will know that one is making a consistent application of its name. But will it also be possible to have a *false* memory impression? On the private-language hypothesis, what would *show* that your memory impression is false—or true? Another memory impression? Would this imply that memory is a court from which there is no appeal? But, as a matter of fact, that is *not* our concept of memory.

> Imagine that you were supposed to paint a particular color "C," which was the color that appeared when the chemical substances X and Y combined.— Suppose that the color struck you as brighter on one day than on another; would you not sometimes say: "I must be wrong, the color is certainly the same as yesterday"? This shows that we do not always resort to what memory tells us as the verdict of the highest court of appeal [56].

There is, indeed, such a thing as checking one memory against another, e.g., I check my recollection of the time of departure of a train by calling up a memory image of how a page of the time-table looked—but "this process has got to produce a memory which is actually *correct.* If the mental image of the time-table could not itself be *tested* for correctness, how could it confirm the correctness of the first memory?" (265).

If I have a language that is really private (i.e., it is a logical impossibility that anyone else should understand it or should have any basis for knowing whether I am using a particular name consistently), my assertion that my memory tells me so and so will be utterly empty. 'My memory' will not even mean—my memory *impression.* For by a memory impression we understand something that is either accurate or inaccurate; whereas there would not be, in the private language, any *conception* of what would establish a memory impression as correct, any conception of what 'correct' would mean here.

The Same

One wants to say, 'Surely there can't be a difficulty in knowing whether a feeling of mine is or isn't the *same* as the feeling I now have. I will call this feeling "pain" and will thereafter call the *same* thing "pain" whenever it occurs. What could be easier than to follow that rule?' To understand Wittgenstein's reply to this attractive proposal we must come closer to his treatment of rules and of what it is to follow a rule. (Here he forges a remarkably illuminating connection between the philosophy of psychology and the philosophy of mathematics.) Consider his example of the pupil who has been taught to write down a cardinal number series of the form '0, n, 2n, 3n . . .' at an order of the form '+n,' so that at the order '+1' he writes down the series of natural numbers (185). He has successfully done exercises and tests up to the number 1,000. We then ask him to continue the series '+2' beyond 1,000; and he writes 1,000, 1,004, 1,008, 1,012. We tell him that this is wrong. His instructive reply is, "But I went on in the same way" (185). There was nothing in the previous explanations, examples, and exercises that made it *impossible* for him to regard that as the continuation of the series. Repeating *those* examples and explanations won't help him. One must say to him, in effect, 'That isn't what we *call* going on in the *same* way.' It is a fact, and a fact of the kind whose importance Wittgenstein constantly stresses, that it is *natural* for human beings to continue the series in the manner 1,002, 1,004, 1,006, given the previous training. But that is merely what it is—a fact of human nature.

One is inclined to retort, 'Of course he can misunderstand the instruction and misunderstand the order "+2"; but if he *understands* it he must go on in the right way.' And here one has the idea that "The understanding itself is a state which is the *source* of the correct use" (146)—that the correct continuation of the series, the right application of the rule or formula, springs from one's understanding of the rule. But the question of whether one understands the rule cannot be divorced from the question of whether one will go on in that one particular way that we call 'right.' The correct use is a criterion of understanding. If you say that knowing the formula is a state of the mind and that making this and that application of the formula is merely a *manifestation* of the knowledge, then you are in a difficulty: for you are postulating a mental apparatus that explains the manifestations, and so you ought to have (but do not have) a knowledge of the construction of the apparatus, quite apart from what it does (149). You would like to think that your understanding of the formula determines in advance the steps to be taken, that when you understood or meant the formula in a certain way "your mind as it were flew ahead and took all the steps before you physically arrived at this or that one" (188). But how you meant it is not independent of how in

fact you use it. "We say, for instance, to someone who uses a sign unknown to us: 'If by *"x!2"* you mean x^2, then you get *this* value for y, if
you mean *2x, that* one.'—Now ask yourself: how does one *mean* the one
thing or the other by *'x!2'?"* (190). The answer is that his putting down
this value for y shows whether he meant the one thing and not the other:
"*That* will be how meaning it can determine the steps in advance" (190).
How he meant the formula determines his subsequent use of it, only in
the sense that the latter is a criterion of—how he meant it.

It is easy to suppose that when you have given a person the order 'Now
do the *same* thing,' you have pointed out to him the way to go on. But
consider the example of the man who obtains the series 1, 3, 5, 7 . . . by
working out the formula $2x + 1$ and then asks himself, "Am I always
doing the same thing, or something different every time?" (226). One
answer is as good as the other; it doesn't matter which he says, so long as
he continues in the right way. If we could not observe his work, his mere
remark 'I am going on in the same way' would not tell us what he was
doing. If a child writing down a row of 2's obtained '2, 2, 2' from the
segment '2, 2' by adding '2' once, he might deny that he had gone on in
the *same* way. He might declare that it would be doing the same thing
only if he went from '2, 2' to '2, 2, 2, 2' in *one* jump, i.e., only if he
doubled the original segment (just as it doubled the original single '2').
That could strike one as a *reasonable* use of 'same.' This connects up
with Wittgenstein's remark: "If you have to have an intuition in order
to develop the series 1 2 3 4 . . . you must also have one in order to
develop the series 2 2 2 2 . . ." (214). One is inclined to say of the latter
series, 'Why, all that is necessary is that you keep on doing the *same*
thing.' But isn't this just as true of the other series? In both cases one has
already *decided* what the correct continuation is, and one calls that
continuation, and no other, 'doing the same thing.' As Wittgenstein says:
"One might say to the person one was training: 'Look, I always do the
same thing: I . . .'" (223). And then one proceeds to show him what
'the same' *is*. If the pupil does not acknowledge that what you have
shown him is the *same,* and if he is not persuaded by your examples and
explanations to carry on as you wish him to—then you have reached bed-
rock and will be inclined to say "This is simply what I do" (217). You
cannot give him more reasons than you yourself have for proceeding in
that way. Your reasons will soon give out. And then you will proceed,
without reasons (211).

Private Rules

All of this argument strikes at the idea that there can be such a thing
as my following a rule in my private language—such a thing as naming
something of which only I can be aware, 'pain,' and then going on to
call the same thing, 'pain,' whenever it occurs. There is a charm about the

expression 'same' which makes one think that there cannot be any difficulty or any chance of going wrong in deciding whether A is the *same* as B—as if one did not have to be *shown* what the 'same' is. This may be, as Wittgenstein suggests, because we are inclined to suppose that we can take the identity of a thing *with itself* as "an infallible paradigm" of the *same* (215). But he destroys this notion with one blow: "Then are two things the same when they are what *one* thing is? And how am I to apply what the *one* thing shows me to the case of two things?" (215).

The point to be made here.is that when one has given oneself the private rule 'I will call this same thing "pain" whenever it occurs,' one is then free to do anything or nothing. That 'rule' does not point in any direction. On the private-language hypothesis, no one can teach me what the correct use of 'same' is. I shall be the sole arbiter of whether this is the *same* as that. What I choose to call the 'same' will *be* the same. No restriction whatever will be imposed upon my application of the word. But a sound that I can use *as I please* is not a *word*.

How would you teach someone the meaning of 'same'? By example and practice: you might show him, for instance, collections of the same colors and same shapes and make him find and produce them and perhaps get him to carry on a certain ornamental pattern uniformly (208). Training him to form collections and produce patterns is teaching him what Wittgenstein calls "techniques." Whether he has mastered various techniques determines whether he understands 'same.' The exercise of a technique is what Wittgenstein calls a "practice." Whether your pupil has understood any of the rules that you taught him (e.g., the rule: this is the 'same' color as that) will be shown in his practice. But now there cannot be a 'private' practice, i.e., a practice that cannot be exhibited. For there would then be no distinction between believing that you have that practice and having it. 'Obeying a rule' is itself a practice. "And to *think* one is obeying a rule is not to obey a rule. Hence it is not possible to obey a rule 'privately'; otherwise thinking one was obeying a rule would be the same thing as obeying it" (202, cf. 380).

If I recognize that my mental image is the 'same' as one that I had previously, how am I to know that this public word 'same' describes what I recognize? "Only if I can express my recognition in some other way, and if it is possible for someone else to teach me that 'same' is the correct word here" (378). The notion of the private language doesn't admit of there being 'some other way.' It doesn't allow that my behavior and circumstances can be so related to my utterance of the word that another person, by noting my behavior and circumstances, can discover that my use of the word is correct or incorrect. Can I discover this for myself, and how do I do it? That discovery would presuppose that I have a conception of correct use which comes from outside my private language and against which I measure the latter. If this were admitted, the private language would lose its privacy and its point. So it isn't admitted. But now the notion of 'correct' use that will exist within the private language will be such that if I *believe* that my use is correct then it is correct; the rules will be only impressions of rules; my 'language' will not be a language, but merely the impression of a language. The most that can be said for it is that I *think* I understand it (cf. 269).

Sensations of Others

The argument that I have been outlining has the form of *reductio ad absurdum:* postulate a 'private' language; then deduce that it is not *language.* Wittgenstein employs another argument that is an external, not an internal, attack upon private language. What is attacked is the assumption that once I know from my *own* case what pain, tickling, or consciousness is, then I can transfer the ideas of these things to objects outside myself (283). Wittgenstein says:

> If one has to imagine someone else's pain on the model of one's own, this is none too easy a thing to do: for I have to imagine pain which I *do not feel* on the model of the pain which I *do feel.* That is, what I have to do is not simply to make a transition in imagination from one place of pain to another. As, from pain in the hand to pain in the arm. For I am not to imagine that I feel pain in some region of his body. (Which would also be possible.) [302]

The argument that is here adumbrated is, I think, the following: If I were to learn what pain is from perceiving my own pain then I should, necessarily, have learned that pain is something that exists only when *I* feel pain. For the pain that serves as my paradigm of pain (i.e., my own) has the property of existing only when *I* feel it. That property is essential, not accidental; it is nonsense to suppose that the pain I feel could exist when I did not feel it. So if I obtain my *conception* of pain from pain that I experience, then it will be part of my conception of pain that *I* am the only being that can experience it. For me it will be a *contradiction* to speak of *another's* pain. This strict solipsism is the necessary outcome of the notion of private language. I take the phrase "this is none too easy" to be a sarcasm.

One is tempted at this point to appeal to the 'same' again: "But if I suppose that someone has a pain, then I am simply supposing that he has just the same as I have so often had" (350). I will quote Wittgenstein's brilliant counterstroke in full:

> That gets us no further. It is as if I were to say: "You surely know what 'It is 5 o'clock here' means; so you also know what 'It's 5 o'clock on the sun' means. It means simply that it is just the same time there as it is here when it is 5 o'clock."—The explanation by means of *identity* does not work here. For I know well enough that one can call 5 o'clock here and 5 o'clock

there "the same time," but what I do not know is in what cases one is to speak of its being the same time here and there.

In exactly the same way it is no explanation to say: the supposition that he has a pain is simply the supposition that he has the same as I. For *that* part of the grammar is quite clear to me: that is, that one will say that the stove has the same experience as I, *if* one says: it is in pain and I am in pain [350].

Expressions of Sensation

Wittgenstein says that he destroys "houses of cards" ("Luftgebaüde": 118) and that his aim is to show one how to pass from disguised to obvious nonsense (464). But this is not all he does or thinks he does. For he says that he changes one's *way of looking at things* (144). What is it that he wishes to substitute for that way of looking at things that is represented by the idea of private language? One would *like* to find a continuous exposition of his own thesis, instead of mere hints here and there. But this desire reflects a misunderstanding of Wittgenstein's philosophy. He rejects the assumption that he should put forward a *thesis* (128). "We may not advance any kind of theory" (109). A philosophical problem is a certain sort of confusion. It is like being lost; one can't see one's way (123). Familiar surroundings suddenly seem strange. We need to command a view of the country, to get our bearings. The country is well known to us, so we need only to be *reminded* of our whereabouts. "The work of the philosopher consists in assembling reminders for a particular purpose" (127). "The problems are solved, not by giving new information, but by arranging what we have always known" (109). When we describe (remind ourselves of) certain functionings of our language, what we do must have a definite bearing on some particular confusion, some "deep disquietude" (111), that ensnares us. Otherwise our work is irrelevant—to *philosophy*. It is philosophically pointless to formulate a general theory of language or to pile up descriptions for their own sake. "This description gets its light, that is to say its purpose—from the philosophical problems" (109). Thus we may not complain at the absence from the *Investigations* of elaborate theories and classifications.

Wittgenstein asks the question "How do words *refer* to sensations?" transforms it into the question "How does a human being learn the meaning of the names of sensations?" and gives this answer: "Words are connected with the primitive, the natural expressions of the sensation and used in their place. A child has hurt himself and he cries; and then the adults talk to him and teach him exclamations and, later, sentences. They teach the child new pain-behavior" (244). Wittgenstein must be talking about how it is that a human being learns to refer with words to his *own* sensations—about how he learns to use 'I am in pain'; not about how he learns to use 'He is in pain.' What Wittgenstein is saying is indeed radically different from the notion that I learn what 'I am in pain' means by fixing my attention on a 'certain' sensation and calling it 'pain.' But is he saying that what I do instead is to fix my attention on my *expressions* of pain and call them 'pain'? Is he saying that the word 'pain' means crying? "On the contrary: the verbal expression of pain replaces crying and does not describe it" (244). My words for sensations are used *in place of* the behavior that is the natural expression of the sensations; they do not *refer* to it.

Wittgenstein does not expand this terse reminder. He repeats at least once that my words for sensations are "tied up with my natural expressions of sensation" (256) and frequently alludes to the importance of the connection between the language for sensations and the behavior which is the expression of sensation (e.g., 288, 271). The following questions and objections will arise:

(1) What shows that a child has made this 'tie up'? I take Wittgenstein to mean that the child's utterances of the word for a sensation must, in the beginning, be frequently concurrent with some nonverbal, natural expression of that sensation. This concomitance serves as the criterion of his understanding the word. Later on, the word can be uttered in the absence of primitive expressions. ('It hurts' can be said without cries or winces.)

(2) In what sense does the verbal expression 'replace' the nonverbal expression? In the sense, I think, that other persons will react to the child's mere words in the same way that they previously reacted to his nonverbal sensation-behavior; they will let the mere words serve as a *new* criterion of his feelings.

(3) I feel inclined to object: 'But has the child *learned* what the words *mean*? Hasn't he merely picked up the *use* of the word from his parents?' My objection probably arises from assimilating the learning of the meaning of words to the labeling of bottles—a tendency that is easily decried but not easily resisted. 'Learning *ought* to consist in attaching the right name to the right object,' I should like to say (cf. 26). The example of 'the beetle in the box' is pertinent here (see 293). The aim of this fantasy is to prove that attending to a private object can have nothing to do with learning words for sensations. Suppose you wanted to teach a child what a tickling feeling is. You tickle him in the ribs, and he laughs and jerks away. You say to him, 'That's what the feeling of tickling is.' Now imagine that he felt something that you can't know anything about. Will this be of any interest to you when you decide from his subsequent use of the word 'tickling' whether he understands it? Others understand the word too. If each one has something that only he can know about, then all the somethings may be different. The something could even be nothing! Whatever it is, it can have no part in determining whether the

person who has it understands the word. "If we construe the grammar of the expression of sensation on the model of 'object and name' the object drops out of consideration as irrelevant" (293, cf. 304).

My previous objection could be put like this: the teaching and learning of names of sensations cannot stop at the mere expressions of sensation; the names must be brought *right up* to the sensations themselves, must be applied *directly* to the sensations! Here we can imagine Wittgenstein replying, "Like *what*, e.g.?" as he replies to an analogous objection in a different problem (191). In *what* sense is Wittgenstein denying that names are applied directly to sensations? Do I have a model of what it would be to apply the name 'directly'? No. I have this picture—that learning the meaning of 'pain' is applying the sign 'pain' to pain itself. I have that picture, to be sure, but what does it teach me, what is its "application"? When shall I say that what it pictures has taken place, i.e., that someone has learned the meaning of 'pain'? It doesn't tell me; it is *only* a picture. It cannot conflict with, cannot refute, Wittgenstein's reminder of what it is that determines whether a child has learned the word for a sensation.

(4) Wittgenstein says that the verbal expressions of sensation can take the place of the nonverbal expressions and that in learning the former one learns "new pain-behavior." This seems to mean that the words (and sentences) for sensations are related to sensations in the same way as are the primitive expressions of sensations. I am inclined to object again. I want to say that the words are used to *report* the occurrence of a sensation and to inform others of it. The natural expressions, on the contrary, are not used to inform others; they are not 'used' at all; they have no purpose, no function; they *escape* from one. But I have oversimplified the difference, because (a) a sentence can be forced from one, can escape one's lips ('My God, it hurts!'), and (b) a natural expression of sensation can be used to inform another, e.g., you moan to let the nurse know that your pain is increasing (you would have suppressed the moan if she hadn't entered the room), yet the moan is genuine. Perhaps my objection comes to this: I don't *learn* to moan; I do learn the words. But this is the very distinction that is made by saying that moaning is a "natural," a "primitive," expression of sensation.

It is a mistake to suppose that Wittgenstein is saying that the utterance 'My leg hurts' is *normally called* an 'expression of sensation.' (Of course it isn't. For that matter, only a facial expression, not a groan, is called an *'expression* of pain.' But this is of no importance.) He is not reporting ordinary usage, but drawing our attention to an *analogy* between the groan of pain and the utterance of those words. The important similarity that he is trying to bring to light (here I may misinterpret him) is that the verbal utterance and the natural pain-behavior are each (as I shall express it) 'incorrigible.' A man cannot be in *error* as to whether he is in pain; he cannot say, 'My leg hurts,' by mistake, any more than he can groan by mistake. It is senseless to suppose that he has wrongly identified a tickle as pain or that he falsely believes that it is in his leg when in fact it is in his shoulder. True, he may be un-decided as to whether it is best described as an 'ache' or a 'pain' (one is often hard put to give satisfactory descriptions of one's feelings); but his very indecision *shows* us what his sensation is, i.e., something between ar ache and a pain. His hesitant observation, 'I'm not sure whether it is a pain or an ache,' is itself an *expression* of sensation. What it expresses is an indefinite, an ambiguous sensation. The point about the incor-rigibility of the utterance 'I'm in pain' lies behind Wittgenstein's reiter-ated remark that 'I *know* I'm in pain' and 'I don't know whether I'm in pain' are both senseless (e.g., 246, 408).[2] Wherever it is *meaningless* to speak of 'false belief,' it is also meaningless to speak of 'knowledge'; and wherever you cannot say 'I don't know . . .' you also cannot say 'I know. . . .' Of course, a philosopher can say of me that I *know* I am in pain. But "What is it supposed to mean—except perhaps that I *am* in pain?" (246).

There are many 'psychological' sentences, other than sentences about sensations, that are incorrigible, e.g., the *truthful* report of a dream is a criterion for the occurrence of the dream and, unless some other criterion is introduced, "the question cannot arise" as to whether the dreamer's memory deceives him (pp. 222-223). If one who has a mental image were asked whom the image is of, "his answer would be decisive," just as it would be if he were asked whom the drawing represents that he has just made (p. 177). When you say, 'It will stop soon,' and are asked whether you *meant* your pain or the sound of the piano-tuning, your truthful answer is the answer (666-684).

When Wittgenstein says that learning the words for sensations is learn-ing "new pain-behavior" and that the words "replace" the natural ex-pressions, he is bringing to light the arresting fact that my sentences about my present sensations have the same logical status as my outcries and facial expressions. And thus we are helped to "make a radical break with the idea that language always functions in one way, always serves the same purpose: to convey thoughts—which may be about houses, pains, good and evil, or anything else you please" (304).

This is not to deny that first-person sentences about sensations may, in other respects, be more or less like natural expressions of sensation. Wittgenstein's examples of the use of 'I am afraid' (pp. 187-188) show how the utterance of that sentence can be a cry of fear, a comparison, an attempt to tell someone how I feel, a confession, a reflection on my state of mind, or something in between. "A cry is not a description. But there are transitions. And the words 'I am afraid' may approximate more, or less, to being a cry. They may come quite close to this and also

---

[2] It is interesting to note that as long ago as 1930 Wittgenstein had remarked that it has no sense to speak of *verifying* 'I have a too+thache.' (See G. E. Moore, "Wittgen-stein's Lectures in 1930-33," *Mind*, LXIV [1955], 14.)

be *far* removed from it" (p. 189). The words 'I am in pain' "may be a cry of complaint, and may be something else" (p. 189); and 'it makes me shiver' may be a "shuddering reaction" or may be said "as a piece of information" (p. 174). If we pursue these hints, it is not hard to construct a list of examples of the use of the words 'My head hurts,' in which the variety is as great as in Wittgenstein's list for 'I am afraid.' E.g., compare 'Oh hell, how my head hurts!' with 'If you want to know whether to accept the invitation for tonight then I must tell you that my head hurts again.' In one case the sentence 'My head hurts' belongs to an exclamation of pain, not in the other. In saying that in *both* cases it is an 'expression' of pain, Wittgenstein stretches ordinary language and in so doing illuminates the hidden continuity between the utterance of that sentence and—expressions of pain.

Criterion

That the natural pain-behavior and the utterance 'It hurts' are each incorrigible is what makes it possible for each of them to be a criterion of pain. With some reluctance I will undertake to say a little bit about this notion of 'criterion,' a most difficult region in Wittgenstein's philosophy. Perhaps the best way to elucidate it is to bring out its connection with *teaching* and *learning* the use of words. "When I say the ABC to myself, what is the criterion of my doing the same as someone else who silently repeats it to himself? It might be found that the same thing took place in my larynx and in his. (And similarly when we both think of the same thing, wish the same, and so on.) But then did we learn the use of the words, 'to say such-and-such to oneself,' by someone's pointing to a process in the larynx or the brain?" (376). Of course we did not, and this means that a physiological process is not our 'criterion' that *A* said such-and-such to himself. Try to imagine, realistically and in detail, how you would teach someone the meaning of 'saying the ABC silently to oneself.' This, you may think, is merely psychology. But if you have succeeded in bringing to mind what it is that would show that he *grasped* your teaching, that he *understood* the use of the words, then you have elicited the 'criterion' for their use—and that is not psychology. Wittgenstein exhorts us, over and over, to bethink ourselves of how we learned to use this or that form of words or of how we should teach it to a child. The purpose of this is not to bring philosophy down to earth (which it does), but to bring into view those features of someone's circumstances and behavior that *settle* the question of whether the words (e.g., 'He is calculating in his head') rightly apply to him. Those features constitute the 'criterion' of calculating in one's head. It is logically possible that someone should have been born with a knowledge of the use of an expression or that it should have been produced in him by a drug; that his knowledge came about by way of the normal process of teaching is not necessary. What is necessary is that there should be something on the basis of which we *judge* whether he *has* that knowledge. To undertake to describe this may be called a 'logical' investigation, even though one should arrive at the description by reflecting on that logically inessential process of teaching and learning.

If someone says, e.g., 'I feel confident . . . ,' a question can arise as to whether he understands those words. Once you admit the untenability of 'private ostensive definition' you will see that there must be a *behavioral* manifestation of the feeling of confidence (579). There must be behavior against which his words, 'I feel confident . . . ,' can be checked, if it is to be possible to judge that he does or does not understand them. Even if you picture a feeling of confidence as an "inner process," still it requires "outward criteria" (580).

Wittgenstein contrasts 'criterion' with 'symptom,' employing both words technically. The falling barometer is a 'symptom' that it is raining; its looking like *that* outdoors (think how you would teach the word 'rain' to a child) is the 'criterion' of rain (354). A process in a man's brain or larynx might be a symptom that he has an image of red; the criterion is "what he says and does" (377, 376). What makes something into a symptom of *y* is that experience teaches that it is always or usually associated with *y*; that so-and-so is the criterion of *y* is a matter, not of experience, but of "definition" (354). The satisfaction of the criterion of *y* establishes the existence of *y* beyond question; it repeats the kind of case in which we were taught to say '*y*.' The occurence of a symptom of *y* may also establish the existence of *y* 'beyond question'—but in a different sense. The observation of a brain process may make it certain that a man is in pain—but not in the same way that his pain behavior makes it certain. Even if physiology has established that a specific event in the brain accompanies bodily pain, still it *could* happen (it makes sense to suppose) that a man might be in pain without that brain event occurring. But if the criterion of being in pain is satisfied then he *must* be in pain. Sometimes, and especially in science, we *change* our criteria: "what today counts as an observed concomitant of a phenomenon will tomorrow be used to define it" (79).

The preceding remarks point up the following question: Do the propositions that describe the criterion of his being in pain *logically imply* the proposition 'He is in pain'? Wittgenstein's answer is clearly in the negative. Pain-behavior is a criterion of pain only in *certain circumstances*. If we come upon a man exhibiting violent pain-behavior, couldn't something show that he is not in pain? Of course. For example, he is rehearsing for a play; or he has been hypnotized and told, 'You will act as if you are in pain, although you won't be in pain,' and when he is released from the hypnotic state he has no recollection of having been in pain; or his pain-behavior suddenly ceases and he reports in apparent bewilderment that it was as if his body had been possessed—

tor his movements had been entirely involuntary, and during the 'seizure' he had felt no pain; or he has been narrowly missed by a car and as soon as a sum for damages has been pressed into his hand, his pain-behavior ceases and he laughs at the hoax; or . . . , etc. The expressions of pain are a criterion of pain in *certain* "surroundings," not in others (cf. 584).

Now one would like to think that one can still formulate a logical implication by taking a description of his pain-behavior and conjoining it with the negation of every proposition describing one of those circumstances that would count against saying he is in pain. Surely, the conjunction will logically imply 'He is in pain'! But this assumes there is a *totality* of those circumstances such that if none of them were fulfilled, and he was also pain-behaving, then he *could not but* be in pain (cf. 183). There is no totality that can be exhaustively enumerated, as can the letters of the alphabet. It is quite impossible to list six or nine such circumstances and then to say 'That is all of them; no other circumstances can be imagined that would count against his being in pain.' The list of circumstances has no 'all,' in that sense; the list is, not infinite, but *indefinite*. Therefore, entailment-conditions cannot be formulated; there are none.

The above thought is hard to accept. It is not in line with our *ideal* of what language should be. It makes the 'rules' for the use of 'He is in pain,' too vague, too loose, not really *rules*. Wittgenstein has deep and difficult things to say about the nature of this 'ideal': "We want to say that there can't be any vagueness in logic. The idea now absorbs us, that the ideal *'must'* be found in reality. Meanwhile we do not as yet see *how* it occurs there, nor do we understand the nature of this 'must.' We think it must be in reality; for we think we already see it there" (101). "The strict and clear rules of the logical structure of propositions appear to us as something in the background—hidden in the medium of the understanding" (102). "The more narrowly we examine actual language, the sharper becomes the conflict between it and our requirement. (For the crystalline purity of logic was, of course, not a *result of investigation:* it was a requirement.)" (107) What we need to do is to remove from our noses the logical glasses through which we look at reality (103). We must study the phenomenon of language, as it is, without preconceived ideas. One thing this study will teach us is that the criteria for the use of third-person psychological statements are not related to the latter by an entailment-relation.

Wittgenstein suggests that propositions describing the fulfillment of behavioral criteria are related to third-person psychological statements in the way that propositions describing sense-impressions are related to physical-object statements (compare 486 and p. 180). It does not *follow* from the propositions describing my sense-impressions that there is a chair over there (486). The relation cannot be reduced to a *simple* formula (p. 180). *Why* doesn't it follow? Wittgenstein does not say, but the reason would appear to be of the same sort as in the example of 'He is in pain.' The propositions describing my sense-impressions would have to be conjoined with the proposition that I am not looking in a mirror, or at a painted scenery, or at a movie film, or . . . , etc. Here too there cannot be an exhaustive enumeration of the negative conditions that would have to be added to the description of sense-impressions *if* 'There's a chair over there' *were* to be logically implied.

The puzzling problem now presents itself: if it does not *follow* from his behavior and circumstances that he is in pain, then how can it ever be *certain* that he is in pain? "I can be as *certain* of someone else's sensations as of any fact," says Wittgenstein (p. 224). How can this be so, since there is not a definite set of six or eight conditions (each of which would nullify his pain-behavior) to be checked off as not fulfilled? It *looks* as if the conclusion ought to be that we cannot 'completely verify' that he is in pain. This conclusion is wrong, but it is not easy to see why. I comprehend Wittgenstein's thought here only dimly. He says:

> A doctor asks: "How is he feeling?" The nurse says: "He is groaning." A report on his behavior. But need there be any question for them whether the groaning is really genuine, is really the expression of anything? Might they not, for example, draw the conclusion "If he groans, we must give him more analgesic"—without suppressing a middle term? Isn't the point the service to which they put the description of behavior [p. 179]?

One hint that I take from this is that there can be situations of real life in which a question as to whether someone who groans is pretending, or rehearsing, or hypnotized, or . . . , simply does not exist. "Just try—in a real case—to doubt someone else's fear or pain" (303). A doubt, a question, would be rejected as absurd by anyone who knew the actual surroundings. 'But might there not be still further surroundings, unknown to you, that would change the whole aspect of the matter?' Well, we go only *so* far—and then we are certain. "Doubting has an end" (p. 180). Perhaps we can *imagine* a doubt; but we do not take it seriously (cf. 84). Just as it becomes certain to us that there is a chair over there, although we can imagine a *possible* ground of doubt. There is a concept of certainty in these language-games only because we stop short of what is conceivable.

" 'But, if you are *certain,* isn't it that you are shutting your eyes in face of doubt?'—They are shut" (p. 224). This striking remark suggests that what we sometimes do is draw a boundary around *this* behavior in *these* circumstances and say, 'Any additional circumstances that might come to light will be irrelevant to whether this man is in pain.' Just as we draw a line and say, 'No further information will have any bearing on whether there is a chair in the corner—that is settled.' If your friend is struck down by a car and writhes with a broken leg, you do not think:

Perhaps it was prearranged in order to alarm me; possibly his leg was anaesthetized just before the 'accident' and he isn't suffering at all. Someone *could* have such doubts whenever another person was ostensibly in pain. Similarly: "I can easily imagine someone always doubting before he opened his front door whether an abyss did not yawn behind it; and making sure about it before he went through the door (and he might on some occasion prove to be right)—but that does not make me doubt in the same case" (84).

The man who doubts the other's pain may be neurotic, may 'lack a sense of reality,' but his reasoning is perfectly sound. *If* his doubts are true then the injured man is *not* in pain. His reaction is abnormal but not illogical. The certainty that the injured man is in pain (the normal reaction) ignores the endless doubts that *could* be proposed and investigated.

And it is important to see that the abnormal reaction *must* be the exception and not the rule. For if someone *always* had endless doubts about the genuineness of expressions of pain, it would mean that he was not using *any criterion* of another's being in pain. It would mean that he did not accept anything as an *expression* of pain. So what could it mean to say that he even had the *concept* of another's being in pain? It is senseless to suppose that he has this concept and yet always doubts.

Third-Person Sensation-Sentences

Wittgenstein assimilates first-person, not third-person, sensation-sentences to *expressions* of sensation. I will say one or two things more about his conception of the use of third-person sensation-sentences.

(1) "Only of a living human being and what resembles (behaves like) a living human being can one say: it has sensations; it sees; is blind; hears; is deaf; is conscious or unconscious" (281). The *human* body and *human* behavior are the *paradigm* to which third-person attributions of consciousness, sensations, feelings, are related. (The use of first-person sensation-sentences is governed by *no* paradigm.) Thus there cannot occur in ordinary life a question as to whether other human beings ever possess consciousness, and I can have this question when I philosophize only if I forget that I use that paradigm in ordinary life. It is by analogy with the human form and behavior that I attribute consciousness (or unconsciousness) to animals and fish, the more remote the analogy the less sense in the attribution. (Just as it is by analogy with our ordinary language that anything is called 'language') (494). In order to imagine that a pot or a chair has thoughts or sensations one must give it, in imagination, something like a human body, face, and speech (282, 361). A child says that its doll has stomach-ache, but this is a "secondary" use of the concept of pain. "Imagine a case in which people ascribed pain *only* to inanimate things; pitied *only* dolls" (282, cf. 385, p. 216)!

Wittgenstein means, I think, that this is an impossible supposition be-cause we should not want to say that those people *understood* ascriptions of pain. If they did not ever show pity for human beings or animals or expect it for themselves, then their treatment of dolls would not be *pity*. (2) My criterion of another's being in pain is, first, his behavior and circumstances and, second, his words (after they have been found to be connected in the right way with his behavior and circumstances). Does it follow that my interest is in his behavior and words, not in his pain? Does 'He is in pain' *mean* behavior? In lectures Wittgenstein imagined a tribe of people who had the idea that their slaves had no feelings, no souls—that they were automatons—despite the fact that the slaves had human bodies, behaved like their masters, and even spoke the same language. Wittgenstein undertook to try to give sense to that idea. When a slave injured himself or fell ill or complained of pains, his master would try to heal him. The master would let him rest when he was fatigued, feed him when he was hungry and thirsty, and so on. Further-more, the masters would apply to the slaves our usual distinctions be-tween genuine complaints and malingering. So what could it mean to say that they had the idea that the slaves were automatons? Well, they would *look* at the slaves in a peculiar way. They would observe and com-ment on their movements *as if* they were machines. ('Notice how smoothly his limbs move.') They would discard them when they were worn and useless, like machines. If a slave received a mortal injury and twisted and screamed in agony, no master would avert his gaze in horror or prevent his children from observing the scene, any more than he would if the ceiling fell on a printing press. Here is a difference in 'attitude' that is not a matter of believing or expecting different facts.

So in the *Investigations,* Wittgenstein says, "My attitude towards him is an attitude towards a soul. I am not of the *opinion* that he has a soul" (p. 178). I do not *believe* that the man is suffering who writhes before me—for to what facts would a 'belief' be related, such that a change in the facts would lead me to alter it? I *react* to his suffering. I look at him with compassion and try to comfort him. If I complain of headache to someone and he says 'It's not so bad,' does this prove that he believes in something *behind* my outward expression of pain? "His attitude is a proof of his attitude. Imagine not merely the words 'I am in pain' but also the answer 'It's not so bad' replaced by instinctive noises and ges-tures" (310). The thought that behind someone's pain-behavior is the pain itself does not enter into our use of 'He's in pain,' but what does enter into it is our sympathetic, or unsympathetic, reaction to him. The fact that the latter does enter into our use of that sentence (but might not have) gives sense to saying that the sentence 'He is in pain' does not just *mean* that his behavior, words, and circumstances are such and such—although these are the criterion for its use.

When he groans we do not *assume,* even tacitly, that the groaning expresses pain. We fetch a sedative and try to put him at ease. A totally different way of reacting to his groans would be to make exact records of their volume and frequency—and do nothing to relieve the sufferer! But our reaction of seeking to comfort him does not involve a presupposition, for, "Doesn't a presupposition imply a doubt? And doubt may be entirely lacking" (p. 180).

Form of Life

The gestures, facial expressions, words, and activities that constitute pitying and comforting a person or a dog are, I think, a good example of what Wittgenstein means by a "form of life." One could hardly place too much stress on the importance of this latter notion in Wittgenstein's thought. It is intimately related to the notion "language-game." His choice of the latter term is meant to "bring into prominence the fact that the *speaking* of language is part of an activity, or of a form of life" (23; cf. 19). If we want to understand any concept we must obtain a view of the human behavior, the activities, the natural expressions, that surround the words for that concept. What, for example, is the concept of *certainty* as applied to *predictions?* The nature of my certainty that fire will burn me comes out in the fact that "Nothing could induce me to put my hand into a flame" (472). That reaction of mine to fire shows the *meaning* of certainty in this language-game (474). (Of course, it is *different* from the concept of certainty in, e.g., mathematics. "The kind of certainty is the kind of language-game" [p. 124].) But is my certainty justified? Don't I need reasons? Well, I don't normally think of reasons, I can't produce much in the way of reasons, and I don't feel a need of reasons (cf. 477). Whatever was offered in the way of reasons would not strengthen my fear of fire, and if the reasons turned out to be weak I still wouldn't be induced to put my hand on the hot stove.

As far as 'justification' is concerned, "What people accept as a justification—is shown by how they think and live" (325). If we want to elucidate the concept of justification we must take note of what people *accept* as justified; and it is clearly shown in our lives that we accept as justified both the certainty that fire will burn and the certainty that this man is in pain—even without reasons. Forms of life, embodied in language-games, teach us what justification is. As philosophers we must not attempt to justify the forms of life, to give reasons for *them*—to argue, for example, that we pity the injured man because we believe, assume, presuppose, or know that in addition to the groans and writhing, there is pain. The fact is, we pity him! "What has to be accepted, the given, is —so one could say—*forms of life*" (p. 226). What we should say is: "*This language-game is played*" (654).

From this major theme of Wittgenstein's thought one passes easily to **another** major theme—that "Philosophy simply puts everything before us, and neither explains nor deduces anything" (126). "It leaves everything as it is" (124).

Strawson's Criticism

Mr. Peter Strawson's critical notice[3] of the *Investigations* contains misunderstandings that might obtain currency. To Strawson it appears that, for Wittgenstein, "No word whatever stands for or names a special experience," [4] "no words name sensations (or 'private experiences'); and in particular the word 'pain' does not." [5] Wittgenstein "has committed himself to the view that one cannot sensibly be said to recognize or identify anything, unless one uses *criteria;* and, as a consequence of this, that one cannot recognize or identify sensations." [6] His "obsession with the *expression* of pain" leads him "to deny that sensations can be recognized and bear names." [7] Wittgenstein is hostile to "the idea of what is not observed (seen, heard, smelled, touched, tasted), and in particular to the idea that what is not observed can in any sense be recognized or described or reported" [8]—although at one place in the book (p. 189) "it looks as if he were almost prepared to acknowledge" that 'I am in pain' "may be just a report of my sensations." [9] His "prejudice against 'the inner' " leads him to deny that it is possible for a person to report the words that went through his mind when he was saying something to himself in his thoughts.[10] Strawson attributes Wittgenstein's errors not only to prejudice and, possibly, to "the old verificationist horror of a claim that cannot be checked," [11] but also to various confusions and muddles.[12]

It is important to see how very erroneous is this account of Wittgenstein. The latter says, "Don't we talk about sensations every day, and give them names?" and then asks, "How does a human being learn the names of sensations?—of the word 'pain' for example?" (244) So Wittgenstein does not deny that we *name* sensations. It is a howler to accuse Wittgenstein of "hostility to the idea of what is not observed" ("observed" apparently means 'perceived by one of the five senses') and of "hostility to the idea that what is not observed can in any sense be recognized or described or reported." [13] Dreams and mental pictures are not observed, in Strawson's sense; yet Wittgenstein discusses *reports* of dreams (p. 222; also p. 184) and *descriptions* of mental pictures (e.g., 367). Consider this general remark: "Think how many different kinds of things are called 'description': description of a body's position by means of its co-ordinates; description of a facial expression; *description of a*

---

[3] P. F. Strawson, "Critical Notice: *Philosophical Investigations,*" *Mind,* LXIII (1954), 70-99. (References to Strawson will be placed in footnotes, references to Wittgenstein will remain in the text.)
[4] P. 83.   [5] P. 84.   [6] P. 86.   [7] P. 87.   [8] P. 90.   [9] P. 94.   [10] P. 91.   [11] P. 92.
[12] See p. 86 and p. 98.   [13] P. 90.

sensation of touch; of a mood" (24, my italics). And at many places in the *Investigations,* Wittgenstein *gives* descriptions of various sensations, although sensations are not observed, in Strawson's sense. Strawson's belief that Wittgenstein thinks that "one cannot sensibly be said to recognize or identify anything, unless one uses criteria," [14] is proved false by the remarks about mental images: I have *no* criterion for saying that two images of mine are the same (377); yet there is such a thing as *recognition* here, and a correct use of 'same' (378). How can it be maintained that Wittgenstein has a prejudice against 'the inner' when he allows that in our ordinary language a man *can* write down or give vocal expression to his "inner experiences—his feelings, moods, and the rest —for his private use" (243)? Wittgenstein does not deny that there are *inner* experiences any more than he denies that there are *mental* occurrences. Indeed, he gives examples of things that he calls *"seelische Vorgänge,"* e.g., "a pain's growing more or less," and in contrast with which a thing like *understanding a word* is not, he argues, a *"seelischen Vorgang"* (154). Either to deny that such occurrences exist or to claim that they cannot be named, reported, or described is entirely foreign to Wittgenstein's outlook. For what would the denial amount to other than an attempt to "reform language," which is not his concern? It may *look* as if he were trying to reform language, because he is engaged in "giving prominence to distinctions which our ordinary forms of language easily make us overlook" (132). For example, Wittgenstein suggests that when we think about the philosophical problem of sensation the word 'describe' *tricks* us (290). Of course he does not mean that it is a mistake to speak of 'describing' a sensation. He means that the similarity in "surface grammar" (664) between 'I describe my sensations' and 'I describe my room' may mislead, may cause us to fail "to call to mind the differences between the language-games" (290).

Strawson rightly avers, "To deny that 'pain' is the name of a (type of) sensation is comparable to denying that 'red' is the name of a color." [15] I suppose that, conversely, to affirm that 'pain' is the name of a sensation is like affirming that 'red' is the name of a color, and also that 'o' is the name of a number. This classification tells us nothing of philosophical interest. What we need to notice is the *difference* between the way that 'o' and '2,' say, function, although both are 'names of numbers' (think how easily one may be tempted to deny that o is a number), and the difference between the way 'red' and 'pain' function, although both are 'names.' "We call very different things 'names'; the word 'name' is used to characterize many different kinds of use of a word, related to one another in many different ways" (38). To suppose that the uses of 'pain' and 'red,' as *names,* are alike is just the sort of error that Wittgenstein wants to expose. If one thinks this, one will want

[14] P. 86. [15] P. 87.

to by-pass the *expression* of pain and will wonder at Wittgenstein's "obsession" with it. Not that Strawson does by-pass it, but he seems to attach the wrong significance to it. He appears to think that the fact that there is a characteristic pain-behavior is what makes possible a *common* "language of pain," and he seems to imply that if we did not care to have a *common* language of pain each of us would still be able to name and describe his pains in "a private language-game," even if there were no characteristic pain-behavior.[16] It looks as if he thinks that with his private language he could step between pain and its expression, and apply names to the bare sensations themselves (cf. 245).

For Strawson the conception of a private language possesses no difficulty. A man "might simply be struck by the recurrence of a certain sensation and get into the habit of making a certain mark in a different place every time it occurred. The making of the marks would help to impress the occurrence on his memory." [17] Just as, I suppose, he might utter a certain sound each time a cow appeared. But we need to ask, what makes the latter sound a *word,* and what makes it the word for *cow?* Is there no difficulty here? Is it sufficient that the sound is uttered when and only when a cow is present? Of course not. The sound might refer to anything or nothing. What is necessary is that it should play a part in various activities, in calling, fetching, counting cows, distinguishing cows from other things and pictures of cows from pictures of other things. If the sound has no fixed place in activities ("language-games") of this sort, then it isn't a word for *cow.* To be sure, I can sit in my chair and talk about cows and not be engaged in any of those activities—but what makes my words *refer* to cows is the fact that I have already mastered those activities; they lie in the background. The kind of way that 'cow' refers is the kind of language-game to which it belongs. If a mark or sound is to be a word for a *sensation* it, too, must enter into language-games, although of a very different sort. What sort? Well, such things as showing the location of the sensation, exhibiting different reactions to different intensities of stimulus, seeking or avoiding causes of the sensation, choosing one sensation in preference to another, indicating the duration of the sensation, and so on. Actions and reactions of that sort constitute the sensation-behavior. They are the "outward criteria" (580) with which the sign must be connected if it is to be a sign for a sensation *at all,* not merely if it is to be a sign in a *common* language. In the mere supposition that there is a man who is "struck by the recurrence of a certain sensation" and who gets into the habit of "making a certain mark in a different place every time it occurred," no ground *whatever* has been given for saying that the mark is a sign for a sensation. The necessary surroundings have not been supplied. Strawson sees no problem here. He is surprised that "Wittgenstein gives himself

[16] See pp. 84-88.   [17] P. 85.

considerable trouble over the question of how a man would *introduce* a name for a sensation into this private language." [18] It is as if Strawson thought: There is no difficulty about it; the man just *makes* the mark refer to a sensation. How the man does it puzzles Strawson so little that he is not even inclined to feel that the connection between the name and the sensation is queer, occult (cf. 38)—which it would be, to say the least, if the name had no fixed place in those activities and reactions that constitute sensation-behavior, for that, and not a magical act of the mind, is what *makes* it refer to a sensation.

The conception of private language that Wittgenstein attacks is not the conception of a language that only the speaker does understand, but of a language that no other person *can* understand (243). Strawson thinks that Wittgenstein has not refuted the conception of a private language but has only shown that certain conditions must be satisfied if a common language is to exist. Strawson appears to believe (I may misunderstand him) that each of us not only can have but does have a private language of sensations, that if we are to understand one another when we speak of our sensations there must be criteria for the use of our sensation-words, and that therefore the words with which we *refer* to our sensations must, in addition, contain "allusions" either to behavior or to material substances that are "associated" with the sensations. [19] The allusions must be to things that can be perceived by us all. By virtue of this the use of sensation-words can be taught and misuses corrected, and so those words will belong to a common language. There is another feature of their use (namely, their reference) that cannot be taught. Thus sensation-words will have both a public and a private meaning. Strawson's view appears to be accurately characterized by Wittgenstein's mock conjecture: "Or is it like this: the word 'red' means something known to everyone; and in addition, for each person, it means something known only to him? (Or perhaps rather: it *refers* to something known only to him.)" (273)

But if my words, *without* these allusions, can refer to my sensations, then what is alluded to is only *contingently* related to the sensations. Adding the "allusions to what can be seen and touched" [20] will not help one little bit in making us understand one another. For the behavior that is, for me, contingently associated with 'the sensation of pain' may be, for you, contingently associated with 'the sensation of tickling'; the piece of matter that produces in you what you call 'a metallic taste' may produce in me what, if you could experience it, you would call 'the taste of onions'; my 'sensation of red' may be your 'sensation of blue'; we do not know and cannot know whether we are talking about the same things; we cannot *learn* the essential thing about one another's use of sensation-words—namely, their reference. The language in which the private referring is done cannot be turned into a common language by having some-

[18] *Ibid.*   [19] P. 86.   [20] *Ibid.*

thing grafted on to it. Private language cannot be the understructure of the language we all understand. It is as if, in Strawson's conception, the sensation-words were supposed to perform two functions—to refer and to communicate. But if the reference is incommunicable, then the trappings of allusion will not communicate it, and what they do communicate will be irrelevant.

Strawson's idea that expressions like 'jabbing pain,' 'metallic taste,' mean something known to everyone and, in addition, for each person, refer to something known only to him, is responsible, I believe, for his failure to understand Wittgenstein on the topic of recognizing and identifying sensations. There is *a* sense of 'recognize' and 'identify' with respect to which Wittgenstein does deny that we can recognize or identify our own sensations, feelings, images. Consider, for example, that although a man understands the word 'alcohol' he may fail to identify the alcohol in a bottle as alcohol, because the bottle is marked 'gasoline' or because the cork smells of gasoline; or, although he understands 'rabbit' and is familiar with rabbits, he may fail to recognize a rabbit as a rabbit, taking it for a stump instead; or, he may be in doubt and say, 'I don't know whether this is alcohol,' 'I'm not sure whether that is a rabbit or a stump.' But can a man who understands the word 'pain' be in doubt as to whether he has pain? Wittgenstein remarks:

> If anyone said "I do not know if what I have got is a pain or something else," we should think something like, he does not know what the English word "pain" means; and we should explain it to him.—How? Perhaps by means of gestures, or by pricking him with a pin and saying: "See, that's what pain is!" This explanation, like any other, he might understand right, wrong, or not at all. And he will show which he does by his use of the word, in this as in other cases.
>
> If he now said, for example: "Oh, I know what 'pain' means; what I don't know is whether *this,* that I have now, is pain"—we should merely shake our heads and be forced to regard his words as a queer reaction which we have no idea what to do with [288].

That a man wonders whether what he has is pain can only mean that he does not understand the word 'pain'; he cannot both understand it and have that doubt. Thus there is a sense of 'identify' that has no application to sensations. One who understands the word 'alcohol' may fail to identify *this* as alcohol or may be in doubt as to its identity or may correctly identify it. These possibilities have no meaning in the case of pain. There is not over and above (or underneath) the understanding of the word 'pain' a further process of correctly identifying or failing to identify *this* as pain. There would be if Strawson's conception was right. But there is not, and this is why "That expression of doubt ['Oh, I know what "pain" means; what I don't know is whether *this,* that

I have now, is pain'] has no place in the language-game" (288). (Strawson does not have, but in consistency should have, an inclination to dispute this last remark of Wittgenstein's.)[21] The fact that there is no *further* process of identifying a particular sensation is a reason why "the object drops out of consideration as irrelevant" when "we construe the grammar of the expression of sensation on the model of 'object and name' " (293) —a remark that Strawson misunderstands as the thesis that "no words name sensations." [22] If my use of a sensation-word satisfies the normal outward criteria and if I truthfully declare that I have that sensation, then I *have* it—there is not a further problem of my applying the word right or wrong within myself. If a man used the word 'pain' in accordance with "the usual symptoms and presuppositions of pain" then it would have no sense to suppose that perhaps his memory did not retain *what* the word 'pain' refers to, "so that he constantly called different things by that name" (271). If my use of the word fits those usual criteria there is not an added problem of whether I accurately pick out the objects to which the word applies. In this sense of 'identify,' the hypothesis that I identify my sensations is "a mere ornament, not connected with the mechanism at all" (270).

It does not follow nor, I think, does Wittgenstein mean to assert that there is *no* proper use of 'identify' or 'recognize' with sensations. He acknowledges a use of 'recognize' with mental images, as previously noted. It would be a natural use of language, I believe, if someone who upon arising complained of an unusual sensation were to say, 'Now I can identify it! It is the same sensation that I have when I go down in an elevator.' Wittgenstein, who has no interest in reforming language, would not dream of calling this an incorrect use of 'identify.' He attacks a philosophical use of the word only, the use that belongs to the notion of the private object. In this example of a nonphilosophical use, if the speaker employed the rest of the sensation-language as we all do, and if his behavior in this case was approximately what it was when he was affected by the downward motion of an elevator, then his declaration that he was feeling the elevator-sensation would be decisive; and also his declaration that it was *not* the elevator-sensation would be decisive. It is *out of the question* that he should have made a mistake in identifying the sensation. His identification of his sensation is an *expression* of sensation (in Wittgenstein's extended sense of this phrase). The identification is 'incorrigible.' We have here a radically different use of 'identify' from that illustrated in the examples of alcohol and rabbit.

The philosophical use of 'identify' seems to make possible the committing of *errors* of identification of sensations and inner experiences. The idea is that my sensation or my image is an object that I cannot show to anyone and that I identify it and from it derive its description

(374). But if this is so, why cannot my identification and description go wrong, and not just sometimes but always? Here we are in a position to grasp the significance of Wittgenstein's maneuver: "Always get rid of the idea of the private object in this way: assume that it constantly changes, but that you do not notice the change because your memory constantly deceives you" (p. 207). We are meant to see the *senselessness* of this supposition: for what in the world would *show* that I was deceived constantly or even once? Do I look again—and why can't I be deceived that time, too? The supposition is a knob that doesn't turn anything (cf. 270). Understanding this will perhaps remove the temptation to think that I have something that I cannot show to you and from which I derive a knowledge of its identity. This is what Wittgenstein means in saying that when I related to another what I just said to myself in my thoughts " 'what went on within me' is not the point at all" (p. 222). He is not declaring, as Strawson thinks, that I cannot report what words went through my mind.[23] He is saying that it is a report "whose truth is guaranteed by the special criteria of truthfulness" (p. 222). It is *that* kind of report. So it is not a matter of trying faithfully to observe something within myself and of trying to produce a correct account of it, of trying to do something at which I might unwittingly fail.

The influence of the idea of the private object on Strawson's thinking is subtly reflected, I believe, in his declaration that a metallic taste is "quite certainly recognizable and identifiable in itself" and in his remark that "if the question 'What is the criterion of identity here?' is pushed, one can only answer: 'Well, the taste itself' (cf. 'the sensation itself')."[24] Strawson realizes that we don't identify a sensation by means of criteria (e.g., a metallic taste by means of the metallic material that produces it). He is inclined to add that we identify it by 'the sensation itself.' This seems to me to misconstrue the "grammar" of 'identify' here. It may be to the point to consider again the comparison of colors and sensations. Wittgenstein says, "How do I know that this color is red?—It would be an answer to say 'I have learned English' " (381). One thing this answer does is to deny that I have *reasons* for saying that this color before me is red. We might put this by saying that I identify it as red by 'the color itself,' not by anything else. The cases of red and pain (or metallic taste) so far run parallel. Equally, I don't have reasons for saying that this color is red or that this sensation is pain. But it *can* happen that I should fail to identify this color correctly, even though I have learned English (e.g., the moonlight alters its appearance). Here the parallel ends. Nothing can alter the 'appearance' of the sensation. Nothing counts as mistaking its identity. If we assimilate identifying sensations to identifying colors, because in neither instance reasons are relevant, we conceal the philosophically more important difference. To

[23] See pp. 90, 91.   [24] P. 86.

insist that the parallel is perfect, that one identifies sensations in the same sense that one identifies colors, is like saying that "there must also be something boiling in the pictured pot" (297). Identifying one's own sensation is nothing that is either in error or *not* in error. It is not, in *that* sense, *identifying*. When I identify my sensation, I do not *find out* its identity, not even from 'the sensation itself.' My identification, one could say, *defines* its identity.

We use a man's identification of his sensation as a criterion of what his sensation is. But this is a *dependent* criterion. We do not isolate it from the rest of his behavior. His verbal reports and identifications would not *be* a criterion unless they were grounded in the primitive sensation-behavior that is the primary and independent criterion of his sensations. If we cut out human behavior from the language-game of sensations (which Strawson does in defending the 'private language-game'), one result will be that a man's identifying a sensation as the 'same' that he had a moment before will no longer be a criterion of its being the same. Not only the speaker but *no one* will have a criterion of identity. Consequently, for no one will it have any meaning to speak of a man's being "struck by the *recurrence* of a certain sensation." [25] I hope that I will be forgiven if I have misunderstood Mr. Strawson.

Conclusion

I have discussed only one strand of this complex, difficult, and exciting book. Countless other riches are there: a powerful attack upon Wittgenstein's own *Tractatus;* deep inquiries into the notions of *concept* and *proposition;* investigations of *naming, thinking, meaning, intending, understanding, imagining;* a remarkable study of *seeing as,* a notion that is important to Gestalt psychology; a revolutionary account of the nature of philosophy. All this, and far more, is presented with the passion and profundity of genius, in language of never-failing force.

[*] P 85, my italics.

V ⤳ Is Consciousness a Brain Process?

U. T. Place

The thesis that consciousness is a process in the brain is put forward as a reasonable scientific hypothesis, not to be dismissed on logical grounds alone. The conditions under which two sets of observations are treated as observations of the same process, rather than as observations of two independent correlated processes, are discussed. It is suggested that we can identify consciousness with a given pattern of brain activity, if we can explain the subject's introspective observations by reference to the brain processes with which they are correlated. It is argued that the problem of providing a physiological explanation of introspective observations is made to seem more difficult than it really is by the "phenomenological fallacy," the mistaken idea that descriptions of the appearances of things are descriptions of the actual state of affairs in a mysterious internal environment.

I. Introduction

The view that there exists a separate class of events, mental events, which cannot be described in terms of the concepts employed by the physical sciences no longer commands the universal and unquestioning acceptance among philosophers and psychologists which it once did. Modern physicalism, however, unlike the materialism of the seventeenth and eighteenth centuries, is behavioristic. Consciousness on this view is either a special type of behavior, "sampling" or "running-back-and-forth" behavior as Tolman has it,[1] or a disposition to behave in a certain way, an itch for example being a temporary propensity to scratch. In the case of cognitive concepts like "knowing," "believing," "understanding," "remembering," and volitional concepts like "wanting" and "intending," there can be little doubt, I think, that an analysis in terms of dispositions to behave is fundamentally sound.[2] On the other hand, there would seem to be an intractable residue of concepts clustering around the notions of consciousness, experience, sensation, and mental imagery, where some sort of inner process story is unavoidable.[3] It is

---

[1] E. C. Tolman, *Purposive Behavior in Animals and Men* (Berkeley: University of California Press, 1932).

[2] L. Wittgenstein, *Philosophical Investigations* (Oxford: Blackwell, 1953); G. Ryle, *The Concept of Mind* (London: Hutchinson's University Library, 1949).

[3] U. T. Place, "The Concept of Heed," *British Journal of Psychology*, XLV (1954), 243-55.

possible, of course, that a satisfactory behavioristic account of this conceptual residuum will ultimately be found. For our present purposes, however, I shall assume that this cannot be done and that statements about pains and twinges, about how things look, sound, and feel, about things dreamed of or pictured in the mind's eye, are statements referring to events and processes which are in some sense private or internal to the individual of whom they are predicated. The question I wish to raise is whether in making this assumption we are inevitably committed to a dualist position in which sensations and mental images form a separate category of processes over and above the physical and physiological processes with which they are known to be correlated. I shall argue that an acceptance of inner processes does not entail dualism and that the thesis that consciousness is a process in the brain cannot be dismissed on logical grounds.

II. The "Is" of Definition and the "Is" of Composition

I want to stress from the outset that in defending the thesis that consciousness is a process in the brain, I am not trying to argue that when we describe our dreams, fantasies, and sensations we are talking about processes in our brains. That is, I am not claiming that statements about sensations and mental images are reducible to or analyzable into statements about brain processes, in the way in which "cognition statements" are analyzable into statements about behavior. To say that statements about consciousness are statements about brain processes is manifestly false. This is shown (a) by the fact that you can describe your sensations and mental imagery without knowing anything about your brain processes or even that such things exist, (b) by the fact that statements about one's consciousness and statements about one's brain processes are verified in entirely different ways, and (c) by the fact that there is nothing self-contradictory about the statement "X has a pain but there is nothing going on in his brain." What I do want to assert, however, is that the statement "Consciousness is a process in the brain," although not necessarily true, is not necessarily false. "Consciousness is a process in the brain," on my view is neither self-contradictory nor self-evident; it is a reasonable scientific hypothesis, in the way that the statement "Lightning is a motion of electric charges" is a reasonable scientific hypothesis.

The all but universally accepted view that an assertion of identity between consciousness and brain processes can be ruled out on logical grounds alone, derives, I suspect, from a failure to distinguish between what we may call the "is" of definition and the "is" of composition. The distinction I have in mind here is the difference between the function of the word "is" in statements like "A square is an equilateral rectangle," "Red is a color," "To understand an instruction is to be able to act appropriately under the appropriate circumstances," and its function in statements like "His table is an old packing case," "Her hat is a bundle of straw tied together with string," "A cloud is a mass of water droplets or other particles in suspension." These two types of "is" statements have one thing in common. In both cases it makes sense to add the qualification "and nothing else." In this they differ from those statements in which the "is" is an "is" of predication; the statements "Toby is 80 years old and nothing else," "Her hat is red and nothing else" or "Giraffes are tall and nothing else," for example, are nonsense. This logical feature may be described by saying that in both cases both the grammatical subject and the grammatical predicate are expressions which provide an adequate characterization of the state of affairs to which they both refer.

In another respect, however, the two groups of statements are strikingly different. Statements like "A square is an equilateral rectangle" are necessary statements which are true by definition. Statements like "His table is an old packing case," on the other hand, are contingent statements which have to be verified by observation. In the case of statements like "A square is an equilateral rectangle" or "Red is a color," there is a relationship between the meaning of the expression forming the grammatical predicate and the meaning of the expression forming the grammatical subject, such that whenever the subject expression is applicable the predicate must also be applicable. If you can describe something as red then you must also be able to describe it as colored. In the case of statements like "His table is an old packing case," on the other hand, there is no such relationship between the meanings of the expressions "his table" and "old packing case"; it merely so happens that in this case both expressions are applicable to and at the same time provide an adequate characterization of the same object. Those who contend that the statement "Consciousness is a brain process" is logically untenable base their claim, I suspect, on the mistaken assumption that if the meanings of two statements or expressions are quite unconnected, they cannot both provide an adequate characterization of the same object or state of affairs: if something is a state of consciousness, it cannot be a brain process, since there is nothing self-contradictory in supposing that someone feels a pain when there is nothing happening inside his skull. By the same token we might be led to conclude that a table cannot be an old packing case, since there is nothing self-contradictory in supposing that someone has a table, but is not in possession of an old packing case.

III. The Logical Independence of Expressions and the Ontological Independence of Entities

There is, of course, an important difference between the table/packing case case and the consciousness/brain process case in that the statement "His table is an old packing case" is a particular proposition which refers only to one particular case, whereas the statement "Consciousness is a process in the brain" is a general or universal proposition applying to all states of consciousness whatever. It is fairly clear, I think, that if we lived in a world in which all tables without exception were packing cases, the concepts of "table" and "packing case" in our language would not have their present logically independent status. In such a world a table would be a species of packing case in much the same way that red is a species of color. It seems to be a rule of language that whenever a given variety of object or state of affairs has two characteristics or sets of characteristics, one of which is unique to the variety of object or state of affairs in question, the expression used to refer to the characteristic or set of characteristics which defines the variety of object or state of affairs in question will always entail the expression used to refer to the other characteristic or set of characteristics. If this rule admitted of no exception it would follow that any expression which is logically independent of another expression which uniquely characterizes a given variety of object or state of affairs, must refer to a characteristic or set of characteristics which is not normally or necessarily associated with the object or state of affairs in question. It is because this rule applies almost universally, I suggest, that we are normally justified in arguing from the logical independence of two expressions to the ontological independence of the states of affairs to which they refer. This would explain both the undoubted force of the argument that consciousness and brain processes must be independent entities because the expressions used to refer to them are logically independent and, in general, the curious phenomenon whereby questions about the furniture of the universe are often fought and not infrequently decided merely on a point of logic.

The argument from the logical independence of two expressions to the ontological independence of the entities to which they refer breaks down in the case of brain processes and consciousness, I believe, because this is one of a relatively small number of cases where the rule stated above does not apply. These exceptions are to be found, I suggest, in those cases where the operations which have to be performed in order to verify the presence of the two sets of characteristics inhering in the object or state of affairs in question can seldom if ever be performed simultaneously. A good example here is the case of the cloud and the mass of droplets or other particles in suspension. A cloud is a large semi-transparent mass with a fleecy texture suspended in the atmosphere whose shape is subject to continual and kaleidoscopic change. When observed at close quarters, however, it is found to consist of a mass of tiny particles, usually water droplets, in continuous motion. On the basis of this second observation we conclude that a cloud is a mass of tiny particles and nothing else. But there is no logical connection in our language between a cloud and a mass of tiny particles; there is nothing self-contradictory in talking about a cloud which is not composed of tiny particles in suspension. There is no contradiction involved in supposing that clouds consist of a dense mass of fibrous tissue; indeed, such a consistency seems to be implied by many of the functions performed by clouds in fairy stories and mythology. It is clear from this that the terms "cloud" and "mass of tiny particles in suspension" mean quite different things. Yet we do not conclude from this that there must be two things, the mass of particles in suspension and the cloud. The reason for this, I suggest, is that although the characteristics of being a cloud and being a mass of tiny particles in suspension are invariably associated, we never make the observations necessary to verify the statement "That is a cloud" and those necessary to verify the statement "This is a mass of tiny particles in suspension" at one and the same time. We can observe the microstructure of a cloud only when we are enveloped by it, a condition which effectively prevents us from observing those characteristics which from a distance lead us to describe it as a cloud. Indeed, so disparate are these two experiences that we use different words to describe them. That which is a cloud when we observe it from a distance becomes a fog or mist when we are enveloped by it.

IV. When Are Two Sets of Observations Observations of the Same Event?

The example of the cloud and the mass of tiny particles in suspension was chosen because it is one of the few cases of a general proposition involving what I have called the "is" of composition which does not involve us in scientific technicalities. It is useful because it brings out the connection between the ordinary everyday cases of the "is" of composition like the table/packing case example and the more technical cases like "Lightning is a motion of electric charges" where the analogy with the consciousness/brain process case is most marked. The limitation of the cloud/tiny particles in suspension case is that it does not bring out sufficiently clearly the crucial problem of how the identity of the states of affairs referred to by the two expressions is established. In the cloud case the fact that something is a cloud and the fact that something is a mass of tiny particles in suspension are both verified by the normal processes of visual observation. It is arguable, moreover, that the identity of the entities referred to by the two expressions is established by the continuity between the two sets of observations as the observer moves towards or away from the cloud. In the case of brain processes and consciousness there is no such continuity between the two sets of observations involved. A closer introspective scrutiny will never reveal the passage of nerve impulses over a thousand synapses in the way that a closer scrutiny of a cloud will reveal a mass of tiny particles in suspension. The operations required to verify statements about consciousness and statements about brain processes are fundamentally different.

To find a parallel for this feature we must examine other cases where an identity is asserted between something whose occurrence is verified by the ordinary processes of observation and something whose occurrence is established by special scientific procedures. For this purpose I have chosen the case where we say that lightning is a motion of electric charges. As in the case of consciousness, however closely we scrutinize the lightning we shall never be able to observe the electric charges, and just as the operations for determining the nature of one's state of consciousness are radically different from those involved in determining the nature of one's brain processes, so the operations for determining the occurrence of lightning are radically different from those involved in determining the occurrence of a motion of electric charges. What is it, therefore, that leads us to say that the two sets of observations are observations of the same event? It cannot be merely the fact that the two sets of observations are systematically correlated such that whenever there is lightning there is always a motion of electric charges. There are innumerable cases of such correlations where we have no temptation to say that the two sets of observations are observations of the same event. There is a systematic correlation, for example, between the movement of the tides and the stages of the moon, but this does not lead us to say that records of tidal levels are records of the moon's stages or vice versa. We speak rather of a causal connection between two independent events or processes.

The answer here seems to be that we treat the two sets of observations as observations of the same event in those cases where the technical scientific observations set in the context of the appropriate body of scientific theory provide an immediate explanation of the observations made by the man in the street. Thus we conclude that lightning is nothing more than a motion of electric charges, because we know that a motion of electric charges through the atmosphere, such as occurs when lightning is reported, gives rise to the type of visual stimulation which would lead an observer to report a flash of lightning. In the moon/tide case, on the other hand, there is no such direct causal connection between the stages of the moon and the observations made by the man who measures the height of the tide. The causal connection is between the moon and the tides, not between the moon and the measurement of the tides.

V. The Physiological Explanation of Introspection and the Phenomenological Fallacy

If this account is correct, it should follow that in order to establish the identity of consciousness and certain processes in the brain, it would be necessary to show that the introspective observations reported by the subject can be accounted for in terms of processes which are known to have occurred in his brain. In the light of this suggestion it is extremely interesting to find that when a physiologist as distinct from a philosopher finds it difficult to see how consciousness could be a process in the brain, what worries him is not any supposed self-contradiction involved in such an assumption, but the apparent impossibility of accounting for the reports given by the subject of his conscious processes in terms of the known properties of the central nervous system. Sir Charles Sherrington has posed the problem as follows:

> The chain of events stretching from the sun's radiation entering the eye to, on the one hand, the contraction of the pupillary muscles, and on the other, to the electrical disturbances in the brain-cortex are all straightforward steps in a sequence of physical "causation," such as, thanks to science, are intelligible. But in the second serial chain there follows on, or attends, the stage of brain-cortex reaction an event or set of events quite inexplicable to us, which both as to themselves and as to the causal tie between them and what preceded them science does not help us; a set of events seemingly incommensurable with any of the events leading up to it. The self "sees" the sun; it senses a two-dimensional disc of brightness, located in the "sky," this last a field of lesser brightness, and overhead shaped as a rather flattened dome, coping the self and a hundred other visual things as well. Of hint that this is within the head there is none. Vision is saturated with this strange property called "projection," the unargued inference that what it sees is at a "distance" from the seeing "self." Enough has been said to stress that in the sequence of events a step is reached where a physical situation in the brain leads to a psychical, which however contains no hint of the brain or any other bodily part. . . . The supposition has to be, it would seem, two continuous series of events, one physicochemical, the other psychical, and at times interaction between them.[4]

Just as the physiologist is not likely to be impressed by the philosopher's contention that there is some self-contradiction involved in supposing consciousness to be a brain process, so the philosopher is unlikely to be impressed by the considerations which lead Sherrington to conclude that there are two sets of events, one physicochemical, the other psychical. Sherrington's argument for all its emotional appeal depends on a fairly simple logical mistake, which is unfortunately all too frequently made by psychologists and physiologists and not infrequently in the past by the philosophers themselves. This logical mistake, which I shall refer to as the "phenomenological fallacy," is the mistake of supposing that when the subject describes his experience, when he describes how things look, sound, smell, taste, or feel to him, he is describing the literal properties of objects and events on a peculiar sort of internal cinema or television screen, usually referred to in the modern psychological literature as the "phenomenal field." If we assume, for example,

[4] Sir Charles Sherrington, *The Integrative Action of the Nervous System* (Cambridge: Cambridge University Press, 1947), pp. xx-xxi.

that when a subject reports a green after-image he is asserting the occurrence inside himself of an object which is literally green, it is clear that we have on our hands an entity for which there is no place in the world of physics. In the case of the green after-image there is no green object in the subject's environment corresponding to the description that he gives. Nor is there anything green in his brain; certainly there is nothing which could have emerged when he reported the appearance of the green after-image. Brain processes are not the sort of things to which color concepts can be properly applied.

The phenomenological fallacy on which this argument is based depends on the mistaken assumption that because our ability to describe things in our environment depends on our consciousness of them, our descriptions of things are primarily descriptions of our conscious experience and only secondarily, indirectly, and inferentially descriptions of the objects and events in our environments. It is assumed that because we recognize things in our environment by their look, sound, smell, taste, and feel, we begin by describing their phenomenal properties, i.e., the properties of the looks, sounds, smells, tastes, and feels which they produce in us, and infer their real properties from their phenomenal properties. In fact, the reverse is the case. We begin by learning to recognize the real properties of things in our environment. We learn to recognize them, of course, by their look, sound, smell, taste, and feel; but this does not mean that we have to learn to describe the look, sound, smell, taste, and feel of things before we can describe the things themselves. Indeed, it is only after we have learned to describe the things in our environment that we can learn to describe our consciousness of them. We describe our conscious experience not in terms of the mythological "phenomenal properties" which are supposed to inhere in the mythological "objects" in the mythological "phenomenal field," but by reference to the actual physical properties of the concrete physical objects, events, and processes which normally, though not perhaps in the present instance, give rise to the sort of conscious experience which we are trying to describe. In other words when we describe the after-image as green, we are not saying that there is something, the after-image, which is green; we are saying that we are having the sort of experience which we normally have when, and which we have learned to describe as, looking at a green patch of light.

Once we rid ourselves of the phenomenological fallacy we realize that the problem of explaining introspective observations in terms of brain processes is far from insuperable. We realize that there is nothing that the introspecting subject says about his conscious experiences which is inconsistent with anything the physiologist might want to say about the brain processes which cause him to describe the environment and his consciousness of that environment in the way he does. When the subject describes his experience by saying that a light which is in fact stationary, appears to move, all the physiologist or physiological psychologist has to do in order to explain the subject's introspective observations, is to show that the brain process which is causing the subject to describe his experience in this way, is the sort of process which normally occurs when he is observing an actual moving object and which therefore normally causes him to report the movement of an object in his environment. Once the mechanism whereby the individual describes what is going on in his environment has been worked out, all that is required to explain the individual's capacity to make introspective observations is an explanation of his ability to discriminate between those cases where his normal habits of verbal description are appropriate to the stimulus situation and those cases where they are not and an explanation of how and why, in those cases where the appropriateness of his normal descriptive habits is in doubt, he learns to issue his ordinary descriptive protocols preceded by a qualificatory phrase like "it appears," "seems," "looks," "feels," etc.[5]

[5] I am greatly indebted to my fellow-participants in a series of informal discussions on this topic which took place in the Department of Philosophy, University of Adelaide, in particular to Mr. C. B. Martin for his persistent and searching criticism of my earlier attempts to defend the thesis that consciousness is a brain process, to Prof. D. A. T. Gasking, of the University of Melbourne, for clarifying many of the logical issues involved, and to Prof. J. J. C. Smart for moral support and encouragement in what often seemed a lost cause.

VI ❧ Emotions

Errol Bedford

The concept of emotion gives rise to a number of philosophical problems. The most important of these, I think, concern the function of statements about emotions and the criteria for their validity. A solution to these problems is offered by what I shall call the traditional theory of the emotions, and I should like to begin by discussing some aspects of this. According to this view[1] an emotion is a feeling, or at least an experience of a special type which involves a feeling. Logically, this amounts to regarding emotion words as the names of feelings. It is assumed that to each word there corresponds a qualitatively distinct experience which may, although it need not, find "expression" in outward behavior. If it does, this behavior entitles us to infer the existence of the inner feeling, and therefore to assert, with some degree of probability, statements of the form "He is angry." Looked at in this way, emotions naturally come to be thought of as inner forces that move us, in combination with, or in opposition to other forces, to act as we do. Briefly, anger is a specific feeling which leads the angry man to show the signs of anger (e.g., striking someone) unless he is willing to, and able to, suppress them. It follows, I take it, that to explain behavior by saying that a man acted as he did because he was angry, is to give a causal explanation, although, admittedly, a causal explanation of a special sort.

This is the accepted view of the older psychological textbooks. Stout distinguishes, indeed, between "emotional dispositions" (e.g., liking and disliking, hate and love) and "emotions," but he affirms that the emotion

---

[1] The details vary. For example, it is very commonly held that every emotion must have an object, and therefore that it is an experience involving a "cognitive" element, not a pure state of feeling. "We must hold," writes McTaggart, "that the cogitation of that to which the emotion is directed, and the emotion towards it, are the same mental state, which has both the quality of being a cogitation of it, and the quality of being an emotion directed towards it" (*The Nature of Existence* [Cambridge: Cambridge University Press, 1921 and 1927], II, 146). (I think it is important to ask what "directed towards" could mean here.) Russell claims that emotions also involve bodily movements. In *The Analysis of Mind* (London: George Allen & Unwin, 1921) he says that "An emotion—rage, for example—(is) a certain kind of process . . . The ingredients of an emotion are only sensations and images and bodily movements succeeding each other according to a certain pattern" (p. 284). To discuss the details of these theories would complicate, without affecting, my argument, which is meant to show that an emotion is not any sort of experience or process.

itself in which an emotional disposition is actualized is "always an actual state of consciousness" that, besides sensations and conative tendencies, "also involves specific kinds of feeling which cannot be explained away as resultants or complications of more simple elements." [2] Even James thinks that an emotion is a feeling, although he identifies the feeling with somatic sensations. In the famous passage in his *Principles of Psychology* he tells us that his theory is "that the bodily changes follow directly the perception of the exciting fact, and that our feeling of the same changes as they occur IS the emotion." [3]

I am going to argue that this involves a fundamental mistake: the logical mistake of treating emotion words as names, which leads in turn to a misconception of their function. There might, all the same, be more to be said for this view if it were less inadequate at the psychological level, if it did not presuppose a richness and clarity in the "inner life" of feeling that it does not possess. What evidence is there for the existence of a multitude of feelings corresponding to the extensive and subtle linguistic differentiation of our vocabulary for discussing emotions? This assumption gains no support from experience. Indignation and annoyance are two different emotions; but, to judge from my own case, the feelings that accompany indignation appear to differ little, if at all, from those that accompany annoyance. I certainly find no feeling, or class of feelings, that marks off indignation from annoyance, and enables me to distinguish them from one another. The distinction is of a different *sort* from this. (Perhaps I do not remember very clearly—but then is not this part of the difficulty, that the words "indignation" and "annoyance" do *not* call up recollections of two distinct feelings?) I might add that at the present time this is psychological orthodoxy. The author of the chapter on "Feeling and Emotion" in a standard textbook (Boring, Langfeld, and Weld's *Foundations of Psychology* [New York: Wiley, 1948]) remarks that "there is little evidence that a peculiar, unique type of consciousness accompanies and identifies the different emotions" (p 100).

In any case, does the truth of such a statement as "He is afraid" logically require the existence of a specific feeling? I imagine that it would nowadays be generally conceded that emotion words are commonly used without any implication that the person they refer to is having a particular experience at any given time. But it may be said, granting this, that such expressions as "is afraid," "is angry," nevertheless gain their whole meaning from an indirect reference that they make to experiences, and can only be defined in terms of feelings. A man can feel angry as well as be angry; the expression "is angry" may not name an experi-

[2] G. F. Stout, *A Manual of Psychology*, 5th ed. (London: W. B. Clive, 1938), pp. 375 and 371.

[3] William James, *The Principles of Psychology* (New York: Henry Holt and Co., 1890), II, 449. James prints the passage in italics.

ence, but "feels angry" surely does, and all that can be meant by saying that someone is angry is that he is liable to, and sometimes does, feel angry. I do not think, however, that this argument can prove what it sets out to prove, i.e., that anger necessarily involves a specific feeling. In the first place, "feels angry" is often able to serve instead of "is angry." We can say, "I felt angry about it for days afterwards." A more important point is that one cannot understand what it is to feel angry without first understanding what it is to be angry. If we can assume the meaning of "is angry," or teach it (ostensively or by a descriptive account), we can go on to explain "feels angry" by saying that it is to feel as people often feel who are angry. But how could we explain the expression "feels angry" without presupposing that the person we are explaining it to understands "is angry"? The only possible method open to us would seem to be this: to make him angry, e.g., by insulting him, and then to say to him, "Well, feeling angry is feeling as you feel now." The difficulty is that, if the view I am criticizing is correct, we cannot ensure in this way that we have taught him the meaning of the expression. We have to be certain that he has experienced a specific feeling. Yet it is logically possible that the insult (or other stimulus, and it is a crucial point that there is no *specific* stimulus) has failed in its object—it may have produced no feeling, or the wrong feeling, or so confused a mixture of feelings that he cannot discriminate the essential from the inessential (the matter is, if anything, even more difficult from his point of view). We cannot exclude this by arguing "He is angry, therefore he feels angry," for how are we to know that he is angry? *Ex hypothesi* his behavior is no proof of this. And having as yet no guarantee that he has grasped what the question means, we obviously cannot ask him whether he feels angry. Nor can we discover that he has understood the meaning of the expression by observing that he uses it in the same way as we do, for, *ex hypothesi* again, this will not prove that he means the same by it. The conclusion to be drawn, if I am right, is that being angry is logically prior to feeling angry, and therefore that being angry does not entail feeling angry, and a fortiori does not entail having any other feeling.

Now it may seem that this does not accord with the confidence we have in our beliefs about our own and other people's emotions respectively. But is this really so? We do not first ascertain that a man feels angry, and then conclude that he is angry. On the contrary, we realize that he is angry, and assume (perhaps wrongly) that he feels angry. Behavioral evidence for a statement about emotions is evidence in its own right, so to speak, and not because it entitles us to infer to private experiences. For if we have good grounds for the assertion that a person is jealous, we do not withdraw this assertion on learning that he does not feel jealous, although we may accept this as true. It is, after all, notorious that we can be mistaken about our own emotions, and that in this matter a man is not the final court of appeal in his own case; those who are jealous are often the last, instead of the first, to recognize that they are. This is scarcely consistent with the view that the criterion for identifying an emotion is the recognition of the special qualities of an experience; it is intelligible if the criteria are different from, and more complex than this. I am going to discuss these criteria shortly. For the moment, I only want to suggest that the traditional answer to the question "How do we identify our own emotions?" namely, "By introspection," cannot be correct. It seems to me that there is every reason to believe that we learn about our own emotions essentially in the same way as other people learn about them. Admittedly, it is sometimes the case that we know our own emotions better than anyone else does, but there is no need to explain this as being due to the introspection of feelings. One reason for this is that it is hardly possible for a man to be completely ignorant, as others may be, of the context of his own behavior. Again, thoughts may cross his mind that he does not make public. But the fact that he prefers to keep them to himself is incidental; and if they were known they would only be corroborative evidence, not indispensable evidence of a radically different sort from that which is available to other people. It is only in some respects, then, that each of us is in a better position to understand himself than anyone else is. Against this must be set the possibility of self-deception and a reluctance to admit that we are, for instance, vain or envious.

I must now meet what is, I think, the most serious objection that is likely to be made to this—the alleged impossibility of distinguishing, from an external observer's point of view, between real anger, say, and the pretence of it. It is sometimes claimed that although someone might behave as if he were angry, and give every appearance that he would persist in this behavior, there would still be a sense in which he might be shamming. What then is the difference between being angry and merely pretending to be? It may be held that it can only lie in the fact that the man who is pretending is not in the appropriate state of inner feeling. Now this objection plainly rests on the attempt to assimilate being angry to other cases of "being so-and-so" in which the only decisive evidence for whether someone is pretending or not is what he feels. One line of reply to it, therefore, would be to deny that there are any such cases. But it is doubtful whether this could be sustained. Pain is a specific sensation (or class of similar sensations) and it seems clear that being in pain does entail having that sensation, since "I am in pain but I don't feel anything" is self-contradictory. If so, it is possible for someone consistently to pretend to be in pain, and yet to be deceiving us. We might, of course, be unwilling to believe anyone who after showing all the signs of pain confessed that he felt no pain; but the point is, that *if* what he says is true, it entails the falsity of "He was in pain." Can we say that being angry is similar to being in pain in this respect? Let us contrast the cases of a man who is angry and another, behaving in a similar way, who is only pretending to be. Now it may well be true that the former feels angry, whereas the latter does not, but in any case it is not this that constitutes the difference between the fact that the one is angry and the fact that the other is only pretending to be. The objection rests on a misconception of what pretence is. There is necessarily involved in pretence, or shamming, the notion of a limit which must not be overstepped; pretence is always insulated, as it were, from reality. Admittedly, this limit may be vague, but it must exist. It is a not unimportant point that it is usually *obvious* when someone is pretending. If a man who is behaving as if he were angry goes so far as to smash the furniture or commit an assault, he has passed the limit; he is not *pretending*, and it is useless for him to protest afterwards that he did not feel angry. Far from his statement being *proof* that he was not angry, it would be discounted even if it were accepted as true. "He was angry, but he did not feel angry" is not self-contradictory, although it is no doubt normally false. If in a particular case it is difficult—as it may be —to settle the question, "Pretended or real?" that can only be because the relevant public evidence is inadequate to settle it. What we want is more evidence of the same kind, not a special piece of evidence of a different kind. Our difficulty in resolving the question "Is he really in pain?" on the other hand, arises from the fact that the only decisive evidence is evidence that he alone is in a position to give. (I think that even in the case of pretending to be in pain there is a limit, only it is exceptional in depending on a subjective condition. It is decisively passed if a person truly says "I feel pain." There may, of course, be inductive evidence for accepting or rejecting his statement.)

This is confirmed by the difference between the two questions "Do I really feel pain?" and "Do I really feel angry?" Since there is little room for doubt about the answer, the former is not a query that anyone is very likely to put to himself; it may even be said that it is a meaningless question. But I am inclined to think that it could be asked as a classificatory question, as roughly equivalent to "Is this pain or rather discomfort?" It is to be answered, if at all, by comparing the present feeling with other feelings definitely counted as pains, and considering whether it is sufficiently similar to be classed with them. One cannot resolve it by answering the question "Am I really in pain?" since the answer to that question must depend on the answer given to the first. By contrast, "Do I really feel angry?" is one of a class of similar questions that are common in everyday life. This question does not concern the comparison of feelings; in answering it one is trying to decide whether one is angry or not, and the answer "Yes" can be mistaken in a way that a similar answer to the question "Do I really feel pain?" cannot be.

II

Having, I hope, cleared the ground a little by putting some preliminary arguments against the traditional theory, I now want to consider whether an adequate alternative to it is provided by a dispositional theory of emotions, and to discuss the criteria for the use of emotion words. Can the concept of an emotion be fully elucidated without using non-behavioral, indeed non-psychological, concepts? I will try to justify the negative answer that I think should be given to this question.

To begin with, statements about emotions cannot be said to describe behavior; they interpret it.[4] The situation seems to be that emotional behavior, so to speak, is far from being homogeneous. The behavioral evidence for "He was angry" varies with the person and the occasion; in different cases it is not the same, and possibly it may not even be partially the same. Conversely, the same, or similar, behavior, can be differently, yet correctly, interpreted in different circumstances, for example as anger, indignation, annoyance, exasperation, or resentment. Accordingly, categorical descriptive statements, e.g., (1) "He raised his voice and began to thump the table," and hypothetical descriptive statements, e.g., (2) "If I had gone on teasing him he would have thrown something at me," are evidence for such statements as (3) "He was very angry," but they are not part of what these statements mean. Clearly, on hearing (3), it would be proper to ask for details, and such details could be given in (1) and (2). (1) and (2) would therefore give additional information to that already given in (3). To put the matter another way, (1), (2), and (3) are independent of one another in respect of truth and falsity. (1) may be true when (3) is false (a man can thump the table and raise his voice—to emphasize a point—without being angry), and (3) may be true although (1) is false (for not all angry men thump tables). The same holds of the relationships of (2) and (3). The truth of (2) is perfectly compatible with joining in the fun; anger, on the other hand, is consistent with not being prepared to throw things. I think that this would still hold if other statements were substituted for (1) and (2). It does not seem to be possible, therefore, to analyze (3) into a set, however complex, of categorical and hypothetical statements that describe individual behavior. (3) does not sum up, but goes beyond, the behavioral evidence for it, and it would always be logically possible to accept the evidence and deny the conclusion. Although when we say (3) we are in a sense

---

[4] This is not to say that we do not also use the word "description" in such a way that (3) (immediately below) might form part of a description of some incident. When I say that (3) does not describe I am making what could be looked on as a technical distinction between description and interpretation, which is meant to indicate a difference of order between (3) and (1) or (2). Higher order statements explain and interpret what lower order statements describe.

talking about the behavior on which its truth rests, anger is not merely a disposition, and cannot be reduced to a pattern of behavior, actual or potential.[5] All that can be said about the logical relationships between (3) and such statements as (1) and (2) is that it is a necessary, but not a sufficient, condition for the truth of (3) that some statements such as (1) and (2) should be true, without it being possible to specify which.

This last assertion may be challenged in at least two ways. It might be said, first, that the phrase "necessary, but not a sufficient, condition" ought to be changed to "neither a necessary nor a sufficient condition." But since the only ground on which this could be maintained appears to be the traditional view, I shall not discuss it any further. I will only add that I do not believe that we either do, or should, take any notice of anyone's protestations that, for instance, he loves his wife, if his conduct offers no evidence whatever that he does. At the other extreme, those who want to be thoroughly behavioristic about emotions will argue that the phrase "necessary but not sufficient" should be amended to "both necessary and sufficient." What I am suggesting is that people who share the same information and the same expectations about another person's behavior may possibly place different emotional interpretations on that behavior, if their knowledge is confined to descriptive statements about it. It may be urged that this difference of opinion can be eliminated as further evidence of the same type comes to light, and that it can only be eliminated in this way. The assumption underlying this—that the criteria for assertions about emotions are purely behavioral—is not, however, borne out by an examination of the way in which we actually use emotion words. These words, when used without qualification, carry implications, not merely about behavior, but also about its social context. Consider the distinction between two emotions that have a close similarity, shame and embarrassment. The behavior of an embarrassed man is often not noticeably different from that of one who is ashamed; but there is an important difference between the respective situations they are in. In a newspaper article last year, Mr. Peter Davies, the publisher, was said to be "to his mild embarrassment" the original of Peter Pan. The embarrassment is understandable, and the epithet appropriate, whether its application is correct or not. Yet we can say at once that if the writer of the article had alleged that Mr. Davies was "to his shame" the original of Peter Pan, this would have been incorrect; it is scarcely conceivable that it could be true. The reason for this is obvious, and it is logical, not psychological, since it has nothing to do with Mr. Davies' behavior, still less with his feelings. It is simply that the fact that Barrie modeled Peter Pan on him is not his *fault*—it was not due to an act of his, and there is nothing reprehensible about it anyway. In

---

[5] Let me give an analogy. "Jones is responsible for this muddle" is a statement about the behavior its truth is dependent on, although it is not shorthand for a set of statements describing that behavior.

general, it is only true to say of someone "He is ashamed of so-and-so" if what is referred to is something that he can be criticized for (the criticism is commonly, though not perhaps necessarily, moral). It is, in other words, a necessary condition for the truth of the statement that he should be at fault. The word "embarrassed" is not connected in the same way with blame and responsibility; the claim that it makes is the vaguer and weaker one that the situation is awkward or inconvenient or something of that kind. "He was embarrassed" may impute a fault to someone else, but not to the person of whom it is said. (I do not mean that we may not also impute a fault to someone of whom we say this. Sometimes one puts oneself into an embarrassing situation, sometimes one finds oneself in it. I mean that we do not impute it *in* saying "He was embarrassed," in the way we do if we say "He was ashamed.") It may be pointed out that we can, after all, be ashamed of the faults of others. But I do not believe that this is true unless we accept the fault as our own; when, for instance, our children, or even our friends, commit antisocial acts in houses that we introduce them to. It is most unusual to be ashamed of the deeds of total strangers, although it is possible provided that responsibility is accepted through identification with the stranger in virtue of a common characteristic—"I was ashamed to see an Englishman lying dead drunk on the pavement." A Frenchman would be unlikely to say this, although rising to a still higher level of generality he might change "Englishman" to "European." (It is beside the point that such acceptance of responsibility may be irrational.) The connection between shame and responsibility is not, of course, ignored in the traditional theory of emotions. It appears as the doctrine that every emotion must have an appropriate object; that it is impossible (psychologically) to experience the feeling specific to shame unless you recognize that you are open to criticism. But there are no limits to what men may feel; we can only set limits to what they can say. This is merely the misrepresentation of a logical point as a piece of implausible a priori psychology.

The point of the example is to show that although knowledge of facts that is quite independent of knowledge of behavior cannot by itself establish a given interpretation of that behavior, it can be sufficient definitely to exclude it. I suggest, then, that it is possible to rebut the contention that, e.g., A is jealous of B's relationship with C, by showing that the claim that such an assertion makes about the situation which A is in, viz., that he is in a certain marital, professional, or other relationship (depending on the context) with B, is not satisfied. Certainly the contention that A is jealous is as a rule rebutted by evidence about his behavior which is inconsistent with its truth. The reason why the claim that A is in a certain relationship with B is usually unquestioned, is that it is very rarely false; the assertion that A is jealous is not usually made unless it is already known that the claim is satisfied, although it is frequently made on inadequate behavioral evidence. In general, then, this

criterion is relevant to the *assertion* of statements, rather than the justification or rebuttal of statements that have *already* been asserted—it
leads us to pick one word rather than another. For example, the decision
whether to say that the driver of a car which has broken down for lack
of water is indignant, or merely annoyed or angry, depends on whether
the radiator is empty through (let us say) the carelessness of a garage
mechanic who undertook to fill it for him, or through his own carelessness ("annoyed with myself" but not "indignant with myself"). Indignation, but not annoyance, seems to imply unfairness, particularly unfair
accusation, or breach of an agreement. Thus, if the garage mechanic is
later taxed with his carelessness, it could not be said that he was indignant, unless he was in a position to reply "But you said you would do
it yourself, sir" or something similar.

Statements about emotions may also involve another, and somewhat
different, type of commitment, which has an even closer bearing on the
elucidation of their function. It can be illustrated in the contrast between hope and expectation, and I think this throws some light on the
question why one is, and the other is not, usually counted as an emotion. The most apparent difference between them is that hoping for
and expecting an event express different degrees of confidence that the
event will happen. To expect something is to believe that it is more
likely than not to happen. In the case of hope it is only necessary that
it should not be an impossibility. This is, however, not the only, nor the
most crucial, difference. Phrases which express a low degree of confidence, e.g., "I think it may . . . ," "Perhaps it will . . ." cannot be
substituted without loss for "I hope that . . . ." The expression "I hope
that . . ." implies, in addition to a very vague estimate of probability,
an *assessment* of whatever is referred to in the clause that follows. I
think it is clear that one cannot hope for something, although one can
expect something, without judging it favorably in some respect, or from
some point of view. Compare (1) "I don't favor a higher purchase tax
but I expect it will be raised," with (2) "I don't favor a higher purchase
tax, but I hope it will be raised." (1) Creates no surprise; (2) demands
further explanation. Does he think it bad for the country, but profitable
to him personally because he has a large stock of goods on which he has
already paid tax? Does he regard it as unsound fiscal policy in general,
but advisable temporarily in an inflationary economy? Failing an answer to questions such as these (2) is surely a puzzling remark, and (3)
"I don't favor a higher purchase tax in any respect, but I hope it will be
raised" seems to me to be self-contradictory. (Since—to mention one reason—one can only favor events under human control, and hope is not
restricted in this way. "I favor . . ." does not precisely represent the
implication of "I hope that . . . ," but it will do for the purpose of the
present example. I need hardly say that it is not my intention in this
paper to give an exhaustive—or, indeed, a more than roughly accurate—

account of the particular concepts that I use as examples.) It is a psychological truism that men do not, with some exceptions, hope that their opponents will win; it is a truth of logic that they cannot hope that their opponents will win without approving of this in *some* respect. Thus "I hope that . . ." is commonly used to declare, or to commit oneself to, an allegiance, and although disagreement *about* hopes is disagreement about the interpretation of facts, disagreement *in* hopes is not—it is one of the forms that disagreement about value may take (e.g., "I hope the Socialists will get in." "Well, I don't. I think it would be a disaster for the country.") This is a further reason why it would be absurd to say that questions of the form "Do I feel regret for . . . ?" "Do I really hope that . . . ?" could be settled by introspection. "Do I really hope that the Tories will get in?" is plainly a question a wavering Tory supporter might put to himself. This may amount to asking himself whether, granted that he thinks a Tory government better than a Labour one, he is concerned enough about the election result, or whether he is not too indifferent to say, if he is honest, that he *hopes* for a Tory victory. If so, he will not answer it by searching his feelings, for they have nothing to do with the matter, but by reflecting, for example, that when the party's policy was attacked, he did not bother to defend it, or by remembering that after all he has agreed to do some canvassing. But it is just as likely, if not more likely, that the answer to the question will be a *decision* about his allegiance, reached by reconsidering the merits of the two parties. (Contrast "Do I really feel pain?" discussed above.)

To generalize from this example: emotion words form part of the vocabulary of appraisal and criticism, and a number of them belong to the more specific language of moral criticism. Normally, the verbs in their first-person use imply the speaker's assessment of something, and in their third-person use they carry an implication about an assessment by the person they refer to.[6] It is perhaps worth mentioning that there are certain cases in which a third-person statement gives the speaker's verdict on that person; a factor which certainly complicates discussions of character. Such terms as "vain," "envious," and "resentful" are terms of censure.[7] There is an overlap between the lists of emotions, and the lists of virtues and vices that are given by philosophers. The overlap is not complete; some virtues (e.g., veracity) are not connected with emotions, and some emotions (e.g., regret) cannot be treated as elements of character and are not merits or defects.

So far I have discussed the conditions which appear to govern the truth and falsity of statements about emotions. While emotion concepts do not form an altogether homogeneous group, I believe that this is cor-

---

[6] But the words "right," "unreasonable," etc., when used to qualify third person statements sometimes serve as endorsements of, or refusals to endorse, this assessment on the speaker's part. I discuss this point below

[7] A point noted in respect of envy by Aristotle at *Eth. Nic.* 1107a.

rect as a broad outline. But there is one respect in which it needs to be supplemented. This concerns the sense in which emotions (as opposed to statements about emotions) can be justified or unjustified, reasonable or unreasonable. It is fairly obvious, to begin with, that the behavioral criteria for the use of emotion words are not connected with the application of these predicates. The way in which a man behaves will determine whether he is or is not angry. But *if* he is angry, the behavioral evidence for this is not in itself relevant to the question whether his anger is justified or unjustified. On the other hand, if the claim that an emotion word makes about a situation is not satisfied, this is often indicated by saying that the emotion is unjustified or unreasonable. The attribution of the emotion, that is to say, is not withdrawn, but qualified. An example will make this clearer. Suppose that B does something that is to A's advantage, although A thinks that it is to his disadvantage (e.g., B, a solicitor administering A's affairs, sells some shares that A believes [wrongly] will appreciate in value). Now it would be misleading to say simply, except to a fully informed audience, "A resents what B did"—this surely carries the incorrect implication that B has injured A. To guard against this it is necessary to add "but his resentment is quite unjustified," or some equivalent expression. A's belief that B has done something that affects him adversely is, however, a necessary condition if the word "resentment" is to be used at all. The distinction between what the situation is, and what it is believed to be, is normally unimportant, and for this reason emotion words make an objective claim unless special precautions are taken to exclude or cancel it (e.g., "He was afraid but no one else was" [there was no real danger], "Your surprise is quite unjustified" [the event was only to be expected]).

But this is not the whole story and the question whether an emotion is justified or not does not always turn on an issue of fact. There is a second group of emotions (not, I think, necessarily exclusive of the first) in respect of which the qualifications "unjustified," "unreasonable" refer to a different implication, and have quite a different force. Contempt, disgust, and pride are typical of this group. If I were to say that a music critic's contempt for Bartók was unjustified, I should not be asserting a fact; I should be challenging his assessment of Bartók. It is impossible to give any simple paraphrase of this remark, but it could be taken, in part, as more or less equivalent to saying that Bartók is a better composer than the critic allows. While the critic's assessment of Bartók determines, among other considerations, whether I shall assert or deny that he is contemptuous of Bartók, it does not determine whether I shall say that his contempt is justified or not; *that* depends on my opinion about his assessment.

How far can these distinctions be accounted for by theories in which emotion concepts are treated as psychological concepts? I am inclined to think that if an emotion were a feeling no sense could be made of them at all. It may be said that an emotion is unjustified when a feeling is inappropriate or unfitting to a situation. But I find this unintelligible. Feelings do not have a character that makes this relationship possible. In any case, the interpretation suggested is not what is meant by saying that, e.g., a critic's contempt is unjustified. In general, I do not think it can be maintained that logical predicates apply either to feelings or to sensations. What reasons could be given for or against a feeling, or for or against its "inappropriateness" to a situation? If someone were to say "I felt a pang this afternoon," it would be meaningless to ask whether it was a reasonable or unreasonable pang. The matter is different if he says "pang of regret," but the phrase "of regret" does not *name* the feeling, as I have already argued, and the pang of regret is justified, if it is, not as a feeling, but because his regret is justified. Nor do these predicates apply to bodily sensations, such as feeling giddy or having a pain in one's leg. This, I think, explains the fact that while we often say "You ought (or ought not) to be (or feel) ashamed (etc.),", we cannot say this of feelings[8]; a point that has created difficulties for moral philosophers who adhere to the traditional theory about emotions. Sir David Ross, for instance, recognizes that "ought" does not apply to feelings, and he assumes that from this it follows that it has no application to emotions, except in an "improper use." According to him "we cannot seriously say" e.g., "You ought to feel ashamed." [9] He is therefore constrained to interpret this remark as meaning that a certain feeling is "right or fitting" in the circumstances, which, as I shall argue shortly, misconstrues its point. If, however, we do not presuppose that the primary function of "I feel ashamed" is to report a feeling, there is no objection to allowing—what is surely the case—that "You ought to feel ashamed" employs "ought" in a perfectly "proper" sense, indeed in the same sense as in "You ought to apologize."

A dispositional theory of emotions may be thought to be on stronger ground, since it can be argued that behavior may be unreasonable or unjustified. To use a previous example again, to say that someone has an unjustified contempt for Bartók is to say, I take it, on this view, that certain categorical and hypothetical statements are true of him, and that these statements describe behavior that is unjustified. In other words, the assertion that contempt for Bartók is unjustified means that a certain pattern of preferential behavior is unjustified. But what is this pattern

[8] In the same, i.e., moral, sense. A doctor might maintain that his patient ought not to feel any pain, when the physical condition is not as a rule painful or when he has given a dose of morphine that would alleviate the pain of most patients. "Ought not to" here means (roughly) "would not normally." He might equally be prepared to give a reason why a patient feels giddy, i.e., a causal explanation. This is not a reason *for* feeling giddy, which is an impossibility.

[9] Sir David Ross, *Foundations of Ethics* (London: Oxford University Press, 1939), pp. 45 and 55.

of behavior? Presumably it will consist in doing (or being prepared to do) things of this sort: switching off when Bartók's music is announced on the Third Programme, wasting free tickets for a concert of his music, never buying records of Bartók, going for a walk when a neighbor plays his music on the violin, and so on; in short, choosing against this composer whenever a choice presents itself. Now let us suppose that contempt for Bartók is unjustified, as it undoubtedly is. Even so, this behavior may be perfectly reasonable or justified, and therefore cannot constitute an unjustified contempt for Bartók. It is open to a different interpretation, that the person who behaves in this way is simply uninterested in this composer's music, or in modern music generally. Consistently to choose against something is not necessarily to condemn it, or to be contemptuous of it, because this choice is susceptible of rational explanation in other ways.

III

I must now amplify what I have said in passing about the functions performed by statements that refer to emotions. It is generally assumed that these functions are to report feelings, or to report, predict or explain behavior. Now although some statements containing emotion words are used in these ways, and particularly as explanations, the force of the qualifications "unjustified" and "unreasonable" in itself suggests that this is much less common than might be thought, and my contention is that it would be a mistake to imagine that the primary function of these statements is to communicate psychological facts. Their principal functions are judicial, not informative, and when they are informative, it is often not merely psychological information that they give. Consider the following remarks, as they might be used in suitable contexts in everyday life:

(1) "They are very jealous of one another"
(2) "I envy Schnabel's technique"
(3) "I feel ashamed about it now"
(4) "I never feel the slightest pang of regret for what I did"
(5) "I am quite disgusted with the literary men" (Keats)
(6) "Well, I hope you are ashamed of yourself"
(7) "His pride in the Company's record is unjustified"
(8) "He is very disappointed in you."

I think these are all typical examples, and they have been chosen at random, except that I have taken care to ensure that in each case it is clear that the operative word is the emotion word, i.e., I have avoided such instances as "He is very disappointed by your failure to get there in time." Of these examples, the first is different from the rest, its point, I assume, being to inform the hearer that a certain relationship exists between the persons referred to, e.g., in a suitable context, that they are rivals in their profession. The other remarks have what I have termed, for want of a better word, a judicial function. (2) Praises Schnabel; it resembles, say, "Schnabel has a brilliant technique," although it is more tentative and personal, and implies more than this—it would only be said by another pianist. (3) is an admission of responsibility, or perhaps a plea in mitigation, and (4) is the justification of a choice. (5) and (6) imply highly unfavorable assessments. In (5) Keats condemns literary men, and he goes on (Letter of 8th October, 1817) to give part of his reasons for feeling disgusted by telling an anecdote about Leigh Hunt. The force of (6) seems to lie in its mixture of blame with imputation of responsibility—there are two general lines of reply to it, either (*a*) "No, I think I was quite right" or (*b*) "No, it wasn't my fault." (7) is either a way of saying that the person referred to is taking more credit than he deserves, or of saying that the Company's record is not as good as he believes. The normal conversational point of (8), I think, would be to convey blame.

In general then, the affinities of (1) to (8) are not with descriptive statements about what people feel and do, but with a different type of statement altogether. (4), for instance, is very close to "My choice was quite correct (sound, justified)" and (8) to "You have not done as well as he expected." These are not put forward as exact paraphrases; I only wish to suggest that they do not miss the point in the way that any psychological interpretation does. We do not counter such statements as (1) to (8), if we disagree, by challenging an alleged fact. If this is accepted, it can only be consistent with a psychological analysis of emotion concepts if either (*a*) a naturalistic theory of value is presupposed, or (*b*) these usages are treated as non-literal.

(*a*) It may be said that a judgment of value is a report or expression of an individual's feelings, and that it would not be surprising, therefore, if emotion words (reporting or expressing feelings) had a function somewhat similar to that of value words. I can only make one or two remarks about this here. Earlier on I discussed a moral emotion, shame, and tried to show that the concept of shame is logically dependent on the moral notion of wrong action. I believe, then, that there are specifically moral emotions in this sense only: that the use of some emotion words ("remorse," "shame," etc.) presupposes moral concepts. There are not specifically moral (or for that matter, aesthetic) experiences, and consequently no judgment of value can be a report, or an expression, of an experience. In the case of example (3), no statement that merely reported a feeling could be equivalent to it, since such a statement would not be an admission of responsibility. To accept responsibility for a past action (in the ordinary sense in which it is the opposite of taking credit for something), one has to admit that one did the action and to concede that it was wrong. But there is no experience which, taken in itself, is inconsistent with refusing to admit the one or concede the other. Even if there were a specific experience which always accompanied the admission of responsibility, this would be something logically accidental.

(*b*) It could be argued that although such words as "regret" and "pride" name emotions in their primary sense, they are used in a different sense in the examples. This will no doubt be turned by some into the objection that a consideration of such usages can throw no light on the nature of the emotions. What does this amount to? There exist uses of emotion words that are unquestionably figurative or metaphorical, e.g., "angry masses of cloud," "the raging waves of the sea foaming out their own shame." Statements (1) to (8) are precisely the literal uses that would be contrasted with these, and no one is likely to maintain, therefore, that they are figurative in the strict sense. It may more plausibly be argued that they are extended or derivative senses of emotion words. But what, then, are the senses from which they are extended or derived? No use of, e.g., "envy," "ashamed," or "pang of regret" appears to exist which is more basic, primary, or literal than that of the examples. There is perhaps a temptation to suppose, because we associate emotion with violent feelings and behavior, that the word "disgusted" is somehow being used more literally when it is used by or of a man who is actually feeling nausea, than it is by Keats in the sentence I have quoted. But all that this proves, it seems to me, is that the experiences of those who are disgusted are different on different occasions. No doubt, to be disgusted with the literary men is not the same as being disgusted with the state of the kitchen sink; the one criticism is moral, and the other is not; but there is a very close and intelligible connection between them which should not be obscured by treating one sense as more primary than the other.

IV

What kind of an explanation of behavior are we giving when we account for it in terms of emotions? I should like, in conclusion, to sketch the general lines on which I think this question ought to be answered. As this is no more than a corollary of the preceding discussion I can put it very briefly.

The traditional theory gives the answer that emotion words explain behavior by specifying its cause, i.e., a certain feeling or inner experience. But surely, when we ask what caused someone to do something, we usually neither expect nor receive an answer in terms of feelings. The answer takes the form of a reference to some external circumstance, if that is relevant, or to some thought, memory, observation, etc., that accounts for the action. If we refer to feelings at all, this appears to be a type of explanation that we fall back on as a last resort, because it is unilluminating and only one step removed from saying that the action is unaccountable. What seems to me to be wrong, then, on this score, with the traditional view is that it does not do justice to the explanatory power of emotion words. For the fact is that to know the feeling that may have preceded an action is not to understand it, or to understand it only very imperfectly. One can remember an action that one did many years ago, an action that one no longer understands, and the question "Why did I do it?" can remain in the face of the clearest recollection of what it felt like to do it. If emotion words merely named some inner experience that preceded or accompanied behavior, to explain behavior by using them would not give the insight that it does.

A quite different answer to this question is proposed by Professor Ryle in *The Concept of Mind*. Referring to what he calls "inclinations" or "motives," Professor Ryle writes, "The imputation of a motive for a particular action is not a causal inference to an unwitnessed event but the subsumption of an episode proposition under a law-like proposition" (p. 90). Again, "To explain an action as done from a certain motive is not to correlate it with an occult cause, but to subsume it under a propensity or behavior-trend" (p. 110). And as I understand him, explanation in terms of mood-words is of a generally similar character. Mood and motive explanations, despite their differences, have this in common, that they are explanations by reference to types of disposition (p. 97). Now although I have been simply following Professor Ryle in what he here denies, I find the positive side of this less adequate. It does not seem to me that emotion words explain merely in the relatively superficial way that dispositional words explain, if "the glass broke because it was brittle" is to be taken as a model, however rough, of this kind of explanation. To refer to a man's laziness or fondness for gardening is to account for what he does on a particular occasion by removing the need for a *special* explanation of it; by showing that his conduct is not in any way surprising or unusual, but part of the regular pattern of things that he does or is likely to do. To assimilate emotion words closely to dispositional words is to give an incomplete account of their explanatory function; they explain behavior more fully than could be done by saying, in effect, that it was only to be expected. ("To say that he did something from that motive is to say that this action, done in its particular circumstances, was just the sort of thing that that was an inclination to do. It is to say 'he *would* do that.' " *Ibid.* pp. 92-93.) I would suggest that emotion words go beyond this sort of explanation in two ways. First, they set the action to be explained, not merely in the context of the rest of an individual's behavior, but in a social context. "He was rude to you because he was jealous" resembles "I helped him because he was a friend" in accounting for his behavior by the reference it makes to his relationship with other people. Secondly, emotion words explain by giving one sort of reason for an action, i.e., by giving a justification, or partial justification, for it. "He refused an interview because of his contempt for journalists" explains the refusal by connecting it with an assessment made by the person whose behavior is referred to. In this respect it has some analogy with, for instance, "He reads Gibbon because he thinks highly of his style." Emotion concepts, I have argued, are not purely psychological: they presuppose concepts of social relationships and institutions, and concepts belonging to systems of judgment, moral, aesthetic, and legal. In using emotion words we are able, therefore, to relate behavior to the complex background in which it is enacted, and so to make human actions intelligible.

VII ✌ Persons

P. F. Strawson

I

In the *Tractatus* (5.631-5.641), Wittgenstein writes of the I which occurs in philosophy, of the philosophical idea of the subject of experiences. He says first: "The thinking, presenting subject—there is no such thing." Then, a little later: "*In an important sense* there is no subject." This is followed by: "The subject does not belong to the world, but is a limit of the world." And a little later comes the following paragraph: "There is [therefore] really a sense in which in philosophy we can talk nonpsychologically of the I. The I occurs in philosophy through the fact that the 'world is my world.' The philosophical I is not the man, not the human body, or the human soul of which psychology treats, but the metaphysical subject, the limit—not a part of the world." These remarks are impressive, but also puzzling and obscure. Reading them, one might think: Well, let's settle for the human body and the human soul of which psychology treats, and which is a part of the world, and let the metaphysical subject go. But again we might think: No, when I talk of myself, I do after all talk of that which has all of my experiences, I do talk of the subject of my experiences—and yet also of something that is part of the world in that it, but not the world, comes to an end when I die. The limit of *my* world is not—and is not so thought of by me— the limit of *the* world. It may be difficult to explain the idea of something which is both a subject of experiences and a part of the world. But it is an idea we have: it should be an idea we can explain.

Let us think of some of the ways in which we ordinarily talk of ourselves, of some of the things which we ordinarily ascribe to ourselves. They are of many kinds. We ascribe to ourselves *actions* and *intentions* (I am doing, did, shall do this); *sensations* (I am warm, in pain); *thoughts* and *feelings* (I think, wonder, want this, am angry, disappointed, contented); *perceptions* and *memories* (I see this, hear the other, remember that). We ascribe to ourselves, in two senses, position: *location* (I am on the sofa) and *attitude* (I am lying down). And of course we ascribe to ourselves not only temporary conditions, states, and situations, like most of these, but also enduring characteristics, including such physical characteristics as height, coloring, shape, and weight. That is to say, among the things we ascribe to ourselves are things of a kind that we also ascribe to material bodies to which we would not dream of ascribing others of the things that we ascribe to ourselves. Now there seems nothing needing explanation in the fact that the particular height, coloring, and physical position which we ascribe to ourselves, should be ascribed to *something or other;* for that which one calls one's body is, at least, a body, a material thing. It can be picked out from others, identified by ordinary physical criteria and described in ordinary physical terms. But it can seem, and has seemed, to need explanation that one's states of consciousness, one's thoughts and sensations, are ascribed *to the very same thing* as that to which these physical characteristics, this physical situation, is ascribed. Why are one's states of consciousness ascribed to the very same thing as certain corporeal characteristics, a certain physical situation, etc.? And once this question is raised, another question follows it, viz.: Why are one's states of consciousness ascribed to (said to be of, or to belong to) anything at all? It is not to be supposed that the answers to these questions will be independent of one another.

It might indeed be thought that an answer to both of them could be found in the unique role which each person's body plays in his experience, particularly his perceptual experience. All philosophers who have concerned themselves with these questions have referred to the uniqueness of this role. (Descartes was well enough aware of its uniqueness: "I am *not* lodged in my body like a pilot in a vessel.") In what does this uniqueness consist? Well, of course, in a great many facts. We may summarize some of these facts by saying that for each person there is one body which occupies a certain *causal* position in relation to that person's perceptual experience, a causal position which is in various ways unique in relation to each of the various kinds of perceptual experience he has; and—as a further consequence—that this body is also unique for him as an *object* of the various kinds of perceptual experience which he has. This complex uniqueness of the single body appears, moreover, to be a contingent matter, or rather a cluster of contingent matters; we can, or it seems that we can, imagine many peculiar combinations of dependence and independence of aspects of our perceptual experience on the physical states or situation of more than one body.

Now I must say, straightaway, that this cluster of apparently contingent facts about the unique role which each person's body plays in his experience does not seem to me to provide, *by itself,* an answer to our questions. Of course these facts explain *something.* They provide a very good reason why a subject of experience should have a very *special regard* for just one body, why he should think of it as unique and perhaps more important than any other. They explain—if I may be permitted to put it so—why I feel *peculiarly attached* to what in fact I call my own body; they even might be said to explain why, granted that I am going to speak of one body as *mine,* I should speak of this body (the body that I do speak of as mine) as mine. But they do not explain why I should have the concept of *myself* at all, why I should ascribe my thoughts and experiences to *anything*. Moreover, even if we were satisfied with some other explanation of why one's states of consciousness (thoughts and feelings and perceptions) were ascribed to *something*, and satisfied that the facts in question sufficed to explain why the "possession" of a particular body should be ascribed to the *same* thing (i.e., to explain why a particular body should be spoken of as standing in some special relation, called "being possessed by" to that thing), yet the facts in question still do not explain why we should, as we do, ascribe certain corporeal characteristics not simply to the body standing in this special relation to the thing to which we ascribe thoughts, feelings, etc., but to the thing itself to which we ascribe those thoughts and feelings. (For we say "I am bald" as well as "I am cold," "I am lying on the hearthrug" as well as "I see a spider on the ceiling.") Briefly, the facts in question explain why a subject of experience should pick out one body from others, give it, perhaps, an honored name and ascribe to it whatever characteristics it has; but they do not explain why the experiences should be ascribed to any subject at all; and they do not explain why, if the experiences are to be ascribed to something, they *and* the corporeal characteristics which might be truly ascribed to the favored body, should be ascribed to the same thing. So the facts in question do not explain the use that we make of the word "I," or how any word has the use that word has. They do not explain the concept we have of a person.

II

A possible reaction at this point is to say that the concept we have is wrong or confused, or, if we make it a rule not to say that the concepts we have are confused, that the usage we have, whereby we ascribe, or seem to ascribe, such different kinds of predicate to one and the same thing, is confusing, that it conceals the true nature of the concepts involved, or something of this sort. This reaction can be found in two very important types of view about these matters. The first type of view is Cartesian, the view of Descartes and of others who think like him. Over the attribution of the second type of view I am more hesitant; but there is some evidence that it was held, at one period, by Wittgenstein and possibly also by Schlick. On both of these views, one of the questions we are considering, namely "Why do we ascribe our states of consciousness to the very same thing as certain corporeal characteristics, etc.?" is a question which does not arise; for on both views it is only a linguistic illusion that both kinds of predicate are properly ascribed to one and the same thing, that there is a common owner, or subject, of both types of predicate. And on the second of these views, the other question we are considering, namely "Why do we ascribe our states of consciousness to anything at all?" is also a question which does not arise; for on this view, it is only a linguistic illusion that one ascribes one's states of consciousness at all, that there is any proper subject of these apparent ascriptions, that states of consciousness belong to, or are states of, anything.

That Descartes held the first of these views is well enough known. When we speak of a person, we are really referring to one or both of two distinct substances (two substances of different types), each of which has its own appropriate type of states and properties; and none of the properties or states of either can be a property or state of the other. States of consciousness belong to one of these substances, and not to the other. I shall say no more about the Cartesian view at the moment—what I have to say about it will emerge later on—except to note again that while it escapes one of our questions, it does not escape, but indeed invites, the other: "Why are one's states of consciousness *ascribed* at all, to *any* subject?"

The second of these views I shall call the "no-ownership" or "no-subject" doctrine of the self. Whether or not anyone has explicitly held this view, it is worth reconstructing, or constructing, in outline.[1] For the errors into which it falls are instructive. The "no-ownership" theorist may be presumed to start his explanations with facts of the sort which illustrate the unique causal position of a certain material body in a

[1] The evidence that Wittgenstein at one time held such a view is to be found in the third of Moore's articles in *Mind* on "Wittgenstein's Lectures in 1930-33" (*Mind*, LXIV [1955], especially 13-14). He is reported to have held that the use of "I" was utterly different in the case of "I have a toothache" or "I see a red patch" from its use in the case of "I've got a bad tooth" or "I've got a matchbox." He thought that there were two uses of "I" and that in one of them "I" was replaceable by "this body." So far the view might be Cartesian. But he also said that in the other use (the use exemplified by "I have a toothache" as opposed to "I have a bad tooth"), the "I" *does not denote a possessor,* and that no ego is involved in thinking or in having toothache; and referred with apparent approval to Lichtenberg's dictum that, instead of saying "I think," we (or Descartes!) ought to say "There is a thought" (i.e., "Es denkt"). The attribution of such a view to Schlick would have to rest on his article "Meaning and Verification," Pt. V (in *Readings in Philosophical Analysis,* ed. H. Feigl and W. Sellars [New York: Appleton-Century-Crofts, 1949]). Like Wittgenstein, Schlick quotes Lichtenberg, and then goes on to say: "Thus we see that unless we choose to call our body the owner or bearer of the data [the data of immediate experience]— which seems to be a rather misleading expression—we have to say that the data have no owner or bearer." The full import of Schlick's article is, however, obscure to me, and it is quite likely that a false impression is given by the quotation of a single sentence. I shall say merely that I have drawn on Schlick's article in constructing the case of my hypothetical "no-subject" theorist; but shall not claim to be representing his views.

Lichtenberg's anti-Cartesian dictum is, as the subsequent argument will show, one that I endorse, if properly used. But it seems to have been repeated, without being understood, by many of Descartes' critics.

The evidence that Wittgenstein and Schlick ever held a "no-subject" view seems indecisive, since it is possible that the relevant remarks are intended as criticisms of a Cartesian view rather than as expositions of the true view.

person's experience. The theorist maintains that the uniqueness of this body is sufficient to give rise to the idea that one's experiences can be ascribed to some particular individual thing, can be said to be possessed by, or owned by, that thing. This idea, he thinks, though infelicitously and misleadingly expressed in terms of ownership, would have some validity, would make some sort of sense, so long as we thought of this individual thing, the possessor of the experiences, as the body itself. So long as we thought in this way, then to ascribe a particular state of consciousness to this body, this individual thing, would at least be to say something contingent, something that might be, or might have been, false. It might have been a misascription; for the experience in question might be, or might have been, causally dependent on the state of some other body; in the present admissible, though infelicitous, sense of "belong," it might have belonged to some other individual thing. But now, the theorist suggests, one becomes confused: one slides from this admissible, though infelicitous, sense in which one's experiences may be said to belong to, or be possessed by, some particular thing, to a wholly inadmissible and empty sense of these expressions; and in this new and inadmissible sense, the particular thing which is supposed to possess the experiences is not thought of as a body, but as something else, say an ego.

Suppose we call the first type of possession, which is really a certain kind of causal dependence, "having$_1$," and the second type of possession, "having$_2$"; and call the individual of the first type "B" and the supposed individual of the second type "E." Then the difference is that while it is genuinely a contingent matter that *all my experiences are had$_1$ by B*, it appears as a necessary truth that *all my experiences are had$_2$ by E*. But the belief in E and in having$_2$ is an illusion. Only those things whose ownership is logically transferable can be owned at all. So experiences are not owned by anything except in the dubious sense of being causally dependent on the state of a particular body. This is at least a genuine relationship to a thing, in that they might have stood in it to another thing. Since the whole function of E was to own experiences in a logically non-transferable sense of "own," and since experiences are not owned by anything in this sense, for there is no such sense of "own," E must be eliminated from the picture altogether. It only came in because of a confusion.

I think it must be clear that this account of the matter, though it contains *some* of the facts, is not coherent. It is not coherent, in that one who holds it is forced to make use of that sense of possession of which he denies the existence, in presenting his case for the denial. When he tries to state the contingent fact, which he thinks gives rise to the illusion of the "ego," he has to state it in some such form as "All *my* experiences are had$_1$ by (uniquely dependent on the state of) body B." For any attempt to eliminate the "my," or some other expression with a similar possessive force, would yield something that was not a contingent fact at all. The proposition that *all* experiences are causally dependent on the state of a single body B, for example, is just false. The theorist means to speak of all the experiences *had by a certain person* being contingently so dependent. And the theorist cannot consistently argue that "all the experiences of person P" *means the same thing* as "all experiences contingently dependent on a certain body B"; for then his proposition would not be contingent, as his theory requires, but analytic. He must mean to be speaking of some class of experiences of the members of which it is in fact contingently true that they are all dependent on body B. And the defining characteristic of this class is in fact that they are "*my* experiences" or "the experiences *of* some person," where the sense of "possession" is the one he calls into question.

This internal incoherence is a serious matter when it is a question of denying what prima facie is the case: that is, that one does genuinely ascribe one's states of consciousness to something, viz., oneself, and that this kind of ascription is precisely such as the theorist finds unsatisfactory, i.e., is such that it does not seem to make sense to suggest, for example, that the identical pain which was in fact one's own might have been another's. We do not have to seek far in order to understand the place of this logically non-transferable kind of ownership in our general scheme of thought. For if we think of the requirements of identifying reference, in speech, to *particular* states of consciousness, or private experiences, we see that such particulars cannot be thus identifyingly referred to except as the states or experiences *of* some identified *person*. States, or experiences, one might say, *owe* their identity as particulars to the identity of the person whose states or experiences they are. And from this it follows immediately that if they can be identified as particular states or experiences at all, they must be possessed or ascribable in just that way which the no-ownership theorist ridicules, i.e., in such a way that it is logically impossible that a particular state or experience in fact possessed by someone should have been possessed by anyone else. The requirements of identity rule out logical transferability of ownership. So the theorist could maintain his position only by denying that we could ever refer to particular states or experiences at all. And *this* position is ridiculous.

We may notice, even now, a possible connection between the no-ownership doctrine and the Cartesian position. The latter is, straightforwardly enough, a dualism of two subjects (two types of subject). The former could, a little paradoxically, be called a dualism too: a dualism of one subject (the body) and one non-subject. We might surmise that the second dualism, paradoxically so called, arises out of the first dualism, nonparadoxically so called; in other words, that if we try to think of that to which one's states of consciousness are ascribed as something utterly different from that to which certain corporeal characteristics are ascribed, then indeed it becomes difficult to see why states of conscious-ness should be ascribed, thought of as belonging to, anything at all. And when we think of this possibility, we may also think of another: viz., that both the Cartesian and the no-ownership theorist are profoundly wrong in holding, as each must, that there are two uses of "I" in one of which it denotes something which it does not denote in the other.

III

The no-ownership theorist fails to take account of all the facts. He takes account of some of them. He implies, correctly, that the unique position or role of a single body in one's experience is not a sufficient explanation of the fact that one's experiences, or states of consciousness, are ascribed to something which *has* them, with that peculiar nontrans-ferable kind of possession which is here in question. It may be a necessary part of the explanation, but it is not, by itself, a sufficient explanation. The theorist, as we have seen, goes on to suggest that it is perhaps a sufficient explanation of something else: viz., of our confusedly and mistakenly *thinking* that states of consciousness are to be ascribed to something in this special way. And this suggestion, as we have seen, is incoherent: for it involves the denial that someone's states of conscious-ness are anyone's. We avoid the incoherence of this denial, while agreeing that the special role of a single body in someone's experience does not suffice to explain why that experience should be ascribed to anybody. The fact that there is this special role does not, by itself, give a sufficient reason why what we think of as a subject of experience should have any use for the conception of himself as such a subject.

When I say that the no-ownership theorist's account fails through not reckoning with all the facts, I have in mind a very simple but, in this question, a very central, thought: viz., that it is a necessary condition of one's ascribing states of consciousness, experiences, to oneself, in the way one does, that one should also ascribe them (or be prepared to ascribe them) to others who are not oneself.[2] This means not less than it says.

[2] I can imagine an objection to the unqualified form of this statement, an objection which might be put as follows. Surely the idea of a uniquely applicable predicate (a predicate which in *fact* belongs to only one individual) is not absurd. And, if it is not, then surely the most that can be claimed is that a necessary condition of one's ascribing predicates of a certain class to one individual (oneself) is that one should be prepared, or ready, on appropriate occasions, to ascribe them to other individuals, and hence that one should have a conception of what those appropriate occasions for ascribing them would be; but not, necessarily, that one should actually do so on any occasion.

The shortest way with the objection is to admit it, or at least to refrain from disputing it; for the lesser claim is all that the argument strictly requires, though it is *slightly* simpler to conduct it on the basis of the larger claim. But it is well to point out further that we are not speaking of a single predicate, or merely of some group or other of predicates, but of the whole of an enormous class of predicates such that the

It means, for example, that the ascribing phrases should be used in just the same sense when the subject is another, as when the subject is oneself. Of course the thought that this is so gives no trouble to the nonphilosopher: the thought, for example, that "in pain" means the same whether one says "I am in pain" or "He is in pain." The dictionaries do not give two sets of meanings for every expression which describes a state of consciousness: a first-person meaning, and a second- and third-person meaning. But to the philosopher this thought has given trouble; indeed it has. How could the sense be the same when the method of verification was so different in the two cases—or, rather, when there *was* a method of verification in the one case (the case of others) and not, properly speaking, in the other case (the case of oneself)? Or, again, how can it be right to talk of *ascribing* in the case of oneself? For surely there can be a question of ascribing only if there is or could be a question of identifying that to which the ascription is made? And though there may be a question of identifying the one who is in pain when that one is another, how can there be such a question when that one is oneself? But this last query answers itself as soon as we remember that we speak primarily to others, for the information of others. In one sense, indeed, there is no question of my having to *tell who it is* who is in pain, when I am. In another sense I may have to *tell who it is,* i.e., to let others know who it is.

What I have just said explains, perhaps, how one may properly be said to ascribe states of consciousness to oneself, given that one ascribes them to others. But how is it that one can ascribe them to others? Well, *one* thing is certain: that *if* the things one ascribes states of consciousness to, in ascribing them to others, are thought of as a set of Cartesian egos to which *only* private experiences can, in correct logical grammar, be ascribed, *then* this question is unanswerable and this problem insoluble. If, in identifying the things to which states of consciousness are to be ascribed, private experiences are to be all one has to go on, then, just for the very same reason as that for which there is, from one's own point of view, no question of telling that a private experience is one's own, there is also no question of telling that a private experience is another's. All private experiences, all states of consciousness, will be mine, i.e., no one's. To put it briefly: one can ascribe states of consciousness to oneself only if one can ascribe them to others; one can ascribe them to others only if one can identify other subjects of experience;

---

applicability of those predicates or their negations determines a major logical type or category of individuals. To insist, at this level, on the distinction between the lesser and the larger claims is to carry the distinction over from a level at which it is clearly correct to a level at which it may well appear idle or, possibly, senseless.

The main point here is a purely logical one: the idea of a predicate is correlative with that of a range of distinguishable individuals of which the predicate can be significantly, though not necessarily truly, affirmed.

and one cannot identify others if one can identify them *only* as subjects of experience, possessors of states of consciousness.

It might be objected that this way with Cartesianism is too short. After all, there is no difficulty about distinguishing bodies from one another, no difficulty about identifying bodies. And does not this give us an indirect way of identifying subjects of experience, while preserving the Cartesian mode? Can we not identify such a subject as, for example, "the subject that stands to that body in the same special relation as I stand to this one"; or, in other words, "the subject of those experiences which stand in the same unique causal relation to body N as *my* experiences stand to body M?" But this suggestion is useless. It requires me to have noted that *my* experiences stand in a special relation to body M, when it is just the right to speak of *my* experiences at all that is in question. (It requires me to have noted that *my* experiences stand in a special relation to body M; but it requires me to have noted this as a condition of being able to identify other subjects of experience, i.e., as a condition of having the idea of myself as a subject of experience, i.e., as a condition of thinking of any experience as *mine*.) So long as we persist in talking, in the mode of this explanation, of experiences on the one hand, and bodies on the other, the most I may be allowed to have noted is that experiences, *all* experiences, stand in a special relation to body M, that body M is unique in just this way, that this is what makes body M unique among bodies. (This "most" is, perhaps, too much—because of the presence of the word "experiences.") The proffered explanation runs: "Another subject of experience is distinguished and identified as the subject of those experiences which stand in the same unique causal relationship to body N as *my* experiences stand to body M." And the objection is: "But what is the word 'my' doing in this explanation? (It could not get on without it.)"

What we have to acknowledge, in order to begin to free ourselves from these difficulties, is the *primitiveness* of the concept of a person. What I mean by the concept of a person is the concept of a type of entity such that *both* predicates ascribing states of consciousness *and* predicates ascribing corporeal characteristics, a physical situation, etc. are equally applicable to a single individual of that single type. And what I mean by saying that this concept is primitive can be put in a number of ways. One way is to return to those two questions I asked earlier: viz., (1) why are states of consciousness ascribed to anything at all? and (2) why are they ascribed to the very same thing as certain corporeal characteristics, a certain physical situation, etc.? I remarked at the beginning that it was not to be supposed that the answers to these questions were independent of each other. And now I shall say that they are connected in this way: that a necessary condition of states of consciousness being ascribed at all is that they should be ascribed to the *very same things* as certain corporeal characteristics, a certain physical situation, etc. That is to say, states of consciousness could not be ascribed at all, *unless* they were ascribed to persons, in the sense I have claimed for this word. We are tempted to think of a person as a sort of compound of two kinds of subject—a subject of experiences (a pure consciousness, an ego), on the one hand, and a subject of corporeal attributes on the other.

Many questions arise when we think in this way. But, in particular, when we ask ourselves how we come to frame, to get a use for, the concept of this compound of two subjects, the picture—if we are honest and careful—is apt to change from the picture of two subjects to the picture of one subject and one nonsubject. For it becomes impossible to see how we could come by the idea of different, distinguishable, identifiable subjects of experiences—different consciousnesses—*if this idea is thought of as logically primitive,* as a logical ingredient in the compound idea of a person, the latter being composed of two subjects. For there could never be any question of assigning an experience, as such, to any subject other than oneself; and therefore never any question of assigning it to oneself either, never any question of ascribing it to a subject at all. So the concept of the pure individual consciousness—the pure ego—is a concept that cannot exist; or, at least, cannot exist as a primary concept in terms of which the concept of a person can be explained or analyzed. It can only exist, if at all, as a secondary, nonprimitive concept, which itself is to be explained, analyzed, in terms of the concept of a person. It was the entity corresponding to this illusory primary concept of the pure consciousness, the ego-substance, for which Hume was seeking, or ironically pretending to seek, when he looked into himself, and complained that he could never discover himself without a perception and could never discover anything but the perception. More seriously—and this time there was no irony, but a confusion, a Nemesis of confusion for Hume—it was this entity of which Hume vainly sought for the principle of unity, confessing himself perplexed and defeated; sought vainly because there is no principle of unity where there is no principle of differentiation. It was this, too, to which Kant, more perspicacious here than Hume, accorded a purely formal ("analytic") unity: the unity of the "I think" that accompanies all my perceptions and therefore might just as well accompany none. And finally it is this, perhaps, of which Wittgenstein spoke when he said of the subject, first, that there is no such thing, and, second, that it is not a part of the world, but its limit.

So, then, the word "I" never refers to this, the pure subject. But this does not mean, as the no-ownership theorist must think and as Wittgenstein, at least at one period, seemed to think, that "I" in some cases does not refer at all. It refers, because I am a person among others. And the predicates which would, *per impossibile,* belong to the pure subject if it could be referred to, belong properly to the person to which "I" does refer.

The concept of a person is logically prior to that of an individual consciousness. The concept of a person is not to be analyzed as that of an animated body or of an embodied anima. This is not to say that the concept of a pure individual consciousness might not have a logically secondary existence, if one thinks, or finds, it desirable. We speak of a dead person—a body—and in the same secondary way we might at least think of a disembodied person, retaining the logical benefit of individuality from having been a person.[3]

IV

It is important to realize the full extent of the acknowledgment one is making in acknowledging the logical primitiveness of the concept of a person. Let me rehearse briefly the stages of the argument. There would be no question of ascribing one's own states of consciousness, or experiences, to anything, unless one also ascribed states of consciousness, or experiences, to other individual entities of the same logical type as that thing to which one ascribes one's own states of consciousness. The condition of reckoning oneself as a subject of such predicates is that one should also reckon others as subjects of such predicates. The condition, in turn, of this being possible, is that one should be able to distinguish from one another (pick out, identify) different subjects of such predicates, i.e., different individuals of the type concerned. And the condition, in turn, of this being possible is that the individuals concerned, including oneself, should be of a certain unique type: of a type, namely, such that to each individual of that type there *must* be ascribed, or ascribable, *both* states of consciousness *and* corporeal characteristics. But this characterization of the type is still very opaque and does not at all clearly bring out what is involved. To bring this out, I must make a rough division, into two, of the kinds of predicates properly applied to individuals of this type. The first kind of predicate consists of those which are also properly applied to material bodies to which we would not dream of applying predicates ascribing states of consciousness. I will call this first kind M-predicates: and they include things like "weighs 10 stone," "is in the drawing room," and so on. The second kind consists of all the other predicates we apply to persons. These I shall call P-predicates. And P-predicates, of course, will be very various. They will include things like "is smiling," "is going for a walk," as well as things like "is in pain," "is thinking hard," "believes in God," and so on.

So far I have said that the concept of a person is to be understood as the concept of a type of entity such that *both* predicates ascribing states of consciousness *and* predicates ascribing corporeal characteristics, a physical situation, etc., are equally applicable to an individual entity of that type. And all I have said about the meaning of saying that this

---

[3] A little further thought will show how limited this concession is. But I shall not discuss the question now.

concept is primitive is that it is not to be analyzed in a certain way or ways. We are not, for example, to think of it as a secondary kind of entity in relation to two primary kinds, viz., a particular consciousness and a particular human body. I implied also that the Cartesian error is just a special case of a more general error, present in a different form in theories of the no-ownership type, of thinking of the designations, or apparent designations, of persons as *not* denoting precisely the same thing, or entity, for all kinds of predicate ascribed to the entity designated. That is, if we are to avoid the general form of this error we must *not* think of "I" or "Smith" as suffering from type-ambiguity. (If we want to locate type-ambiguity somewhere, we would do better to locate it in certain predicates like "is in the drawing room," "was hit by a stone," etc., and say they mean one thing when applied to material objects and another when applied to persons.)

This is all I have so far said or implied about the meaning of saying that the concept of a person is primitive. What has to be brought out further is what the implications of saying this are as regards the logical character of those predicates in which we ascribe states of consciousness. And for this purpose we may well consider P-predicates in general. For though not all P-predicates are what we should call "predicates ascribing states of consciousness" (for example, "going for a walk" is not), they may be said to have this in common, that they imply the possession of consciousness on the part of that to which they are ascribed.

What then are the consequences of this view as regards the character of P-predicates? I think they are these. Clearly there is no sense in talking of identifiable individuals of a special type, a type, namely, such that they possess both M-predicates and P-predicates, unless there is in principle some way of telling, with regard to any individual of that type, and any P-predicate, whether that individual possesses that P-predicate. And, in the case of at least some P-predicates, the ways of telling must constitute in some sense logically adequate kinds of criteria for the ascription of the P-predicate. For suppose in no case did these ways of telling constitute logically adequate kinds of criteria. Then we should have to think of the relation between the ways of telling and what the P-predicate ascribes (or a part of what it ascribes) always in the following way: we should have to think of the ways of telling as *signs* of the presence, in the individual concerned, of this different thing (the state of consciousness). But then we could only know that the way of telling was a sign of the presence of the different thing ascribed by the P-predicate, by the observation of correlations between the two. But this observation we could each make only in one case, namely, our own. And now we are back in the position of the defender of Cartesianism, who thought our way with it was too short. For what, now, does "our own case" mean? There is no sense in the idea of ascribing states of consciousness to oneself, or at all, unless the ascriber already knows how to ascribe at least some states of consciousness to others. So he cannot (or cannot generally) argue "from his own case" to conclusions about how to do this; for unless he already knows how to do this, he has no conception of *his own case,* or any *case* (i.e., any subject of experiences). Instead, he just has evidence that pain, etc., may be expected when a certain body is affected in certain ways and not when others are.

The conclusion here is, of course, not new. What I have said is that one ascribes P-predicates to others on the strength of observation of their behavior; and that the behavior criteria one goes on are not just signs of the presence of what is meant by the P-predicate, but are criteria of a logically adequate kind for the ascription of the P-predicate. On behalf of this conclusion, however, I am claiming that it follows from a consideration of the conditions necessary for any ascription of states of consciousness to anything. The point is not that we must accept this conclusion in order to avoid skepticism, but that we must accept it in order to explain the existence of the conceptual scheme in terms of which the skeptical problem is stated. But once the conclusion is accepted, the skeptical problem does not arise. (And so with the generality of skeptical problems: their statement involves the pretended acceptance of a conceptual scheme and at the same time the silent repudiation of one of the conditions of its existence. This is why they are, in the terms in which they are stated, insoluble.) But this is only half the picture about P-predicates.

Now let us turn to the other half. For of course it is true, at least of some important classes of P-predicates, that when one ascribes them to oneself, one does not do so on the strength of observation of those behavior criteria on the strength of which one ascribes them to others. This is not true of all P-predicates. It is not, in general, true of those which carry assessments of character and capability: these, when self-ascribed, are in general ascribed on the same kind of basis as that on which they are ascribed to others. And of those P-predicates of which it is true that one does not generally ascribe them to oneself on the basis of the criteria on the strength of which one ascribes them to others, there are many of which it is also true that their ascription is liable to correction by the self-ascriber on this basis. But there remain many cases in which one has an entirely adequate basis for ascribing a P-predicate to oneself, and yet in which this basis is quite distinct from those on which one ascribes the predicate to another. (Thus one says, reporting a present state of mind or feeling: "I feel tired, am depressed, am in pain.") How can this fact be reconciled with the doctrine that the criteria on the strength of which one ascribes P-predicates to others are criteria of a logically adequate kind for this ascription?

The apparent difficulty of bringing about this reconciliation may tempt us in many directions. It may tempt us, for example, to deny that these self-ascriptions are really ascriptions at all; to *assimilate* first-person ascriptions of states of consciousness to those other forms of behavior which constitute criteria on the basis of which one person ascribes P-predicates to another. This device seems to avoid the difficulty; it is not, in all cases, entirely inappropriate. But it obscures the facts, and is needless. It is merely a sophisticated form of failure to recognize the special character of P-predicates (or at least of a crucial class of P-predicates). For just as there is not (in general) one primary process of learning, or teaching oneself, an inner private meaning for predicates of this class, then another process of learning to apply such predicates to others on the strength of a correlation, noted in one's own case, with certain forms of behavior, so—and equally—there is not (in general) one primary process of learning to apply such predicates to others on the strength of behavior criteria, and then another process of acquiring the secondary technique of exhibiting a new form of behavior, viz., first-person P-utterances. Both these pictures are refusals to acknowledge the unique logical character of the predicates concerned.

Suppose we write "Px" as the general form of propositional function of such a predicate. Then according to the first picture, the expression which primarily replaces "x" in this form is "I," the first-person singular pronoun; its uses with other replacements are secondary, derivative, and shaky. According to the second picture, on the other hand, the primary replacements of "x" in this form are "he," "that person," etc., and its use with "I" is secondary, peculiar, not a true ascriptive use. But it is essential to the character of these predicates that they have both first- and third-person ascriptive uses, that they are both self-ascribable otherwise than on the basis of observation of the behavior of the subject of them, and other-ascribable on the basis of behavior criteria. To learn their use is to learn both aspects of their use. In order to *have* this type of concept, one must be both a self-ascriber and an other-ascriber of such predicates, and must see every other as a self-ascriber. And in order to *understand* this type of concept, one must acknowledge that there is a kind of predicate which is unambiguously and adequately ascribable *both* on the basis of observation of the subject of the predicate *and* not on this basis (independently of observation of the subject): the second case is the case where the ascriber is also the subject. If there were no concepts answering to the characterization I have just given, we should indeed have no philosophical problem about the soul; but equally we should not have *our* concept of a person.

To put the point—with a certain unavoidable crudity—in terms of one particular concept of this class, say, that of depression, we speak of behaving in a depressed way (of depressed behavior) and also of feeling depressed (of a feeling of depression). One is inclined to argue that feelings can be felt, but not observed, and behavior can be observed, but not felt, and that therefore there must be room here to drive in a logical wedge. But the concept of depression spans the place where one wants to drive it in. We might say, in order for there to be such a concept as that of X's depression, the depression which X has, the concept must cover both what is felt, but not observed, by X and what may be observed, but not felt, by others than X (for all values of X). But it is perhaps better to say: X's depression *is* something, one and the same thing, which is felt but not observed by X and observed but not felt by others than X. (And, of course, what can be observed can also be faked or disguised.) To refuse to accept this is to refuse to accept the structure of the language in which we talk about depression. That is, in a sense, all right. One might give up talking; or devise, perhaps, a different structure in terms of which to soliloquize. What is not all right is simultaneously to pretend to accept that structure and to refuse to accept it; i.e., to couch one's rejection in the language of that structure.

It is in this light that we must see some of the familiar philosophical difficulties in the topic of the mind. For some of them spring from just such a failure to admit, or fully appreciate, the character which I have been claiming for at least some P-predicates. It is not seen that these predicates could not have either aspect of their use (the self-ascriptive and the non-self-ascriptive) without having the other aspect. Instead, one aspect of their use is taken as self-sufficient, which it could not be, and then the other aspect appears as problematical. And so we oscillate between philosophical skepticism and philosophical behaviorism. When we take the self-ascriptive aspect of the use of some P-predicate (say, "depressed") as primary, then a logical gap seems to open between the criteria on the strength of which we say that another is depressed, and the actual state of depression. What we do not realize is that if this logical gap is allowed to open, then it swallows not only his depression, but our depression as well. For if the logical gap exists, then depressed behavior, however much there is of it, is no more than a sign of depression. And it can become a sign of depression only because of an observed correlation between it and depression. But whose depression? Only mine, one is tempted to say. But if *only* mine, then *not* mine at all. The skeptical position customarily represents the crossing of the logical gap as at best a shaky inference. But the point is that not even the syntax of the premises of the inference exists if the gap exists.

If, on the other hand, we take the other-ascriptive uses of these predicates as self-sufficient, we may come to think that all there is in the meaning of these predicates, as predicates, is the criteria on the strength of which we ascribe them to others. Does this not follow from the denial of the logical gap? It does not follow. To think that it does is to forget the self-ascriptive use of these predicates, to forget that we have to do with a class of predicates to the meaning of which it is essential that they should be both self-ascribable and other-ascribable to the same individual, when self-ascriptions are not made on the observational basis on which other-ascriptions are made, but on another basis. It is not that these predicates have two kinds of meaning. Rather, it is essential to the single kind of meaning that they do have that both ways of ascribing them should be perfectly in order.

If one is playing a game of cards, the distinctive markings of a certain card constitute a logically adequate criterion for calling it, say, the Queen of Hearts; but, in calling it this, in the context of the game, one is also ascribing to it properties over and above the possession of those markings. The predicate gets its meaning from the whole structure of the game. So it is with the language which ascribes P-predicates. To say that the criteria on the strength of which we ascribe P-predicates to others are of a logically adequate kind for this ascription is not to say that all there is to the ascriptive meaning of these predicates is these criteria. To say this is to forget that they are P-predicates, to forget the rest of the language-structure to which they belong.

V

Now our perplexities may take a different form, the form of the question "But how can one ascribe to oneself, not on the basis of observation, *the very same thing* that others may have, on the basis of observation, a logically adequate reason for ascribing to one?" And this question may be absorbed in a wider one, which might be phrased: "How are P-predicates possible?" or "How is the concept of a person possible?" This is the question by which we replace those two earlier questions, viz.: "Why are states of consciousness ascribed at all, ascribed to anything?" and "Why are they ascribed to the very same thing as certain corporeal characteristics, etc.?" For the answer to these two initial questions is to be found nowhere else but in the admission of the primitiveness of the concept of a person, and hence of the unique character of P-predicates. So residual perplexities have to frame themselves in this new way. For when we have acknowledged the primitiveness of the concept of a person and, with it, the unique character of P-predicates, we may still want to ask what it is in the natural facts that makes it intelligible that we should have this concept, and to ask this in the hope of a non-trivial answer.[4] I do not pretend to be able to satisfy this demand at all fully. But I may mention two very different things which might count as beginnings or fragments of an answer.

And, first, I think a beginning can be made by moving a certain class of P-predicates to a central position in the picture. They are predicates, roughly, which involve doing something, which clearly imply intention or a state of mind or at least consciousness in general, and which indicate a characteristic pattern, or range of patterns, of bodily movement, while not indicating at all precisely any very definite sensation or expe-

---

[4] I mean, in the hope of an answer which does not *merely* say: Well, there are people in the world.

rience. I mean such things as "going for a walk," "furling a rope," "playing ball," "writing a letter." Such predicates have the interesting characteristic of many P-predicates that one does not, in general, ascribe them to oneself on the strength of observation, whereas one does ascribe them to others on the strength of observation. But, in the case of these predicates, one feels minimal reluctance to concede that what is ascribed in these two different ways is the same. And this is because of the marked dominance of a fairly definite pattern of bodily movement in what they ascribe, and the marked absence of any distinctive experience. They release us from the idea that the only things we can know about without observation, or inference, or both, are private experiences; we can know also, without telling by either of these means, about the present and future movements of a body. Yet bodily movements are certainly also things we can know about by observation and inference.

Among the things that we observe, as opposed to the things we know without observation, are the movements of bodies similar to that about which we have knowledge not based on observation. It is important that we understand such observed movements; they bear on and condition our own. And in fact we understand them, we interpret them, only by seeing them as elements in just such plans or schemes of action as those of which we know the present course and future development without observation of the relevant present movements. But this is to say that we see such movements (the observed movements of others) as *actions*, that we interpret them in terms of intention, that we see them as movements of individuals of a type to which also belongs that individual whose present and future movements we know about without observation; that we see others, as self-ascribers, not on the basis of observations, of what we ascribe to them on this basis.

Of course these remarks are not intended to suggest how the "problem of other minds" could be solved, or our beliefs about others given a general philosophical "justification." I have already argued that such a "solution" or "justification" is impossible, that the demand for it cannot be coherently stated. Nor are these remarks intended as a priori genetic psychology. They are simply intended to help to make it seem intelligible to us, at this stage in the history of the philosophy of this subject, that we have the conceptual scheme we have. What I am suggesting is that it is easier to understand how we can see each other (and ourselves) as persons, if we think first of the fact that we act, and act on each other, and act in accordance with a common human nature. "To see each other as persons" is a lot of things; but not a lot of separate and unconnected things. The class of P-predicates that I have moved into the center of the picture are not unconnectedly there, detached from others irrelevant to them. On the contrary, they are inextricably bound up with the others, interwoven with them. The topic of the mind does **not** divide into unconnected subjects.

I spoke just now of a common human nature. But there is also a sense in which a condition of the existence of the conceptual scheme we have is that human nature should not be common, should not be, that is, a community nature. Philosophers used to discuss the question of whether there was, or could be, such a thing as a "group mind." And for some the idea had a peculiar fascination, while to others it seemed utterly absurd and nonsensical and at the same time, curiously enough, pernicious. It is easy to see why these last found it pernicious: they found something horrible in the thought that people should cease to have toward individual persons the kind of attitudes that they did have, and instead have attitudes in some way analogous to those toward groups; and that they might cease to decide individual courses of action for themselves and instead merely participate in corporate activities. But their finding it pernicious showed that they understood the idea they claimed to be absurd only too well. The fact that we find it natural to individuate as persons the members of a certain class of what might also be individuated as organic bodies does not mean that such a conceptual scheme is inevitable for any class of beings not utterly unlike ourselves.

Might we not construct the idea of a special kind of social world in which the concept of an individual person has no employment, whereas an analogous concept for groups does have employment? Think, to begin with, of certain aspects of actual human existence. Think, for example, of two groups of human beings engaged in some competitive but corporate activity, such as battle, for which they have been exceedingly well trained. We may even suppose that orders are superfluous, though information is passed. It is easy to imagine that, while absorbed in such activity, the members of the groups make no references to individual persons at all, have no use for personal names or pronouns. They do, however, refer to the groups and apply to them predicates analogous to those predicates ascribing purposive activity which we normally apply to individual persons. They may, *in fact,* use in such circumstances the plural forms "we" and "they"; but these are not genuine plurals, they are plurals without a singular, such as we use in sentences like these: "We have taken the citadel," "We have lost the game." They may also refer to elements in the group, to members of the group, but exclusively in terms which get their sense from the parts played by these elements in the corporate activity. (Thus we sometimes refer to what are in fact persons as "stroke" or "tackle.")

When we think of such cases, we see that we ourselves, over a part of our social lives—not, I am thankful to say, a very large part—do operate conceptual schemes in which the idea of the individual person has no place, in which its place is taken, so to speak, by that of a group. But might we not think of communities or groups such that this part of the lives of their members was the dominant part—or was the whole?

It sometimes happens, with groups of human beings, that, as we say, their members think, feel, and act "as one." The point I wish to make is that a condition for the existence, the use, of the concept of an individual person is that this should happen *only sometimes*.

It is absolutely useless to say, at this point: But all the same, even if this happened all the time, every member of the group would have an individual consciousness, would be an individual subject of experience. The point is, once more, that there is no sense in speaking of the individual consciousness just as such, of the individual subject of experience just as such: for there is no way of identifying such pure entities.[5] It is true, of course, that in suggesting this fantasy, I have taken our concept of an individual person as a starting point. It is this fact which makes the useless reaction a natural one. But suppose, instead, I had made the following suggestion: that each part of the human body, each organ and each member, had an individual consciousness, was a separate center of experiences. This, in the same way, but more obviously, would be a useless suggestion. Then imagine all the intermediate cases, for instance these. There is a class of moving natural objects, divided into groups, each group exhibiting the same characteristic pattern of activity. Within each group there are certain differentiations of appearance accompanying differentiations of function, and in particular there is one member of each group with a distinctive appearance. Cannot one imagine different sets of observations which might lead us, in the one case, to think of the particular member as the spokesman of the group, as its mouthpiece; and in the other case to think of him as its mouth, to think of the group as a single *scattered* body? The point is that as soon as we adopt the latter way of thinking then we want to drop the former; we are no longer influenced by the human analogy in its first form, but only in its second; and we no longer want to say: "Perhaps the members have consciousness." To understand the movement of our thought here, we need only remember the startling ambiguity of the phrase "a body and its members."

VI

I shall not pursue this attempt at explanation any further. What I have been mainly arguing for is that we should acknowledge the logical primitiveness of the concept of a person and, with this, the unique logical character of certain predicates. Once this is acknowledged, certain traditional philosophical problems are seen not to be problems at all. In particular, the problem that seems to have perplexed Hume[6] does not exist—the problem of the principle of unity, of identity, of the par-

---

[5] More accurately: their identification is necessarily secondary to the identification of persons.

[6] Cf. the Appendix to the *Treatise of Human Nature*.

ticular consciousness, of the particular subject of "perceptions" (experiences) considered as a primary particular. There is no such problem and no such principle. If there were such a principle, then each of us would have to apply it in order to decide whether any contemporary experience of his was his or someone else's; and there is no sense in this suggestion. (This is not to deny, of course, that one *person* may be unsure of his own identity in some way, may be unsure, for example, whether some particular action, or series of actions, had been performed by him. Then he uses the same methods (the same in principle) to resolve the doubt about himself as anyone else uses to resolve the same doubt about him. And these methods simply involve the application of the ordinary criteria for *personal* identity. There remains the question of what exactly these criteria are, what their relative weights are, etc.; but, once disentangled from spurious questions, this is one of the easier problems in philosophy.)

Where Hume erred, or seems to have erred, both Kant and Wittgenstein had the better insight. Perhaps neither always expressed it in the happiest way. For Kant's doctrine that the "analytic unity of consciousness" neither requires nor entails any principle of unity is not as clear as one could wish. And Wittgenstein's remarks (at one time) to the effect that the data of consciousness are not owned, that "I" as used by Jones, in speaking of his own feelings, etc., does not refer to what "Jones" as used by another refers to, seem needlessly to flout the conceptual scheme we actually employ. It is needlessly paradoxical to deny, or seem to deny, that when Smith says "Jones has a pain" and Jones says "I have a pain," they are talking about the same entity and saying the same thing about it, needlessly paradoxical to deny that Jones can *confirm* that he has a pain. Instead of denying that self-ascribed states of consciousness are really ascribed at all, it is more in harmony with our actual ways of talking to say: For each user of the language, there is just one person in ascribing to whom states of consciousness he does not need to use the criteria of the observed behavior of that person (though he does not necessarily not do so); and that person is himself. This remark at least respects the structure of the conceptual scheme we employ, without precluding further examination of it.

VIII ∾ About Behaviorism
Paul Ziff

"One behaviorist meeting another on the street said 'You feel fine! How do I feel?'" This bad joke embodies two bad arguments against behaviorism. I want to explain why they are bad arguments.

1. I say "I am angry." My statement is true if and only if a certain organism is behaving in certain ways. If I say "George is angry," my statement is true if and only if a certain organism, viz., George, is behaving in certain ways. The only way I can tell whether or not George is angry is by observing George's behavior, verbal or otherwise. (There is nothing else to tell.) But I do not find out whether or not I am angry by observing my own behavior because I do not find out whether or not I am angry. (That I sometimes suddenly realize that I am or that I have become angry is essentially irrelevant here.) To talk of my finding out whether or not I am angry is generally odd: it would not be odd only in peculiar cases.

2. The first bad argument is not particularly interesting. It is this: if my being angry were a matter of my behaving in certain ways then I should be able to find out whether or not I am angry for I can find out whether or not I am behaving in certain ways. Since it is generally odd to speak of my finding out whether or not I am angry, my being angry cannot be a matter of my behaving in certain ways. (Thus: "How do I feel?")

The mistake here is in the assumption that I can find out whether or not I am behaving in the relevant ways. A behaviorist maintains that to be angry is to behave in certain ways. I shall accordingly speak of "anger behavior" and of "anger behaving."

It is generally odd to speak of my finding out whether or not I am angry: it is neither more nor less odd to speak of my finding out whether or not I am anger behaving.

3. It is not always odd to speak of my finding out whether or not I am behaving in a certain way. Suppose I have my hands behind my back, my fingers intermeshed. I am asked to move the third finger of my left hand. I may not know whether or not I am in fact moving that finger.

I may have to look in a mirror to find out. So it is not in every case odd to speak of my finding out whether or not I am behaving in a certain way. It does not follow that it is not sometimes odd.

I am at this moment talking, hence behaving in a certain way. It would be odd to speak of my finding out whether or not I am talking at this moment. No doubt one can think up cases in which it would not be odd to speak of my finding out whether or not I am talking. That is irrelevant. I am not talking about those cases: I am talking about this case, here and now, and here and now I cannot doubt that I am talking. (More can be said about this point, but I shall not try to say it here.)

It would generally be odd to speak of my finding out whether or not I am anger behaving, e.g., gnashing my teeth.

4. The second bad argument is more serious. It is this: if my being angry were a matter of my behaving in certain ways then you should be able to find out whether or not I am angry for you can find out whether or not I am behaving in certain ways. But sometimes you cannot find out whether or not I am angry. Since you can, in principle at least, always find out whether or not I am behaving in certain ways, my being angry cannot be a matter of my behaving in certain ways. (Thus: "You feel fine!")

The mistake here is in the assumption that there is a difference between your finding out whether or not I am anger behaving and your finding out whether or not I am angry. There is no difference.

5. You cannot in fact always find out whether or not I am angry. I may be artful at concealing my anger and I may refuse to tell you. Neither can you in fact always find out whether or not I am behaving in certain ways. You cannot in fact find out whether or not I am flexing my abdominal muscles. I will not tell you and no one else can.

So what you can or cannot in fact find out is beside the point. What is not beside the point?

6. "You can in principle if not in fact always find out whether or not I am behaving in certain ways. But you cannot even in principle always find out whether or not I am angry." This contention will not bear scrutiny.

(I will not cavil over the locution "you can in principle find out." I consider it an instrument of obfuscation. Even so, I shall let it pass: I believe I can more or less grasp what is intended.)

You can in principle always find out whether or not I am angry because I can tell you. Hence you need attend only to my verbal behavior. (I assume that it would generally be odd to speak of my being mistaken about whether or not I am angry.) To suppose that you cannot in principle find out whether or not I am angry would be to suppose that I cannot in principle tell you whether or not I am angry. I find such a supposition unintelligible.

7. The preceding contention can be reformulated as follows: "You can in principle if not in fact always find out whether or not I am behaving in certain ways. In some cases at least, being angry does not involve verbal behavior. Let us restrict our attention to such cases. Then apart from my subsequent verbal behavior, you cannot even in principle always find out whether or not I am angry."

As I said before, I more or less grasp what is intended by the locution "you can in principle find out": I would not pretend I have a firm grasp. (One cannot have a firm grip on a jellyfish.) In so far as I can grasp what is intended, I am inclined to agree that apart from my subsequent verbal behavior you cannot even in principle always find out whether or not I am angry. But I deny that apart from my subsequent verbal behavior you can in principle always find out whether or not I am anger behaving.

8. Let us suppose that in a certain case my anger behavior consists, among other things, in my gnashing my teeth. If we are to suppose that apart from my subsequent verbal behavior you can in principle always find out whether or not I am anger behaving then we must suppose that apart from my subsequent verbal behavior you can in principle always find out whether or not I am gnashing my teeth.

There is a difference between my gnashing my teeth and the gnashing of my teeth. It is conceivable that by supplying the appropriate stimuli directly to the appropriate muscles one could effect the gnashing of my teeth. In the kind of case I envisage, I could not truly say "I was gnashing my teeth" though I could truly say "My teeth were gnashing" and perhaps add "It felt queer."

I would not deny that apart from my subsequent verbal behavior you can in principle always find out whether or not my teeth are gnashing. But I deny that apart from my subsequent verbal behavior you can in principle always find out whether or not I am gnashing my teeth.

9. Can a behaviorist make a distinction between my gnashing my teeth and the gnashing of my teeth? I see no reason why not.

It is true that my teeth are gnashing if and only if it is true that certain teeth and jaws are moving in certain ways. But it is true that I am gnashing my teeth if and only if it is true that a certain organism is behaving in certain ways. If a certain organism is behaving in certain ways then it may be the case that certain teeth and jaws are moving in certain ways. But the converse need not hold: it does not follow that if certain teeth and jaws are moving in certain ways then a certain organism is behaving in certain ways.

10. There is a difference between someone gnashing his teeth and the gnashing of someone's teeth. But the difference is not a difference in behavior: only the former is an instance of behavior; the latter may be a component of behavior.

If George is gnashing his teeth then George's teeth are gnashing. But whether or not a case in which his teeth are gnashing can rightly be characterized as a case in which he is gnashing his teeth depends (not on whether or not the gnashing of his teeth is accompanied by "a movement of the soul" but simply) on contextual and relational matters.

11. I said that whether or not a case in which George's teeth are gnashing can rightly be characterized as a case in which George is gnashing his teeth depends on contextual and relational matters. I am not saying "Whether or not a case in which my teeth are gnashing can rightly be characterized by me as a case in which I am gnashing my teeth depends on contextual and relational matters": that would be odd. It would indicate that I could in general answer the following generally odd question: "Given that your teeth are gnashing, what entitles you to say not merely that your teeth are gnashing but that you are gnashing your teeth, that you are doing it?" (I believe that Wittgenstein once said "The first mistake is to ask the question": the second is to answer it.)

What is in question here is what entitles you to say that I am gnashing my teeth and not merely that my teeth are gnashing. The question whether I am gnashing my teeth or whether my teeth are merely gnashing is a question for you, not for me. It would generally be odd for me to ask "Am I gnashing my teeth or are they merely gnashing?"

12. Whether or not a case in which my teeth are gnashing can rightly be characterized by you as a case in which I am gnashing my teeth depends on contextual and relational matters.

The teeth of a corpse may be gnashing but the corpse cannot (without oddity) be said to be gnashing its teeth. So I must be alive, I must behave in characteristic ways. What more is required? Primarily this: my subsequent behavior, both verbal and otherwise, must be consonant with the claim that I was in fact gnashing my teeth. This is not to say that if I assert "I was not gnashing my teeth," then I was not gnashing my teeth: I may be lying, or forgetful, or confused, etc. But my subsequent behavior, both verbal and otherwise, is clearly relevant.

Therefore I deny that apart from my subsequent verbal behavior you can in principle always find out whether or not I am gnashing my teeth. And in consequence I deny that there is a difference between finding out whether or not I am behaving in certain ways and finding out whether or not I am angry.

Philosophical behaviorism is not a metaphysical theory: it is the denial of a metaphysical theory. Consequently, it asserts nothing.

IX ❧ Knowledge of Other Minds

Norman Malcolm

I

I believe that the argument from analogy for the existence of other minds still enjoys more credit than it deserves, and my first aim in this paper will be to show that it leads nowhere. J. S. Mill is one of many who have accepted the argument and I take his statement of it as representative. He puts to himself the question, "By what evidence do I know, or by what considerations am I led to believe, that there exist other sentient creatures; that the walking and speaking figures which I see and hear, have sensations and thoughts, or in other words, possess Minds?" His answer is the following:

I conclude that other human beings have feelings like me, because, first, they have bodies like me, which I know, in my own case, to be the antecedent condition of feelings; and because, secondly, they exhibit the acts, and other outward signs, which in my own case I know by experience to be caused by feelings. I am conscious in myself of a series of facts connected by an uniform sequence, of which the beginning is modifications of my body, the middle is feelings, the end is outward demeanor. In the case of other human beings I have the evidence of my senses for the first and last links of the series, but not for the intermediate link. I find, however, that the sequence between the first and last is as regular and constant in those other cases as it is in mine. In my own case I know that the first link produces the last through the intermediate link, and could not produce it without. Experience, therefore, obliges me to conclude that there must be an intermediate link; which must either be the same in others as in myself, or a different one: I must either believe them to be alive, or to be automatons: and by believing them to be alive, that is, by supposing the link to be of the same nature as in the case of which I have experience, and which is in all other respects similar, I bring other human beings, as phenomena, under the same generalizations which I know by experience to be the true theory of my own existence.[1]

[1] J. S. Mill, *An Examination of Sir William Hamilton's Philosophy*, 6th ed. (London: Longmans, 1889), pp. 243-44.

I shall pass by the possible objection that this would be very *weak* inductive reasoning, based as it is on the observation of a single instance. More interesting is the following point: suppose this reasoning could yield a conclusion of the sort "It is probable that that human figure (pointing at some person other than oneself) has thoughts and feelings." Then there is a question as to whether this conclusion can *mean* anything to the philosopher who draws it, because there is a question as to whether the sentence "That human figure has thoughts and feelings" can mean anything to him. Why should this be a question? Because the assumption from which Mill starts is that he has *no criterion* for determining whether another "walking and speaking figure" does or does not have thoughts and feelings. If he had a criterion he could apply it, establishing with certainty that this or that human figure does or does not have feelings (for the only plausible criterion would lie in behavior and circumstances that are open to view), and there would be no call to resort to tenuous analogical reasoning that yields at best a probability. If Mill has no criterion for the existence of feelings other than his own then in that sense he does not understand the sentence "That human figure has feelings" and therefore does not understand the sentence "It is *probable* that that human figure has feelings."

There is a familiar inclination to make the following reply: "Although I have no criterion of verification still I *understand*, for example, the sentence 'He has a pain.' For I understand the meaning of 'I have a pain,' and 'He has a pain' means that he has the *same* thing I have when I have a pain." But this is a fruitless maneuver. If I do not know how to establish that someone has a pain then I do not know how to establish that he has the *same* as I have when I have a pain.[2] You cannot improve my understanding of "He has a pain" by this recourse to the notion of "the same," unless you give me a criterion for saying that someone *has* the same as I have. If you can do this you will have no use for the argument from analogy: and if you cannot then you do not understand the supposed conclusion of that argument. A philosopher who purports to rely on the analogical argument cannot, I think, escape this dilemma.

There have been various attempts to repair the argument from analogy. Mr. Stuart Hampshire has argued[3] that its validity as a method of inference can be established in the following way: others sometimes infer that I am feeling giddy from my behavior. Now I have direct, non-inferential knowledge, says Hampshire, of my own feelings. So I can

---

[2] "It is no explanation to say: the supposition that he has a pain is simply the supposition that he has the same as I. For *that* part of the grammar is quite clear to me: that is, that one will say that the stove has the same experience as I, *if* one says: it is in pain and I am in pain" (Wittgenstein, *Philosophical Investigations* [Oxford: Blackwell, 1953], §350).

[3] "The Analogy of Feeling," *Mind*, LXI (1952), 1-12.

check inferences made about me against the facts, checking thereby the accuracy of the "methods" of inference.

> All that is required for testing the validity of any method of factual inference is that each one of us should sometimes be in a position to confront the conclusions of the doubtful method of inference with what is known by him to be true independently of the method of inference in question. Each one of us is certainly in this position in respect of our common methods of inference about the feelings of persons other than ourselves, in virtue of the fact that each one of us is constantly able to compare the results of this type of inference with what he knows to be true directly and non-inferentially; each one of us is in the position to make this testing comparison, whenever he is the designated subject of a statement about feelings and sensations. I, Hampshire, know by what sort of signs I may be misled in inferring Jones' and Smith's feelings, because I have implicitly noticed (though probably not formulated) where Jones, Smith and others generally go wrong in inferring my feelings [pp. 4-5].

Presumably I can also note when the inferences of others about my feelings do not go wrong. Having ascertained the reliability of some inference-procedures I can use them myself, in a guarded way, to draw conclusions about the feelings of others, with a modest but justified confidence in the truth of those conclusions.

My first comment is that Hampshire has apparently forgotten the purpose of the argument from analogy, which is to provide some probability that "the walking and speaking figures which I see and hear, have sensations and thoughts" (Mill). For the reasoning that he describes involves the assumption that other human figures *do* have thoughts and sensations: for they are assumed to *make inferences* about me from *observations* of my behavior. But the philosophical problem of the existence of other minds *is* the problem of whether human figures other than oneself do, among other things, make observations, inferences, and assertions. Hampshire's supposed defense of the argument from analogy is an *ignoratio elenchi*.

If we struck from the reasoning described by Hampshire all assumption of thoughts and sensations in others we should be left with something roughly like this: "When my behavior is such-and-such there come from nearby human figures the sounds 'He feels giddy.' And generally I do feel giddy at the time. Therefore when another human figure exhibits the same behavior and I say 'He feels giddy,' it is probable that he does feel giddy." But the reference here to the sentence-like sounds coming from other human bodies is irrelevant, since I must not assume that those sounds express inferences. Thus the reasoning becomes simply the classical argument from analogy: "When my behavior is such-and-such I feel giddy; so probably when another human figure behaves the same way he feels the same way." This argument, again, is caught in the dilemma about the criterion of the *same*.

The version of analogical reasoning offered by Professor H. H. Price[4] is more interesting. He suggests that "one's evidence for the existence of other minds is derived primarily from the understanding of language" (p. 429). His idea is that if another body gives forth noises one understands, like "There's the bus," and if these noises give one new information, this "provides some evidence that the foreign body which uttered the noises is animated by a mind like one's own. . . . Suppose I am often in its neighborhood, and it repeatedly produces utterances which I can understand, and which I then proceed to verify for myself. And suppose that this happens in many different kinds of situation. I think that my evidence for believing that this body is animated by a mind like my own would then become very strong" (p. 430). The body from which these informative sounds proceed need not be a human body. "If the rustling of the leaves of an oak formed intelligible words conveying new information to me, and if gorse bushes made intelligible gestures, I should have evidence that the oak or the gorse bush was animated by an intelligence like my own" (p. 436). Even if the intelligible and informative sounds did not proceed from a body they would provide evidence for the existence of a (disembodied) mind (p. 435).

Although differing sharply from the classical analogical argument, the reasoning presented by Price is still analogical in form: I know by introspection that when certain combinations of sounds come from me they are "symbols in acts of spontaneous thinking"; therefore similar combinations of sounds, not produced by me, "probably function as instruments to an act of spontaneous thinking, which in this case is not my own" (p. 446). Price says that the reasoning also provides an *explanation* of the otherwise mysterious occurrence of sounds which I understand but did not produce. He anticipates the objection that the hypothesis is nonsensical because unverifiable. "The hypothesis is a perfectly conceivable one," he says, "in the sense that I know very well what the world would have to be like if the hypothesis were true— what sorts of entities there must be in it, and what sorts of events must occur in them. I know from introspection what acts of thinking and perceiving are, and I know what it is for such acts to be combined into the unity of a single mind . . ." (pp. 446-47).

I wish to argue against Price that no amount of intelligible sounds coming from an oak tree or a kitchen table could create any probability that it has sensations and thoughts. The question to be asked is: What would show that a tree or table *understands* the sounds that come from it? We can imagine that useful warnings, true descriptions and predictions, even "replies" to questions, should emanate from a tree, so that it came to be of enormous value to its owner. How should we establish

[4] "Our Evidence for the Existence of Other Minds," *Philosophy*, XIII (1938), 425-56.

that it understood those sentences? Should we "question" it? Suppose that the tree "said" that there was a vixen in the neighborhood, and we "asked" it "What is a vixen?" and it "replied," "A vixen is a female fox." It might go on to do as well for "female" and "fox." This performance might incline us to say that the tree understood the words, in contrast to the possible case in which it answered "I don't know" or did not answer at all. But would it show that the tree understood the words in the same sense that a person could understand them? With a person such a performance would create a presumption that he could make correct *applications* of the word in question: but not so with a tree. To see this point think of the normal teaching of words (e.g., "spoon," "dog," "red") to a child and how one decides whether he understands them. At a primitive stage of teaching one does not require or expect definitions, but rather that the child should *pick out* reds from blues, dogs from cats, spoons from forks. This involves his looking, pointing, reaching for and going to the right things and not the wrong ones. That a child says "red" when a red thing and "blue" when a blue thing is put before him, is indicative of a mastery of those words *only* in conjunction with the other activities of looking, pointing, trying to get, fetching and carrying. Try to suppose that he says the right words but looks at and reaches for the wrong things. Should we be tempted to say that he has mastered the use of those words? No, indeed. The disparity between words and behavior would make us say that he does not understand the words. In the case of a tree there could be no disparity between its words and its "behavior" because it is logically incapable of behavior of the relevant kind.

Since it has nothing like the human face and body it makes no sense to say of a tree, or an electronic computer, that it is looking or pointing at or fetching something. (Of course one can always *invent* a sense for these expressions.) Therefore it would make no sense to say that it did or did not understand the above words. Trees and computers cannot either pass or fail the tests that a child is put through. They cannot even take them. That an object was a source of intelligible sounds or other signs (no matter how sequential) would not be enough by itself to establish that it had thoughts or sensations. How informative sentences and valuable predictions could emanate from a gorse bush might be a grave scientific problem, but the explanation could never be that the gorse bush has a mind. Better no explanation than nonsense!

It might be thought that the above difficulty holds only for words whose meaning has a "perceptual content" and that if we imagined, for example, that our gorse bush produced nothing but pure mathematical propositions we should be justified in attributing thought to it, although not sensation. But suppose there was a remarkable "calculating boy" who could give right answers to arithmetical problems but could not apply numerals to reality in empirical propositions, i.e., he could not *count* any objects. I believe that everyone would be reluctant to say that he *understood* the mathematical signs and truths that he produced. If he could count in the normal way there would not be this reluctance. And "counting in the normal way" involves looking, pointing, reaching, fetching, and so on. That is, it requires the human face and body, and human behavior—or something similar. Things which do not have the human form, or anything like it, not merely do not but *cannot* satisfy the criteria for thinking. I am trying to bring out part of what Wittgenstein meant when he said, "We only say of a human being and what is like one that it thinks" (*Investigations*, §360), and "The human body is the best picture of the human soul" (*ibid.*, p. 178).

I have not yet gone into the most fundamental error of the argument from analogy. It is present whether the argument is the classical one (the analogy between my body and other bodies) or Price's version (the analogy between my language and the noises and signs produced by other things). It is the mistaken assumption that *one learns from one's own case* what thinking, feeling, sensation are. Price gives expression to this assumption when he says: "I know from introspection what acts of thinking and perceiving are . . ." (*op. cit.*, p. 447). It is the most natural assumption for a philosopher to make and indeed seems at first to be the only possibility. Yet Wittgenstein has made us see that it leads first to solipsism and then to nonsense. I shall try to state as briefly as possible how it produces those results.

A philosopher who believes that one must learn what thinking, fear, or pain is "from one's own case," does not believe that the thing to be observed is one's behavior, but rather something "inward." He considers behavior to be related to the inward states and occurrences merely as an accompaniment or possibly an effect. He cannot regard behavior as a *criterion* of psychological phenomena: for if he did he would have no use for the analogical argument (as was said before) and also the priority given to "one's own case" would be pointless. He believes that he notes something in himself that he calls "thinking" or "fear" or "pain," and then he tries to infer the presence of the *same* in others. He should then deal with the question of what his criterion of the *same* in others is. This he cannot do because it is of the essence of his viewpoint to reject circumstances and behavior as a criterion of mental phenomena in others. And what else could serve as a criterion? He ought, therefore, to draw the conclusion that the notion of thinking, fear, or pain in others is in an important sense meaningless. He has no idea of what would count for or against it.[5] "That there should be thinking or pain other than my own is unintelligible," he ought to hold. This would be a rigorous solipsism, and a correct outcome of the assumption that one

---

[5] One reason why philosophers have not commonly drawn this conclusion may be, as Wittgenstein acutely suggests, that they assume that they have "an infallible paradigm of identity in the identity of a thing with itself" (*Investigations*, §215).

can know only from one's own case what the mental phenomena are. An equivalent way of putting it would be: "When I say 'I am in pain,' by 'pain' I mean a certain inward state. When I say 'He is in pain,' by 'pain' I mean *behavior*. I cannot attribute pain to others *in the same sense* that I attribute it to myself."

Some philosophers before Wittgenstein may have seen the solipsistic result of starting from "one's own case." But I believe he is the first to have shown how that starting point destroys itself. This may be presented as follows: one supposes that one inwardly picks out something as thinking or pain and thereafter identifies it whenever it presents itself in the soul. But the question to be pressed is, Does one make *correct* identifications? The proponent of these "private" identifications has nothing to say here. He feels sure that he identifies correctly the occurrences in his soul; but feeling sure is no guarantee of being right. Indeed he has no idea of what being *right* could mean. He does not know how to distinguish between actually making correct identifications and being under the impression that he does. (See *Investigations*, §§258-59.) Suppose that he identified the emotion of anxiety as the sensation of pain? Neither he nor anyone else could know about this "mistake." Perhaps he makes a mistake *every* time! Perhaps all of us do! We ought to see now that we are talking nonsense. We do not know what a *mistake* would be. We have no standard, no examples, no customary practice, with which to compare our inner recognitions. The inward identification cannot hit the bull's-eye, or miss it either, because there is no bull's-eye. When we see that the ideas of correct and incorrect have no application to the supposed inner identification, the latter notion loses its appearance of sense. Its collapse brings down both solipsism and the argument from analogy.

II

This destruction of the argument from analogy also destroys the *problem* for which it was supposed to provide a solution. A philosopher feels himself in a difficulty about other minds because he assumes that first of all he is acquainted with mental phenomena "from his own case." What troubles him is how to make the transition from his own case to the case of others. When his thinking is freed of the illusion of the priority of his own case, then he is able to look at the familiar facts and to acknowledge that the circumstances, behavior, and utterances of others actually are his *criteria* (not merely his evidence) for the existence of their mental states. Previously this had seemed impossible.

But now he is in danger of flying to the opposite extreme of behaviorism, which errs by believing that through observation of one's own circumstances, behavior, and utterances one can find out that one is thinking or angry. The philosophy of "from one's own case" and behaviorism, though in a sense opposites, make the common assumption that the first-person, present-tense psychological statements are verified by self-observation. According to the "one's own case" philosophy the self-observation cannot be checked by others; according to behaviorism the self-observation would be by means of outward criteria that are available to all. The first position becomes unintelligible; the second is false for at least many kinds of psychological statements. We are forced to conclude that the first-person psychological statements are not (or hardly ever) verified by self-observation. It follows that they have no verification at all; for if they had a verification it would have to be by self-observation.

But if sentences like "My head aches" or "I wonder where she is" do not express observations then what do they do? What is the relation between my declaration that my head aches and the fact that my head aches, if the former is not the report of an observation? The perplexity about the existence of *other* minds has, as the result of criticism, turned into a perplexity about the meaning of one's own psychological sentences about oneself. At our starting point it was the sentence "*His* head aches" that posed a problem; but now it is the sentence "*My* head aches" that puzzles us.

One way in which this problem can be put is by the question, "How does *one know when to say* the words 'My head aches'?" The inclination to ask this question can be made acute by imagining a fantastic but not impossible case of a person who has survived to adult years without ever experiencing pain. He is given various sorts of injections to correct this condition, and on receiving one of these one day, he jumps and exclaims, "Now I feel pain!" One wants to ask, "How did he *recognize* the new sensation as a pain?"

Let us note that if the man gives an answer (e.g., "I knew it must be pain because of the way I jumped") then he proves by that very fact that he has not mastered the correct use of the words "I feel pain." They cannot be used to state a *conclusion*. In telling us *how* he did it he will convict himself of a misuse. Therefore the question "How did he recognize his sensation?" requests the impossible. The inclination to ask it is evidence of our inability to grasp the fact that the use of this psychological sentence has nothing to do with recognizing or identifying or observing a state of oneself.

The fact that this imagined case produces an especially strong temptation to ask the "How?" question shows that we have the idea that it must be more difficult to give the right name of one's sensation *the first time*. The implication would be that it is not so difficult *after* the first time. Why should this be? Are we thinking that then the man would have a paradigm of pain with which he could compare his sensations and so be in a position to know right off whether a certain sensation was or was not a pain? But the paradigm would be either something "outer" (behavior) or something "inner" (perhaps a memory impression of the sensation). If the former then he is misusing the first-person sentence. If the latter then the question of whether he compared *correctly* the present sensation with the inner paradigm of pain would be without sense. Thus the idea that the use of the first-person sentences can be governed by paradigms must be abandoned. It is another form of our insistent misconception of the first-person sentence as resting somehow on the identification of a psychological state.

These absurdities prove that we must conceive of the first-person psychological sentences in some entirely different light. Wittgenstein presents us with the suggestion (to which philosophers have not been sufficiently attentive) that the first-person sentences are to be thought of as similar to the natural nonverbal, behavioral expressions of psychological states. "My leg hurts," for example, is to be assimilated to crying, limping, holding one's leg. This is a bewildering comparison and one's first thought is that two sorts of things could not be more unlike. By saying the sentence one can make a *statement;* it has a *contradictory;* it is *true* or *false;* in saying it one *lies* or *tells the truth;* and so on. None of these things, exactly, can be said of crying, limping, holding one's leg. So how can there be any resemblance? But Wittgenstein knew this when he deliberately likened such a sentence to "the primitive, the natural, expressions" of pain, and said that it is "new pain-behavior" (*ibid.,* §244). Although my limits prevent my attempting it here, I think this analogy ought to be explored. For it has at least two important merits: first, it breaks the hold on us of the question "How does one *know when to say* 'My leg hurts'?" for in the light of the analogy this will be as nonsensical as the question "How does one know when to cry, limp, or hold one's leg?"; second, it explains how the utterance of a first-person psychological sentence by another person can have *importance* for us, although not as an identification—for in the light of the analogy it will have the same importance as the natural behavior which serves as our preverbal criterion of the psychological states of others.

X ❧ Sensations and Brain Processes

J. J. C. Smart

This paper[1] takes its departure from arguments to be found in U. T. Place's "Is Consciousness a Brain Process?"[2] I have had the benefit of discussing Place's thesis in a good many universities in the United States and Australia, and I hope that the present paper answers objections to his thesis which Place has not considered and that it presents his thesis in a more nearly unobjectionable form. This paper is meant also to supplement the paper "The 'Mental' and the 'Physical,'" by H. Feigl,[3] which in part argues for a similar thesis to Place's.

Suppose that I report that I have at this moment a roundish, blurry-edged after-image which is yellowish towards its edge and is orange towards its center. What is it that I am reporting? One answer to this question might be that I am not reporting anything, that when I say that it looks to me as though there is a roundish yellowy-orange patch of light on the wall I am expressing some sort of *temptation,* the temptation to say that there *is* a roundish yellowy-orange patch on the wall (though I may know that there is not such a patch on the wall). This is perhaps Wittgenstein's view in the *Philosophical Investigations* (see §§ 367, 370). Similarly, when I "report" a pain, I am not really reporting anything (or, if you like, I am reporting in a queer sense of "reporting"), but am doing a sophisticated sort of wince. (See § 244: "The verbal expression of pain replaces crying and does not describe it." Nor does it describe anything else?)[4] I prefer most of the time

---

[1] This is a very slightly revised version of a paper which was first published in the *Philosophical Review*, LXVIII (1959), 141-56. Since that date there have been criticisms of my paper by J. T. Stevenson, *Philosophical Review*, LXIX (1960), 505-10, to which I have replied in *Philosophical Review*, LXX (1961), 406-7, and by G. Pitcher and by W. D. Joske, *Australasian Journal of Philosophy*, XXXVIII (1960), 150-60, to which I have replied in the same volume of that journal, pp. 252-54.

[2] *British Journal of Psychology*, XLVII (1956), 44-50; reprinted in this volume, pp. 101-09 above. (Page references are to the reprint in this volume.)

[3] *Minnesota Studies in the Philosophy of Science*, Vol. II (Minneapolis: University of Minnesota Press, 1958), pp. 370-497.

[4] Some philosophers of my acquaintance, who have the advantage over me in having known Wittgenstein, would say that this interpretation of him is too behavioristic. However, it seems to me a very natural interpretation of his printed words, and whether or not it is Wittgenstein's real view it is certainly an interesting and important one. I wish to consider it here as a possible rival both to the "brain-process" thesis and to straight-out old-fashioned dualism.

to discuss an after-image rather than a pain, because the word "pain" brings in something which is irrelevant to my purpose: the notion of "distress." I think that "he is in pain" entails "he is in distress," that is, that he is in a certain agitation-condition.[5] Similarly, to say "I am in pain" may be to do more than "replace pain behavior": it may be partly to report something, though this something is quite nonmysterious, being an agitation-condition, and so susceptible of behavioristic analysis. The suggestion I wish if possible to avoid is a different one, namely that "I am in pain" is a genuine report, and that what it reports is an irreducibly psychical something. And similarly the suggestion I wish to resist is also that to say "I have a yellowish-orange after-image" is to report something irreducibly psychical.

Why do I wish to resist this suggestion? Mainly because of Occam's razor. It seems to me that science is increasingly giving us a viewpoint whereby organisms are able to be seen as physicochemical mechanisms:[6] it seems that even the behavior of man himself will one day be explicable in mechanistic terms. There does seem to be, so far as science is concerned, nothing in the world but increasingly complex arrangements of physical constituents. All except for one place: in consciousness. That is, for a full description of what is going on in a man you would have to mention not only the physical processes in his tissues, glands, nervous system, and so forth, but also his states of consciousness: his visual, auditory, and tactual sensations, his aches and pains. That these should be *correlated* with brain processes does not help, for to say that they are *correlated* is to say that they are something "over and above." You cannot correlate something with itself. You correlate footprints with burglars, but not Bill Sikes the burglar with Bill Sikes the burglar. So sensations, states of consciousness, do seem to be the one sort of thing left outside the physicalist picture, and for various reasons I just cannot believe that this can be so. That everything should be explicable in terms of physics (together of course with descriptions of the ways in which the parts are put together—roughly, biology is to physics as radio-engineering is to electromagnetism) except the occurrence of sensations seems to me to be frankly unbelievable. Such sensations would be "nomological danglers," to use Feigl's expression.[7] It is not often realized how odd would be the laws whereby these nomological danglers would dangle. It is sometimes asked, "Why can't there be psychophysical laws which are of a novel sort, just as the laws of electricity and mag-

---

[5] See Ryle, *The Concept of Mind* (London: Hutchinson's University Library, 1949), p. 93.

[6] On this point see Paul Oppenheim and Hilary Putnam, "Unity of Science as a Working Hypothesis," in *Minnesota Studies in the Philosophy of Science*, Vol. II (Minneapolis: University of Minnesota Press, 1958), pp. 3-36.

[7] Feigl, *op. cit.*, p. 428. Feigl uses the expression "nomological danglers" for the laws whereby the entities dangle: I have used the expression to refer to the dangling entities themselves.

netism were novelties from the standpoint of Newtonian mechanics?" Certainly we are pretty sure in the future to come across new ultimate laws of a novel type, but I expect them to relate simple constituents: for example, whatever ultimate particles are then in vogue. I cannot believe that ultimate laws of nature could relate simple constituents to configurations consisting of perhaps billions of neurons (and goodness knows how many billion billions of ultimate particles) all put together for all the world as though their main purpose in life was to be a negative feedback mechanism of a complicated sort. Such ultimate laws would be like nothing so far known in science. They have a queer "smell" to them. I am just unable to believe in the nomological danglers themselves, or in the laws whereby they would dangle. If any philosophical arguments seemed to compel us to believe in such things, I would suspect a catch in the argument. In any case it is the object of this paper to show that there are no philosophical arguments which compel us to be dualists.

The above is largely a confession of faith, but it explains why I find Wittgenstein's position (as I construe it) so congenial. For on this view there are, in a sense, no sensations. A man is a vast arrangement of physical particles, but there are not, over and above this, sensations or states of consciousness. There are just behavioral facts about this vast mechanism, such as that it expresses a temptation (behavior disposition) to say "there is a yellowish-red patch on the wall" or that it goes through a sophisticated sort of wince, that is, says "I am in pain." Admittedly Wittgenstein says that though the sensation "is not a something," it is nevertheless "not a nothing either" (§ 304), but this need only mean that the word "ache" has a use. An ache is a thing, but only in the innocuous sense in which the plain man, in the first paragraph of Frege's *Foundations of Arithmetic,* answers the question "What is the number one?" by "a thing." It should be noted that when I assert that to say "I have a yellowish-orange after-image" is to express a temptation to assert the physical-object statement "There is a yellowish-orange patch on the wall," I mean that saying "I have a yellowish-orange after-image" is (partly) the exercise of the disposition[8] which is the temptation. It is not to *report* that I have the temptation, any more than is "I love you" normally a report that I love someone. Saying "I love you" is just part of the behavior which is the exercise of the disposition of loving someone.

Though for the reasons given above, I am very receptive to the above "expressive" account of sensation statements, I do not feel that it will

[8] Wittgenstein did not like the word "disposition." I am using it to put in a nutshell (and perhaps inaccurately) the view which I am attributing to Wittgenstein. I should like to repeat that I do not wish to claim that my interpretation of Wittgenstein is correct. Some of those who knew him do not interpret him in this way. It is merely a view which I find myself extracting from his printed words and which I think is important and worth discussing for its own sake.

quite do the trick. Maybe this is because I have not thought it out sufficiently, but it does seem to me as though, when a person says "I have
an after-image," he *is* making a genuine report, and that when he says
"I have a pain," he *is* doing more than "replace pain-behavior," and
that "this more" is not just to say that he is in distress. I am not so sure,
however, that to admit this is to admit that there are nonphysical correlates of brain processes. Why should not sensations just be brain processes of a certain sort? There are, of course, well-known (as well as
lesser-known) philosophical objections to the view that reports of sensations are reports of brain-processes, but I shall try to argue that these
arguments are by no means as cogent as is commonly thought to be
the case.

Let me first try to state more accurately the thesis that sensations are
brain-processes. It is not the thesis that, for example, "after-image" or
"ache" means the same as "brain process of sort X" (where "X" is replaced by a description of a certain sort of brain process). It is that, in
so far as "after-image" or "ache" is a report of a process, it is a report
of a process that *happens to be* a brain process. It follows that the thesis
does not claim that sensation statements can be *translated* into statements about brain processes.[9] Nor does it claim that the logic of a sensation statement is the same as that of a brain-process statement. All it
claims is that in so far as a sensation statement is a report of something,
that something is in fact a brain process. Sensations are nothing over
and above brain processes. Nations are nothing "over and above" citizens, but this does not prevent the logic of nation statements being very
different from the logic of citizen statements, nor does it insure the
translatability of nation statements into citizen statements. (I do not,
however, wish to assert that the relation of sensation statements to
brain-process statements is very like that of nation statements to citizen
statements. Nations do not just *happen to be* nothing over and above
citizens, for example. I bring in the "nations" example merely to make
a negative point: that the fact that the logic of A-statements is different
from that of B-statements does not insure that A's are anything over and
above B's.)

Remarks on Identity

When I say that a sensation is a brain process or that lightning is an
electric discharge, I am using "is" in the sense of strict identity. (Just
as in the—in this case necessary—proposition "7 is identical with the
smallest prime number greater than 5.") When I say that a sensation is
a brain process or that lightning is an electric discharge I do not mean
just that the sensation is somehow spatially or temporally continuous
with the brain process or that the lightning is just spatially or tempo-

---

* See Place, *op. cit.*, p. 102. and Feigl, *op. cit.*, p. 390, near top.

rally continuous with the discharge. When on the other hand I say that the successful general is the same person as the small boy who stole the apples I mean only that the successful general I see before me is a time slice[10] of the same four-dimensional object of which the small boy stealing apples is an earlier time slice. However, the four-dimensional object which has the general-I-see-before-me for its late time slice is identical in the strict sense with the four-dimensional object which has the small-boy-stealing-apples for an early time slice. I distinguish these two senses of "is identical with" because I wish to make it clear that the brain-process doctrine asserts identity in the *strict* sense.

I shall now discuss various possible objections to the view that the processes reported in sensation statements are in fact processes in the brain. Most of us have met some of these objections in our first year as philosophy students. All the more reason to take a good look at them. Others of the objections will be more recondite and subtle.

Objection 1. Any illiterate peasant can talk perfectly well about his after-images, or how things look or feel to him, or about his aches and pains, and yet he may know nothing whatever about neurophysiology. A man may, like Aristotle, believe that the brain is an organ for cooling the body without any impairment of his ability to make true statements about his sensations. Hence the things we are talking about when we describe our sensations cannot be processes in the brain.

Reply. You might as well say that a nation of slugabeds, who never saw the Morning Star or knew of its existence, or who had never thought of the expression "the Morning Star," but who used the expression "the Evening Star" perfectly well, could not use this expression to refer to the same entity as we refer to (and describe as) "the Morning Star." [11]

You may object that the Morning Star is in a sense not the very same thing as the Evening Star, but only something spatiotemporally continuous with it. That is, you may say that the Morning Star is not the Evening Star in the strict sense of "identity" that I distinguished earlier.

There is, however, a more plausible example. Consider lightning.[12] Modern physical science tells us that lightning is a certain kind of electrical discharge due to ionization of clouds of water vapor in the atmosphere. This, it is now believed, is what the true nature of lightning is. Note that there are not two things: a flash of lightning and an elec-

---

[10] See J. H. Woodger, *Theory Construction*, International Encyclopedia of Unified Science, II, No. 5 (Chicago: University of Chicago Press, 1939), 38. I here permit myself to speak loosely. For warnings against possible ways of going wrong with this sort of talk, see my note "Spatialising Time," *Mind*, LXIV (1955), 239-41.

[11] Cf. Feigl, *op. cit.*, p. 439.

[12] See Place, *op. cit.*, p. 106; also Feigl, *op. cit.*, p. 438.

trical discharge. There is one thing, a flash of lightning, which is described scientifically as an electrical discharge to the earth from a cloud of ionized water molecules. The case is not at all like that of explaining a footprint by reference to a burglar. We say that what lightning really is, what its true nature as revealed by science is, is an electrical discharge. (It is not the true nature of a footprint to be a burglar.)

To forestall irrelevant objections, I should like to make it clear that by "lightning" I mean the publicly observable physical object, lightning, not a visual sense-datum of lightning. I say that the publicly observable physical object lightning is in fact the electrical discharge, not just a correlate of it. The sense-datum, or rather the having of the sense-datum, the "look" of lightning, may well in my view be a correlate of the electrical discharge. For in my view it is a brain state *caused* by the lightning. But we should no more confuse sensations of lightning with lightning than we confuse sensations of a table with the table.

In short, the reply to Objection 1 is that there can be contingent statements of the form "A is identical with B," and a person may well know that something is an A without knowing that it is a B. An illiterate peasant might well be able to talk about his sensations without knowing about his brain processes, just as he can talk about lightning though he knows nothing of electricity.

Objection 2. It is only a contingent fact (if it is a fact) that when we have a certain kind of sensation there is a certain kind of process in our brain. Indeed it is possible, though perhaps in the highest degree unlikely, that our present physiological theories will be as out of date as the ancient theory connecting mental processes with goings on in the heart. It follows that when we report a sensation we are not reporting a brain-process.

Reply. The objection certainly proves that when we say "I have an after-image" we cannot *mean* something of the form "I have such and such a brain-process." But this does not show that what we report (having an after-image) is not *in fact* a brain process. "I see lightning" does not *mean* "I see an electrical discharge." Indeed, it is logically possible (though highly unlikely) that the electrical discharge account of lightning might one day be given up. Again, "I see the Evening Star" does not *mean* the same as "I see the Morning Star," and yet "The Evening Star and the Morning Star are one and the same thing" is a contingent proposition. Possibly Objection 2 derives some of its apparent strength from a "Fido"– Fido theory of meaning. If the meaning of an expression were what the expression named, then of course it *would* follow from the fact that "sensation" and "brain-process" have different meanings that they cannot name one and the same thing.

Objection 3.[13] Even if Objections 1 and 2 do not prove that sensations are something over and above brain-processes, they do prove that the qualities of sensations are something over and above the qualities of brain-processes. That is, it may be possible to get out of asserting the existence of irreducibly psychic processes, but not out of asserting the existence of irreducibly psychic *properties.* For suppose we identify the Morning Star with the Evening Star. Then there must be some properties which logically imply that of being the Morning Star, and quite distinct properties which entail that of being the Evening Star. Again, there must be some properties (for example, that of being a yellow flash) which are logically distinct from those in the physicalist story.

Indeed, it might be thought that the objection succeeds at one jump. For consider the property of "being a yellow flash." It might seem that this property lies inevitably outside the physicalist framework within which I am trying to work (either by "yellow" being an objective emergent property of physical objects, or else by being a power to produce yellow sense-data, where "yellow," in this second instantiation of the word, refers to a purely phenomenal or introspectible quality). I must therefore digress for a moment and indicate how I deal with secondary qualities. I shall concentrate on color.

First of all, let me introduce the concept of a normal percipient. One person is more a normal percipient than another if he can make color discriminations that the other cannot. For example, if A can pick a lettuce leaf out of a heap of cabbage leaves, whereas B cannot though he can pick a lettuce leaf out of a heap of beetroot leaves, then A is more normal than B. (I am assuming that A and B are not given time to distinguish the leaves by their slight difference in shape, and so forth.) From the concept of "more normal than" it is easy to see how we can introduce the concept of "normal." Of course, Eskimos may make the finest discriminations at the blue end of the spectrum, Hottentots at the red end. In this case the concept of a normal percipient is a slightly idealized one, rather like that of "the mean sun" in astronomical chronology. There is no need to go into such subtleties now. I say that "This is red" means something roughly like "A normal percipient would not easily pick this out of a clump of geranium petals though he would pick it out of a clump of lettuce leaves." Of course it does not exactly mean this: a person might know the meaning of "red" without knowing anything about geraniums, or even about normal percipients. But the point is that a person can be *trained* to say "This is red" of objects which would not easily be picked out of geranium petals by a normal percipient, and so on. (Note that even a color-blind person can reasonably assert that something is red, though of course he needs to use another

[13] I think this objection was first put to me by Professor Max Black. I think it is the most subtle of any of those I have considered, and the one which I am least confident of having satisfactorily met.

human being, not just himself, as his "color meter.") This account of secondary qualities explains their unimportance in physics. For obviously the discriminations and lack of discriminations made by a very complex neurophysiological mechanism are hardly likely to correspond to simple and nonarbitrary distinctions in nature.

I therefore elucidate colors as powers, in Locke's sense, to evoke certain sorts of discriminatory responses in human beings. They are also, of course, powers to cause sensations in human beings (an account still nearer Locke's). But these sensations, I am arguing, are identifiable with brain processes.

Now how do I get over the objection that a sensation can be identified with a brain process only if it has some phenomenal property, not possessed by brain processes, whereby one-half of the identification may be, so to speak, pinned down?

Reply. My suggestion is as follows. When a person says, "I see a yellowish-orange after-image," he is saying something like this: "*There is something going on which is like what is going on when* I have my eyes open, am awake, and there is an orange illuminated in good light in front of me, that is, when I really see an orange." (And there is no reason why a person should not say the same thing when he is having a veridical sense-datum, so long as we construe "like" in the last sentence in such a sense that something can be like itself.) Notice that the italicized words, namely "there is something going on which is like what is going on when," are all quasilogical or topic-neutral words. This explains why the ancient Greek peasant's reports about his sensations can be neutral between dualistic metaphysics or my materialistic metaphysics. It explains how sensations can be brain-processes and yet how a man who reports them need know nothing about brain-processes. For he reports them only very abstractly as "something going on which is like what is going on when. . . ." Similarly, a person may say "someone is in the room," thus reporting truly that the doctor is in the room, even though he has never heard of doctors. (There are not two people in the room: "someone" *and* the doctor.) This account of sensation statements also explains the singular elusiveness of "raw feels"—why no one seems to be able to pin any properties on them.[14] Raw feels, in my view, are colorless for the very same reason that *something* is colorless. This does not mean that sensations do not have plenty of properties, for if they are brain-processes they certainly have lots of neurological properties. It only means that in speaking of them as being like or unlike one another we need not know or mention these properties.

This, then, is how I would reply to Objection 3. The strength of my

---

[14] See B. A. Farrell, "Experience," *Mind*, LIX (1950), 170-98; reprinted in this volume, pp. 23-48 above; see especially p. 27 (of this volume).

reply depends on the possibility of our being able to report that one thing is like another without being able to state the respect in which it is like. I do not see why this should not be so. If we think cybernetically about the nervous system we can envisage it as able to respond to certain likenesses of its internal processes without being able to do more. It would be easier to build a machine which would tell us, say on a punched tape, whether or not two objects were similar, than it would be to build a machine which would report wherein the similarities consisted.

Objection 4. The after-image is not in physical space. The brain-process is. So the after-image is not a brain-process.

Reply. This is an *ignoratio elenchi*. I am not arguing that the after-image is a brain-process, but that the experience of having an after-image is a brain-process. It is the *experience* which is reported in the introspective report. Similarly, if it is objected that the after-image is yellowy-orange, my reply is that it is the experience of seeing yellowy-orange that is being described, and this experience is not a yellowy-orange something. So to say that a brain-process cannot be yellowy-orange is not to say that a brain-process cannot in fact be the experience of having a yellowy-orange after-image. There is, in a sense, no such thing as an after-image or a sense-datum, though there is such a thing as the experience of having an image, and this experience is described indirectly in material object language, not in phenomenal language, for there is no such thing.[15] We describe the experience by saying, in effect, that it is like the experience we have when, for example, we really see a yellowy-orange patch on the wall. Trees and wallpaper can be green, but not the experience of seeing or imagining a tree or wallpaper. (Or if they are described as green or yellow this can only be in a derived sense.)

Objection 5. It would make sense to say of a molecular movement in the brain that it is swift or slow, straight or circular, but it makes no sense to say this of the experience of seeing something yellow.

Reply. So far we have not given sense to talk of experiences as swift or slow, straight or circular. But I am not claiming that "experience" and "brain-process" mean the same or even that they have the same

[15] Dr. J. R. Smythies claims that a sense-datum language could be taught independently of the material object language ("A Note on the Fallacy of the 'Phenomenological Fallacy,'" *British Journal of Psychology*, XLVIII [1957], 141-44). I am not so sure of this: there must be some public criteria for a person having got a rule wrong before we can teach him the rule. I suppose someone might *accidentally* learn color words by Dr. Smythies' procedure. I am not, of course, denying that we can learn a sense-datum language in the sense that we can learn to report our experience. Nor would Place deny it.

logic. "Somebody" and "the doctor" do not have the same logic, but this does not lead us to suppose that talking about somebody telephoning is talking about someone over and above, say, the doctor. The ordinary man when he reports an experience is reporting that something is going on, but he leaves it open as to what sort of thing is going on, whether in a material solid medium or perhaps in some sort of gaseous medium, or even perhaps in some sort of nonspatial medium (if this makes sense). All that I am saying is that "experience" and "brain-process" may in fact refer to the same thing, and if so we may easily adopt a convention (which is not a change in our present rules for the use of experience words but an addition to them) whereby it would make sense to talk of an experience in terms appropriate to physical processes.

Objection 6. Sensations are private, brain processes are *public.* If I sincerely say, "I see a yellowish-orange after-image," and I am not making a verbal mistake, then I cannot be wrong. But I can be wrong about a brain-process. The scientist looking into my brain might be having an illusion. Moreover, it makes sense to say that two or more people are observing the same brain-process but not that two or more people are reporting the same inner experience.

Reply. This shows that the language of introspective reports has a different logic from the language of material processes. It is obvious that until the brain-process theory is much improved and widely accepted there will be no *criteria* for saying "Smith has an experience of such-and-such a sort" *except* Smith's introspective reports. So we have adopted a rule of language that (normally) what Smith says goes.

Objection 7. I can imagine myself turned to stone and yet having images, aches, pains, and so on.

Reply. I can imagine that the electrical theory of lightning is false, that lightning is some sort of purely optical phenomenon. I can imagine that lightning is not an electrical discharge. I can imagine that the Evening Star is not the Morning Star. But it is. All the objection shows is that "experience" and "brain-process" do not have the same meaning. It does not show that an experience is not in fact a brain process.

This objection is perhaps much the same as one which can be summed up by the slogan: "What can be composed of nothing cannot be composed of anything." [16] The argument goes as follows: on the brain-process thesis the identity between the brain-process and the experience is a contingent one. So it is logically possible that there should be no brain-process, and no process of any other sort either (no heart process,

---

[16] I owe this objection to Dr. C. B. Martin. I gather that he no longer wishes to maintain this objection, at any rate in its present form.

no kidney process, no liver process). There would be the experience but no "corresponding" physiological process with which we might be able to identify it empirically.

I suspect that the objector is thinking of the experience as a ghostly entity. So it is composed of something, not of nothing, after all. On his view it is composed of ghost stuff, and on mine it is composed of brain stuff. Perhaps the counter-reply will be[17] that the experience is simple and uncompounded, and so it is not composed of anything after all. This seems to be a quibble, for, if it were taken seriously, the remark "What can be composed of nothing cannot be composed of anything" could be recast as an a priori argument against Democritus and atomism and for Descartes and infinite divisibility. And it seems odd that a question of this sort could be settled a priori. We must therefore construe the word "composed" in a very weak sense, which would allow us to say that even an indivisible atom is composed of something (namely, itself). The dualist cannot really say that an experience can be composed of nothing. For he holds that experiences are something over and above material processes, that is, that they are a sort of ghost stuff. (Or perhaps ripples in an underlying ghost stuff.) I say that the dualist's hypothesis is a perfectly intelligible one. But I say that experiences are not to be identified with ghost stuff but with brain stuff. This is another hypothesis, and in my view a very plausible one. The present argument cannot knock it down a priori.

Objection 8. The "beetle in the box" objection (see Wittgenstein, *Philosophical Investigations*, § 293). How could descriptions of experiences, if these are genuine reports, get a foothold in language? For any rule of language must have public criteria for its correct application.

Reply. The change from describing how things are to describing how we feel is just a change from uninhibitedly saying "this is so" to saying "this looks so." That is, when the naïve person might be tempted to say, "There is a patch of light on the wall which moves whenever I move my eyes" or "A pin is being stuck into me," we have learned how to resist this temptation and say "It *looks as though* there is a patch of light on the wallpaper" or "It *feels as though* someone were sticking a pin into me." The introspective account tells us about the individual's state of consciousness in the same way as does "I see a patch of light" or "I feel a pin being stuck into me": it differs from the corresponding perception statement in so far as it withdraws any claim about what is actually going on in the external world. From the point of view of the psychologist, the change from talking about the environment to talking about one's perceptual sensations is simply a matter of disinhibiting

---

[17] Martin did not make this reply, but one of his students did.

certain reactions. These are reactions which one normally suppresses because one has learned that in the prevailing circumstances they are unlikely to provide a good indication of the state of the environment.[18] To say that something looks green to me is simply to say that my experience is like the experience I get when I see something that really is green. In my reply to Objection 3, I pointed out the extreme openness or generality of statements which report experiences. This explains why there is no language of private qualities. (Just as "someone," unlike "the doctor," is a colorless word.) [19]

If it is asked what is the difference between those brain processes which, in my view, are experiences and those brain processes which are not, I can only reply that it is at present unknown. I have been tempted to conjecture that the difference may in part be that between perception and reception (in D. M. MacKay's terminology) and that the type of brain process which is an experience might be identifiable with MacKay's active "matching response." [20] This, however, cannot be the whole story, because sometimes I can perceive something unconsciously, as when I take a handkerchief out of a drawer without being aware that I am doing so. But at the very least, we can classify the brain processes which are experiences as those brain processes which are, or might have been, causal conditions of those pieces of verbal behavior which we call reports of immediate experience.

I have now considered a number of objections to the brain-process thesis. I wish now to conclude with some remarks on the logical status of the thesis itself. U. T. Place seems to hold that it is a straight-out scientific hypothesis.[21] If so, he is partly right and partly wrong. If the issue is between (say) a brain-process thesis and a heart thesis, or a liver thesis, or a kidney thesis, then the issue is a purely empirical one, and the verdict is overwhelmingly in favor of the brain. The right sorts of things don't go on in the heart, liver, or kidney, nor do these organs possess the right sort of complexity of structure. On the other hand, if the issue is between a brain-or-liver-or-kidney thesis (that is, some form of materialism) on the one hand and epiphenomenalism on the other hand, then the issue is not an empirical one. For there is no conceivable

[18] I owe this point to Place, in correspondence.
[19] The "beetle in the box" objection is, *if it is sound,* an objection to *any* view, and in particular the Cartesian one, that introspective reports are genuine reports. So it is no objection to a weaker thesis that I would be concerned to uphold, namely, that if introspective reports of "experiences" are genuinely reports, then the things they are reports of are in fact brain processes.
[20] See his article "Towards an Information-Flow Model of Human Behaviour," *British Journal of Psychology,* XLVII (1956), 30-43.
[21] *Op. cit.* For a further discussion of this, in reply to the original version of the present paper, see Place's note "Materialism as a Scientific Hypothesis," *Philosophical Review,* LXIX (1960), 101-4.

experiment which could decide between materialism and epiphenome-nalism. This latter issue is not like the average straight-out empirical issue in science, but like the issue between the nineteenth-century English naturalist Philip Gosse[22] and the orthodox geologists and paleontologists of his day. According to Gosse, the earth was created about 4000 B.C. exactly as described in *Genesis,* with twisted rock strata, "evidence" of erosion, and so forth, and all sorts of fossils, all in their appropriate strata, just as if the usual evolutionist story had been true. Clearly this theory is in a sense irrefutable: no evidence can possibly tell against it. Let us ignore the theological setting in which Philip Gosse's hypothesis had been placed, thus ruling out objections of a theological kind, such as "what a queer God who would go to such elaborate lengths to deceive us." Let us suppose that it is held that the universe just *began* in 4004 B.C. with the initial conditions just everywhere as they were in 4004 B.C., and in particular that our own planet began with sediment in the rivers, eroded cliffs, fossils in the rocks, and so on. No scientist would ever entertain this as a serious hypothesis, consistent though it is with all possible evidence. The hypothesis offends against the principles of parsimony and simplicity. There would be far too many brute and inexplicable facts. Why are pterodactyl bones just as they are? No explanation in terms of the evolution of pterodactyls from earlier forms of life would any longer be possible. We would have millions of facts about the world as it was in 4004 B.C. that just have to be *accepted.*

The issue between the brain-process theory and epiphenomenalism seems to be of the above sort. (Assuming that a behavioristic reduction of introspective reports is not possible.) If it be agreed that there are no cogent philosophical arguments which force us into accepting dualism, and if the brain process theory and dualism are equally consistent with the facts, then the principles of parsimony and simplicity seem to me to decide overwhelmingly in favor of the brain-process theory. As I pointed out earlier, dualism involves a large number of irreducible psycho-physical laws (whereby the "nomological danglers" dangle) of a queer sort, that just have to be taken on trust, and are just as difficult to swallow as the irreducible facts about the paleontology of the earth with which we are faced on Philip Gosse's theory.

[22] See the entertaining account of Gosse's book *Omphalos* by Martin Gardner in *Fads and Fallacies in the Name of Science,* 2nd ed. (New York: Dover, 1957), pp. 124-27.

Bibliography

The following list of books and articles on the philosophy of mind includes only some of the more important works on the subject written in English since 1945. No breakdown by topic has been attempted, since many of the works deal with several different topics at once.

The following abbreviations have been used:

A—Analysis
ASP—Aristotelian Society Proceedings
ASSV—Aristotelian Society Supplementary Volume
CBP—Contemporary British Philosophy (Third Series), ed. H. D. Lewis. London: George Allen & Unwin, Ltd., 1956.
DM—Dimensions of Mind, ed. Sidney Hook. New York: New York University Press, 1960.
JP—Journal of Philosophy
M—Mind
MSPS—Minnesota Studies in the Philosophy of Science, Vol. I, *The Foundations of Science and the Concepts of Psychology and Psychoanalysis*, ed. Herbert Feigl and Michael Scriven; Vol. II, *Concepts, Theories, and the Mind-Body Problem*, ed. Herbert Feigl, Michael Scriven, and Grover Maxwell. Minneapolis: University of Minnesota Press, 1956 and 1958.
P—Philosophy
PQ—Philosophical Quarterly
PR—Philosophical Review
RPS—Readings in the Philosophy of Science, ed. Herbert Feigl and May Brodbeck. New York: Appleton-Century-Crofts, Inc., 1953.

BOOKS

Anscombe, G. E. M., *Intention*. Oxford: Basil Blackwell & Mott, Ltd., 1957.
Ayer, A. J., *Thinking and Meaning*. London: H. K. Lewis & Co., Ltd., 1947.
———, *The Problem of Knowledge*. London: Macmillan & Co., Ltd., 1956.
Baier, Kurt, *The Moral Point of View*. Ithaca, N.Y.: Cornell University Press, 1958.
Geach, Peter, *Mental Acts*. London: Routledge & Kegan Paul, Ltd., 1957.
Hamlyn, D. W., *The Psychology of Perception*. London: Routledge & Kegan Paul, Ltd., 1957.
Hampshire, Stuart, *Thought and Action*. London: Chatto and Windus, Ltd., 1959.
———, *Feeling and Expression*. London: H. K. Lewis & Co., Ltd., 1961.
Holloway, John, *Language and Intelligence*. London: Macmillan & Co., Ltd., 1951.
MacIntyre, A. C., *The Unconscious*. London: Routledge & Kegan Paul, Ltd., 1958.
Malcolm, Norman, *Dreaming*. London: Routledge & Kegan Paul, Ltd., 1959.
Melden, A. I., *Free Action*. London: Routledge & Kegan Paul, Ltd., 1961.
Nowell-Smith, P. H., *Ethics*. London: Penguin Books, Ltd., 1954.
Peters, R. S., *The Concept of Motivation*. London: Routledge & Kegan Paul, Ltd., 1958.
Ryle, Gilbert, *The Concept of Mind*. London: Hutchinson's University Library, 1949.
———, *Dilemmas*. Cambridge: Cambridge University Press, 1954.
Von Leyden, W., *Remembering*. London: Gerald Duckworth & Co. Ltd., 1961.
Wisdom, John, *Other Minds*. [A series of articles first published in *M*, XLIX-LII (1940-43)] Oxford: Basil Blackwell & Mott, Ltd., 1952.
Wittgenstein, Ludwig, *The Blue and Brown Books*. Oxford: Basil Blackwell & Mott, Ltd., 1958.
———, *Philosophical Investigations*. Oxford: Basil Blackwell & Mott, Ltd., 1953.

ARTICLES

Aaron, R. I., "Dispensing with Mind," *ASP*, LII (1951-52), 225-42.

Albritton, Rogers, "On Wittgenstein's Use of the Term 'Criterion,' " *JP*, LVI (1959), 845-57.

Alexander, P., "Other People's Experiences," *ASP*, LI (1950-51), 25-46.

——, "Cause and Cure in Psychotherapy," *ASSV*, XXIX (1955), 25-42.

Anscombe, G. E. M., "Pretending," *ASSV*, XXXII (1958), 279-94.

Aune, Bruce, "The Problem of Other Minds," *PR*, LXX (1961), 320-39.

Austin, J. L., "Other Minds," *ASSV*, XX (1946), 148-87; repr. in *Logic and Language* (Second Series), ed. Antony Flew, pp. 123-58. Oxford: Basil Blackwell & Mott, Ltd., 1953.

——, "Ifs and Cans," *Proceedings of the British Academy*, XLII (1956), 109-32.

——, "A Plea for Excuses," *ASP*, LVII (1956-57), 1-30.

——, "Pretending," *ASSV*, XXXII (1958), 261-78.

Ayer, A. J., "Other Minds," *ASSV*, XX (1946), 188-97.

——, "One's Knowledge of Other Minds," *Theoria*, XIX (1953), 1-20; repr. in A. J. Ayer, *Philosophical Essays*, pp. 191-214. London: Macmillan & Co., Ltd., 1954.

——, "Can There Be a Private Language?" *ASSV*, XXVIII (1954), 63-78.

Baier, K., "Decisions and Descriptions," *M*, LX (1951), 181-204.

Barnes, W. H. F., "Talking about Sensations," *ASP*, LIV (1953-54), 261-78.

——, "On Seeing and Hearing," in *CBP*, pp. 65-81.

Bedford, Errol, "Pleasure and Belief," *ASSV*, XXXIII (1959), 73-92.

Benjamin, B. S., "Remembering," *M*, LXV (1956), 312-31.

Bergmann, Gustav, "The Logic of Psychological Concepts," *Philosophy of Science*, XVIII (1951), 93-110.

Black, Max, "Linguistic Method in Philosophy," *Philosophy and Phenomenological Research*, VIII (1947-48), 635-49.

Bouwsma, O. K., "The Expression Theory of Art," in *Philosophical Analysis*, ed. Max Black, pp. 75-101. Ithaca, N.Y.: Cornell University Press, 1950.

Bradley, M. C., "Mr. Strawson and Skepticism," *A*, XX (1959-60), 14-19.

Brandt, Richard B., "Doubts about the Identity Theory," in *DM*, pp. 57-67.

Britton, Karl, "Seeming," *ASSV*, XXVI (1952), 195-214.

——, "Feelings and Their Expression," *P*, XXXII (1957), 97-111.

Brown, D. G., "The Nature of Inference," *PR*, LXIV (1955), 351-69.

Campbell, C. A., "Is 'Freewill' a Pseudo-Problem?" *M*, LX (1951), 441-65.

——, "Self-activity and Its Modes," in *CBP*, pp. 85-115.

Chisholm, Roderick M., "Sentences about Believing," *ASP*, LVI (1955-56), 125-48.

——, and Wilfrid Sellars, "Intentionality and the Mental," in *MSPS*, II, 507-39.

Danto, Arthur C., "Concerning Mental Pictures," *JP*, LV (1958), 12-20.

——, "On Consciousness in Machines," in *DM*, pp. 180-87.

Daveney, T. F., "Wanting," *PQ*, XI (1961), 135-44.

Day, J. P., "Unconscious Perception," *ASSV*, XXXIV (1960), 47-66.

Dilman, Ilham, "The Unconscious," *M*, LXVIII (1959), 446-73.

——, "Dreams," *Review of Metaphysics*, XV (1961-62), 108-17.

Dodwell, P. C., "Causes of Behaviour and Explanation in Psychology," *M*, LXIX (1960), 1-13.

Ebersole, Frank B., "De Somniis," *M*, LXVIII (1959), 336-49.

Evans, J. L., "Knowledge and Behaviour," *ASP*, LIV (1953-54), 27-48.

——, "Choice," *PQ*, V (1955), 301-15.

Ewing, A. C., "Professor Ryle's Attack on Dualism," *ASP*, LIII (1952-53), 47-78.

——, "The Justification of Emotions," *ASSV*, XXXI (1957), 59-74.

Feigl, Herbert, "The Mind-Body Problem in the Development of Logical Empiricism," *Revue Internationale de Philosophie*, IV (1950), 64-83; repr. in *RPS*, pp. 612-26.

——, "The 'Mental' and the 'Physical,' " in *MSPS*, II, 370-497.

——, "Other Minds and the Egocentric Predicament," *JP*, LV (1958), 978-87.
——, "Mind-Body, *Not* a Pseudoproblem," in *DM*, pp. 24-36.
Findlay, J. N., "Is There Knowledge by Acquaintance?" *ASSV*, XXIII (1949), 111-28.
——, "Linguistic Approach to Psycho-Physics," *ASP*, L (1949-50), 43-64.
——, "The Justification of Attitudes," *M*, LXIII (1954), 145-61.
Fleming, Brice Noel, "On Avowals," *PR*, LXIV (1955), 614-25.
——, "Recognizing and Seeing As," *PR*, LXVI (1957), 161-79.
Flew, Annis, "Images, Supposing and Imagining," *P*, XXVIII (1953), 246-54.
Flew, Antony, "Psycho-Analytic Explanation," *A*, X (1949-50), 8-15.
——, "Motives and the Unconscious," in *MSPS*, I, 155-73.
Foot, Philippa, "Moral Beliefs," *ASP*, LIX (1958-59), 83-104.
Furlong, E. J., "Memory," *M*, LVII (1948), 16-44.
——, "Memory and the Argument from Illusion," *ASP*, LIV (1953-54), 131-44.
Gallie, W. B., "Pleasure," *ASSV*, XXVIII (1954), 147-64.
Ginnane, W. J., "Thoughts," *M*, LXIX (1960), 372-90.
Grant, C. K., " 'Good At,' " *ASSV*, XXXII (1958), 173-94.
Grice, H. P., "Meaning," *PR*, LXVI (1957), 377-88.
Grünbaum, Adolf, "Causality and the Science of Human Behavior," *American Scientist*, XL (1952), 665-676; repr. in *RPS*, pp. 766-78.
Hamlyn, D. W., "The Stream of Thought," *ASP*, LVI (1955-56), 63-82.
——, "The Visual Field and Perception," *ASSV*, XXXI (1957), 107-24.
Hampshire, Stuart, "The Concept of Mind. By Gilbert Ryle," *M*, LIX (1950), 237-55.
——, "Freedom of the Will," *ASSV*, XXV (1951), 161-78.
——, "The Analogy of Feeling," *M*, LXI (1952), 1-12.
——, "Self-Knowledge and the Will," *Revue Internationale de Philosophie*, VII (1953), 230-45.
——, "Dispositions," *A*, XIV (1953-54), 5-11.
——, "On Referring and Intending," *PR*, LXV (1956), 1-13.
——, "The Interpretation of Language: Words and Concepts," in *British Philosophy in the Mid-Century*, ed. C. A. Mace, pp. 267-79. London: George Allen and Unwin, Ltd., 1957.
——, and H. L. A. Hart, "Decision, Intention and Certainty," *M*, LXVII (1958), 1-12.
Hanson, Norwood Russell, "On Having the Same Visual Experiences," *M*, LXIX (1960), 340-50.
Hare, R. M., "Freedom of the Will," *ASSV*, XXV (1951), 201-16.
Hart, H. L. A., "The Ascription of Responsibility and Rights," *ASP*, XLIX (1948-49), 171-94; repr. in *Logic and Language* (First Series), ed. Antony Flew, pp. 145-66. Oxford: Basil Blackwell & Mott, Ltd., 1951.
——, "Is There Knowledge by Acquaintance?" *ASSV*, XXIII (1949), 69-90.
——, and Stuart Hampshire, "Decision, Intention and Certainty." *M*, LXVII (1958). 1-12.
Heath, P. L., "Intentions," *ASSV*, XXIX (1955), 147-64.
Hirst, R. J., "The Difference between Sensing and Observing," *ASSV*, XXVIII (1954), 197-218.
Holland, R. F., "The Empiricist Theory of Memory," *M*, LXIII (1954), 464-86.
Hudson, H., "Why We Cannot Witness or Observe What Goes On 'In Our Heads,' " *M*, LXV (1956), 218-30.
——, "Why Are Our Feelings of Pain Perceptually Unobservable?" *A*, XXI (1960-61), 97-100.
Hughes, G. E., "Is There Knowledge by Acquaintance?" *ASSV*, XXIII (1949), 91-110.
Jones, J. R., "Self-Knowledge," *ASSV*, XXX (1956), 120-42.
——, "The Two Contexts of Mental Concepts," *ASP*, LIX (1958-59), 105-24.
Jones, O. R., "Things Known Without Observation," *ASP*, LXI (1960-61), 129-50.
Kneale, M., "What Is the Mind-Body Problem?" *ASP*, L (1949-50), 105-22.
Kneale, W., "Experience and Introspection," *ASP*, L (1949-50), 1-28.

Köhler, Wolfgang, "The Mind-Body Problem," in *DM*, pp. 3-23.
Kremer, Thomas, "The Significance of Solipsism." *ASP*, LX (1959-60), 35-60.
Lloyd, A. C., "Thinking and Language," *ASSV*, XXV (1951), 35-64.
———, "The Visual Field and Perception," *ASSV*, XXXI (1957), 125-44.
McCracken, D. J., "Motives and Causes," *ASSV*, XXVI (1952), 163-78.
Macdonald, Margaret, "Sleeping and Waking," *M*, LXII (1953), 202-15.
Mace, C. A., "Some Implications of Analytical Behaviourism," *ASP*, XLIX (1948-49), 1-16.
———, "Introspection and Analysis," in *Philosophical Analysis*, ed. Max Black, pp. 230-43. Ithaca, N.Y.: Cornell University Press, Inc., 1950.
———, "Abstract Ideas and Images," *ASSV*, XXVII (1953), 137-48.
———, "Some Trends in the Philosophy of Mind," in *British Philosophy in the Mid-Century*, ed. C. A. Mace, pp. 99-112. London: George Allen and Unwin, Ltd., 1957.
McGuinness, B. F., " 'I Know What I Want,' " *ASP*, LVII (1956-57), 305-20.
MacIntyre, A. C., "Cause and Cure in Psychotherapy," *ASSV*, XXIX (1955), 43-58.
———, "Purpose and Intelligent Action," *ASSV*, XXXIV (1960), 79-96.
MacKay, D. M., "Mentality in Machines," *ASSV*, XXVI (1952), 61-86.
Malcolm, Norman, "Knowledge and Belief," *M*, LXI (1952), 178-89.
———, "Direct Perception," *PQ*, III (1953), 301-16.
Mandelbaum, Maurice, "Professor Ryle and Psychology," *PR*, LXVII (1958), 522-30.
Manser, A. R., "Dreams," *ASSV*, XXX (1956), 208-28.
———, "Pleasure," *ASP*, LXI (1960-61), 223-38.
Melden, A. I., "On Promising," *M*, LXV (1956), 49-66.
———, "Action," *PR*, LXV (1956), 523-41.
Mellor, W. W., "Three Problems about Other Minds," *M*, LXV (1956), 200-217.
Miles, T. R., "Self-Knowledge," *ASSV*, XXX (1956), 143-56.
Mitchell, D., "Privileged Utterances," *M*, LXII (1953), 355-66.
Murdoch, Iris, "Thinking and Language," *ASSV*, XXV (1951), 25-34.
———, "Nostalgia for the Particular," *ASP*, LII (1951-52), 243-60.
Nowell-Smith, P. H., "Choosing, Deciding and Doing," *A*, XVIII (1957-58), 63-69.
———, "Purpose and Intelligent Action," *ASSV*, XXXIV (1960), 97-112.
O'Connor, D. J., "Awareness and Communication," *JP*, LII (1955), 505-14.
O'Shaughnessy, B., "The Origin of Pain," *A*, XV (1954-55), 121-30.
———, "The Limits of the Will," *PR*, LXV (1956), 443-90.
Pap, Arthur, "Other Minds and the Principle of Verifiability," *Revue Internationale de Philosophie*, V (1951), 280-306.
———, "Semantic Analysis and Psycho-Physical Dualism," *M*, LXI (1952), 209-21.
Passmore, J. A., "Intentions," *ASSV*, XXIX (1955), 131-46.
Pears, D. F., "The Logical Status of Supposition," *ASSV*, XXV (1951), 83-98.
———, "Professor Norman Malcolm: Dreaming," *M*, LXX (1961), 145-63.
———, "*Individuals.* By P. F. Strawson," *PQ*, XI (1961), 172-85, 262-77.
Penelhum, Terence, "Hume on Personal Identity," *PR*, LXIV (1955), 571-89.
———, "The Logic of Pleasure," *Philosophy and Phenomenological Research*, XVII (1956-57), 488-503.
———, "Personal Identity, Memory, and Survival," *JP*, LVI (1959), 882-903.
Peters, R. S., "Cause, Cure and Motive," *A*, X (1949-50), 103-9.
———, "Observationalism in Psychology," *M*, LX (1951), 43-61.
———, "Motives and Causes," *ASSV*, XXVI (1952), 139-62.
———, "Motives and Motivation," *P*, XXXI (1956), 117-30.
Place, U. T., "The Concept of Heed," *British Journal of Psychology*, XLV (1954), 243-55.
Plantinga, Alvin, "Things and Persons," *Review of Metaphysics*, XIV (1960-61), 493-519.
Pole, David, "Understanding—A Psychical Process," *ASP*, LX (1959-60), 253-68.
Popper, Karl R., "Language and the Body-Mind Problem," in *Proceedings of the XIth International Congress of Philosophy* (1953), VII, 101-7.

———, "A Note on the Body-Mind Problem," *A*, XV (1954-55), 131-35.

Powell, Betty, "Uncharacteristic Actions," *M*, LXVIII (1959), 492-509.

Price, H. H., "Thinking and Language," *ASP*, LI (1950-51), 329-38.

———, "Image Thinking," *ASP*, LII (1951-52), 135-66.

———, "Seeming," *ASSV*, XXVI (1952), 215-34.

———, "Belief and Will," *ASSV*, XXVIII (1954), 1-26.

———, "Some Objections to Behaviourism," in *DM*, pp. 78-84.

Putnam, Hilary, "Psychological Concepts, Explication, and Ordinary Language," *JP*, LIV (1957), 94-100.

———, "Minds and Machines," in *DM*, pp. 148-79.

Quinton, A. M., "Seeming," *ASSV*, XXVI (1952), 235-52.

———, "The Problem of Perception," *M*, LXIV (1955), 28-51.

Rees, W. J., "Continuous States," *ASP*, LVIII (1957-58), 223-44.

Rhees, R., "Can There Be a Private Language?" *ASSV*, XXVIII (1954), 77-94.

Ritchie, A. D., "Agent and Act in Theory of Mind," *ASP*, LII (1951-52), 1-22.

Rollins, C. D., "Personal Predicates," *PQ*, X (1960), 1-11.

Russell, Bertrand, "What Is Mind?" *JP*, LV (1958), 5-12.

Ryle, Gilbert, "Knowing How and Knowing That," *ASP*, XLVI (1945-46), 1-16.

———, "Feelings," *PQ*, I (1950-51), 193-205.

———, "Thinking and Language," *ASSV*, XXV (1951), 65-82.

———, "Pleasure," *ASSV*, XXVIII (1954), 135-46.

———, "Sensation," in *CBP*, pp. 427-43.

———, "On Forgetting the Difference between Right and Wrong," in *Essays in Moral Philosophy*, ed. A. I. Melden, pp. 147-59. Seattle: University of Washington Press, 1958.

———, "A Puzzling Element in the Notion of Thinking," *Proceedings of the British Academy*, XLIV (1958), 129-44.

Scheffler, Israel, "The New Dualism: Psychological and Physical Terms," *JP*, XLVII (1950), 737-52.

Scriven, Michael, "The Mechanical Concept of Mind," *M*, LXII (1953), 230-40.

———, "Modern Experiments in Telepathy," *PR*, LXV (1956), 231-53.

———, "A Study of Radical Behaviorism," in *MSPS*, I, 88-130.

———, "The Compleat Robot: A Prolegomena to Androidology," in *DM*, pp. 118-42.

Sellars, Wilfrid, "Mind, Meaning and Behavior," *Philosophical Studies*, III (1952), 83-95.

———, "A Semantical Solution of the Mind-Body Problem," *Methodos*, V (1953), 45-82.

———, "Empiricism and the Philosophy of Mind," in *MSPS*, I, 253-329.

———, and Roderick M. Chisholm, "Intentionality and the Mental," in *MSPS*, II, 507-39.

Shaffer, Jerome, "Could Mental States Be Brain Processes?" *JP*, LVIII (1961), 813-22.

Shearn, M., "Other People's Sense Data," *ASP*, L (1949-50), 15-26.

Shoemaker, Sydney S., "Personal Identity and Memory," *JP*, LVI (1959), 868-82.

Shorter, J. M., "Imagination," *M*, LXI (1952), 528-42.

Sibley, Frank, "A Theory of the Mind," *Review of Metaphysics*, IV (1950-51), 259-78.

———, "Seeking, Scrutinizing and Seeing," *M*, LXIV (1955), 455-78.

Skinner, B. F., "The Operational Analysis of Psychological Terms," *Psychological Review*, LII (1945), 270-78; repr. in *RPS*, pp. 585-95.

———, "Critique of Psychoanalytic Concepts and Theories," in *MSPS*, I, 77-87.

Smart, J. J. C., "Ryle on Mechanism and Psychology," *PQ*, IX (1959), 349-55.

Spence, Kenneth W., "The Postulates and Methods of 'Behaviorism,'" *Psychological Review*, LV (1948), 67-78; repr. in *RPS*, pp. 571-84.

Spilsbury, R. J., "Mentality in Machines," *ASSV*, XXVI (1952), 27-60.

Strawson, P. F., "*Philosophical Investigations*. By Ludwig Wittgenstein," *M*, LXIII (1954), 70-99.

———, "Professor Ayer's 'The Problem of Knowledge,'" *P*, XXXII (1957), 302-14.

Sutherland, N. S., "Motives as Explanations," *M*, LXVIII (1959), 145-59.

Taylor, D., "Thinking," *M*, LXV (1956), 246-51.

Taylor, James G., "Towards a Science of Mind," *M*, LXVI (1957), 434-52.

Taylor, Paul W., " 'Need' Statements," *A*, XIX (1958-59), 106-11.

Taylor, Richard, " 'I Can,' " *PR*, LXIX (1958), 78-89.

Teichmann, J., "Mental Cause and Effect," *M*, LXX (1961), 36-52.

Thomson, J. F., "The Argument from Analogy and Our Knowledge of Other Minds," *M*, LX (1951), 336-50.

Toulmin, Stephen, "The Logical Status of Psychoanalysis," *A*, IX (1948-49), 23-29.

————, "Knowledge of Right and Wrong," *ASP*, L (1949-50), 139-56.

————, "Concept-Formation in Philosophy and Psychology," in *DM*, pp. 211-25.

Urmson, J. O., "Motives and Causes," *ASSV*, XXVI (1952), 179-94.

————, "Recognition," *ASP*, LVI (1955-56), 259-80.

Vendler, Zeno, "Verbs and Times," *PR*, LXVI (1957), 143-60.

Vesey, G. N. A., "Seeing and Seeing-As," *ASP*, LVI (1955-56), 109-24.

————, "Unconscious Perception," *ASSV*, XXXIV (1960), 67-78.

————, "The Location of Bodily Sensations," *M*, LXX (1961), 25-35.

————, "Volition," *P*, XXXVI (1961), 352-65.

Warnock, G. J., "Seeing," *ASP*, LV (1954-55), 201-18.

Warnock, Mary, "The Justification of Emotions," *ASSV*, XXXI (1957), 43-58.

Watling, John, "Ayer on Other Minds," *Theoria*, XX (1954), 175-80.

Wellman, Carl, "Our Criteria for Third Person Psychological Sentences," *JP*, LVIII (1961), 281-93.

Wheatley, J. M. O., "Wishing and Hoping," *A*, XVIII (1957-58), 121-31.

White, Alan R., "Mr. Hampshire and Professor Ryle on Dispositions," *A*, XIV (1953-54), 111-14.

————, " 'Good At,' " *ASSV*, XXXII (1958), 195-206.

————, "The Language of Motives," *M*, LXVII (1958), 258-63.

————, "Different Kinds of Heed Concepts," *A*, XX (1959-60), 112-16.

————, "The Concept of Care," *PQ*, X (1960), 271-74.

————, "Inclination," *A*, XXI (1960-61), 40-42.

————, "Thinking That and Knowing That," *PQ*, XI (1961), 68-73.

Whiteley, C. H., "Behaviourism," *M*, LXX (1961), 164-74.

Williams, B. A. O., "Personal Identity and Individuation," *ASP*, LVII (1956-57), 229-52.

————, "Pleasure and Belief," *ASSV*, XXXIII (1959), 57-72.

Wisdom, John, "Other Minds," *ASSV*, XX (1946), 122-47.

————, "Philosophy, Metaphysics and Psycho-Analysis," in John Wisdom, *Philosophy and Psycho-Analysis*, pp. 248-82. Oxford: Basil Blackwell & Mott, Ltd., 1953.

Wisdom, J. O., "A New Model for the Mind-Body Relationship," *British Journal for the Philosophy of Science*, II (1951-52), 295-301.

————, "Mentality in Machines," *ASSV*, XXVI (1952), 1-26.

————, "Some Main Mind-Body Problems," *ASP*, LX (1959-60), 187-210.

Wolgast, Elizabeth H., "Perceiving and Impressions," *PR*, LXVII (1958), 226-36.

————, "The Experience in Perception," *PR*, LXIX (1960), 165-82.

Wollheim, Richard, "Privacy," *ASP*, LI (1950-51), 83-104.

————, "Hampshire's Analogy," *M*, LXI (1952), 567-73.

————, "The Difference between Sensing and Observing," *ASSV*, XXVIII (1954), 219-40.

Wright, J. N., "Mind and the Concept of Mind," *ASSV*, XXXIII (1959), 1-22.

Yolton, J. W., "The Dualism of Mind," *JP*, LI (1954), 173-80.

Ziff, Paul, "The Feelings of Robots," *A*, XIX (1958-59), 64-68.

A CATALOG OF SELECTED
DOVER BOOKS
IN ALL FIELDS OF INTEREST

A CATALOG OF SELECTED DOVER
BOOKS IN ALL FIELDS OF INTEREST

DRAWINGS OF REMBRANDT, edited by Seymour Slive. Updated Lippmann, Hofstede de Groot edition, with definitive scholarly apparatus. All portraits, biblical sketches, landscapes, nudes. Oriental figures, classical studies, together with selection of work by followers. 550 illustrations. Total of 630pp. 9⅛ × 12¼.
21485-0, 21486-9 Pa., Two-vol. set $25.00

GHOST AND HORROR STORIES OF AMBROSE BIERCE, Ambrose Bierce. 24 tales vividly imagined, strangely prophetic, and decades ahead of their time in technical skill: "The Damned Thing," "An Inhabitant of Carcosa," "The Eyes of the Panther," "Moxon's Master," and 20 more. 199pp. 5⅜ × 8½. 20767-6 Pa. $3.95

ETHICAL WRITINGS OF MAIMONIDES, Maimonides. Most significant ethical works of great medieval sage, newly translated for utmost precision, readability. Laws Concerning Character Traits, Eight Chapters, more. 192pp. 5⅜ × 8½.
24522-5 Pa. $4.50

THE EXPLORATION OF THE COLORADO RIVER AND ITS CANYONS, J. W. Powell. Full text of Powell's 1,000-mile expedition down the fabled Colorado in 1869. Superb account of terrain, geology, vegetation, Indians, famine, mutiny, treacherous rapids, mighty canyons, during exploration of last unknown part of continental U.S. 400pp. 5⅜ × 8½. 20094-9 Pa. $6.95

HISTORY OF PHILOSOPHY, Julián Marías. Clearest one-volume history on the market. Every major philosopher and dozens of others, to Existentialism and later. 505pp. 5⅜ × 8½. 21739-6 Pa. $9.95

ALL ABOUT LIGHTNING, Martin A. Uman. Highly readable non-technical survey of nature and causes of lightning, thunderstorms, ball lightning, St. Elmo's Fire, much more. Illustrated. 192pp. 5⅜ × 8½. 25237-X Pa. $5.95

SAILING ALONE AROUND THE WORLD, Captain Joshua Slocum. First man to sail around the world, alone, in small boat. One of great feats of seamanship told in delightful manner. 67 illustrations. 294pp. 5⅜ × 8½. 20326-3 Pa. $4.95

LETTERS AND NOTES ON THE MANNERS, CUSTOMS AND CONDITIONS OF THE NORTH AMERICAN INDIANS, George Catlin. Classic account of life among Plains Indians: ceremonies, hunt, warfare, etc. 312 plates. 572pp. of text. 6⅛ × 9¼. 22118-0, 22119-9 Pa. Two-vol. set $15.90

ALASKA: The Harriman Expedition, 1899, John Burroughs, John Muir, et al. Informative, engrossing accounts of two-month, 9,000-mile expedition. Native peoples, wildlife, forests, geography, salmon industry, glaciers, more. Profusely illustrated. 240 black-and-white line drawings. 124 black-and-white photographs. 3 maps. Index. 576pp. 5⅜ × 8½. 25109-8 Pa. $11.95

THE BOOK OF BEASTS: Being a Translation from a Latin Bestiary of the Twelfth Century, T. H. White. Wonderful catalog real and fanciful beasts: manticore, griffin, phoenix, amphivius, jaculus, many more. White's witty erudite commentary on scientific, historical aspects. Fascinating glimpse of medieval mind. Illustrated. 296pp. 5⅜ × 8¼. (Available in U.S. only)   24609-4 Pa. $5.95

FRANK LLOYD WRIGHT: ARCHITECTURE AND NATURE With 160 Illustrations, Donald Hoffmann. Profusely illustrated study of influence of nature—especially prairie—on Wright's designs for Fallingwater, Robie House, Guggenheim Museum, other masterpieces. 96pp. 9¼ × 10¾.   25098-9 Pa. $7.95

FRANK LLOYD WRIGHT'S FALLINGWATER, Donald Hoffmann. Wright's famous waterfall house: planning and construction of organic idea. History of site, owners, Wright's personal involvement. Photographs of various stages of building. Preface by Edgar Kaufmann, Jr. 100 illustrations. 112pp. 9¼ × 10.
23671-4 Pa. $7.95

YEARS WITH FRANK LLOYD WRIGHT: Apprentice to Genius, Edgar Tafel. Insightful memoir by a former apprentice presents a revealing portrait of Wright the man, the inspired teacher, the greatest American architect. 372 black-and-white illustrations. Preface. Index. vi + 228pp. 8¼ × 11.   24801-1 Pa. $9.95

THE STORY OF KING ARTHUR AND HIS KNIGHTS, Howard Pyle. Enchanting version of King Arthur fable has delighted generations with imaginative narratives of exciting adventures and unforgettable illustrations by the author. 41 illustrations. xviii + 313pp. 6⅛ × 9¼.   21445-1 Pa. $6.50

THE GODS OF THE EGYPTIANS, E. A. Wallis Budge. Thorough coverage of numerous gods of ancient Egypt by foremost Egyptologist. Information on evolution of cults, rites and gods; the cult of Osiris; the Book of the Dead and its rites; the sacred animals and birds; Heaven and Hell; and more. 956pp. 6⅛ × 9¼.
22055-9, 22056-7 Pa., Two-vol. set $21.90

A THEOLOGICO-POLITICAL TREATISE, Benedict Spinoza. Also contains unfinished *Political Treatise*. Great classic on religious liberty, theory of government on common consent. R. Elwes translation. Total of 421pp. 5⅜ × 8½.
20249-6 Pa. $6.95

INCIDENTS OF TRAVEL IN CENTRAL AMERICA, CHIAPAS, AND YUCATAN, John L. Stephens. Almost single-handed discovery of Maya culture; exploration of ruined cities, monuments, temples; customs of Indians. 115 drawings. 892pp. 5⅜ × 8½.   22404-X, 22405-8 Pa., Two-vol. set $15.90

LOS CAPRICHOS, Francisco Goya. 80 plates of wild, grotesque monsters and caricatures. Prado manuscript included. 183pp. 6⅞ × 9⅞.   22384-1 Pa. $4.95

AUTOBIOGRAPHY: The Story of My Experiments with Truth, Mohandas K. Gandhi. Not hagiography, but Gandhi in his own words. Boyhood, legal studies, purification, the growth of the Satyagraha (nonviolent protest) movement. Critical, inspiring work of the man who freed India. 480pp. 5⅜ × 8½. (Available in U.S. only)
24593-4 Pa. $6.95

ILLUSTRATED DICTIONARY OF HISTORIC ARCHITECTURE, edited by Cyril M. Harris. Extraordinary compendium of clear, concise definitions for over 5,000 important architectural terms complemented by over 2,000 line drawings. Covers full spectrum of architecture from ancient ruins to 20th-century Modernism. Preface. 592pp. 7½ × 9⅝. 24444-X Pa. $15.95

THE NIGHT BEFORE CHRISTMAS, Clement Moore. Full text, and woodcuts from original 1848 book. Also critical, historical material. 19 illustrations. 40pp. 4⅝ × 6. 22797-9 Pa. $2.50

THE LESSON OF JAPANESE ARCHITECTURE: 165 Photographs, Jiro Harada. Memorable gallery of 165 photographs taken in the 1930's of exquisite Japanese homes of the well-to-do and historic buildings. 13 line diagrams. 192pp. 8⅜ × 11¼. 24778-3 Pa. $8.95

THE AUTOBIOGRAPHY OF CHARLES DARWIN AND SELECTED LETTERS, edited by Francis Darwin. The fascinating life of eccentric genius composed of an intimate memoir by Darwin (intended for his children); commentary by his son, Francis; hundreds of fragments from notebooks, journals, papers; and letters to and from Lyell, Hooker, Huxley, Wallace and Henslow. xi + 365pp. 5⅜ × 8. 20479-0 Pa. $6.95

WONDERS OF THE SKY: Observing Rainbows, Comets, Eclipses, the Stars and Other Phenomena, Fred Schaaf. Charming, easy-to-read poetic guide to all manner of celestial events visible to the naked eye. Mock suns, glories, Belt of Venus, more. Illustrated. 299pp. 5¼ × 8¼. 24402-4 Pa. $7.95

BURNHAM'S CELESTIAL HANDBOOK, Robert Burnham, Jr. Thorough guide to the stars beyond our solar system. Exhaustive treatment. Alphabetical by constellation: Andromeda to Cetus in Vol. 1; Chamaeleon to Orion in Vol. 2; and Pavo to Vulpecula in Vol. 3. Hundreds of illustrations. Index in Vol. 3. 2,000pp. 6⅛ × 9¼. 23567-X, 23568-8, 23673-0 Pa., Three-vol. set $38.85

STAR NAMES: Their Lore and Meaning, Richard Hinckley Allen. Fascinating history of names various cultures have given to constellations and literary and folkloristic uses that have been made of stars. Indexes to subjects. Arabic and Greek names. Biblical references. Bibliography. 563pp. 5⅜ × 8½. 21079-0 Pa. $7.95

THIRTY YEARS THAT SHOOK PHYSICS: The Story of Quantum Theory, George Gamow. Lucid, accessible introduction to influential theory of energy and matter. Careful explanations of Dirac's anti-particles, Bohr's model of the atom, much more. 12 plates. Numerous drawings. 240pp. 5⅜ × 8½. 24895-X Pa. $5.95

CHINESE DOMESTIC FURNITURE IN PHOTOGRAPHS AND MEASURED DRAWINGS, Gustav Ecke. A rare volume, now affordably priced for antique collectors, furniture buffs and art historians. Detailed review of styles ranging from early Shang to late Ming. Unabridged republication. 161 black-and-white drawings, photos. Total of 224pp. 8⅜ × 11¼. (Available in U.S. only) 25171-3 Pa. $12.95

VINCENT VAN GOGH: A Biography, Julius Meier-Graefe. Dynamic, penetrating study of artist's life, relationship with brother, Theo, painting techniques, travels, more. Readable, engrossing. 160pp. 5⅜ × 8½. (Available in U.S. only) 25253-1 Pa. $3.95

HOW TO WRITE, Gertrude Stein. Gertrude Stein claimed anyone could understand her unconventional writing—here are clues to help. Fascinating improvisations, language experiments, explanations illuminate Stein's craft and the art of writing. Total of 414pp. 4⅝ × 6⅜. 23144-5 Pa. $5.95

ADVENTURES AT SEA IN THE GREAT AGE OF SAIL: Five Firsthand Narratives, edited by Elliot Snow. Rare true accounts of exploration, whaling, shipwreck, fierce natives, trade, shipboard life, more. 33 illustrations. Introduction. 353pp. 5⅜ × 8½. 25177-2 Pa. $7.95

THE HERBAL OR GENERAL HISTORY OF PLANTS, John Gerard. Classic descriptions of about 2,850 plants—with over 2,700 illustrations—includes Latin and English names, physical descriptions, varieties, time and place of growth, more. 2,706 illustrations. xlv + 1,678pp. 8½ × 12¼. 23147-X Cloth. $75.00

DOROTHY AND THE WIZARD IN OZ, L. Frank Baum. Dorothy and the Wizard visit the center of the Earth, where people are vegetables, glass houses grow and Oz characters reappear. Classic sequel to *Wizard of Oz.* 256pp. 5⅜ × 8. 24714-7 Pa. $4.95

SONGS OF EXPERIENCE: Facsimile Reproduction with 26 Plates in Full Color, William Blake. This facsimile of Blake's original "Illuminated Book" reproduces 26 full-color plates from a rare 1826 edition. Includes "The Tyger," "London," "Holy Thursday," and other immortal poems. 26 color plates. Printed text of poems. 48pp. 5¼ × 7. 24636-1 Pa. $3.50

SONGS OF INNOCENCE, William Blake. The first and most popular of Blake's famous "Illuminated Books," in a facsimile edition reproducing all 31 brightly colored plates. Additional printed text of each poem. 64pp. 5¼ × 7. 22764-2 Pa. $3.50

PRECIOUS STONES, Max Bauer. Classic, thorough study of diamonds, rubies, emeralds, garnets, etc.: physical character, occurrence, properties, use, similar topics. 20 plates, 8 in color. 94 figures. 659pp. 6⅛ × 9¼. 21910-0, 21911-9 Pa., Two-vol. set $15.90

ENCYCLOPEDIA OF VICTORIAN NEEDLEWORK, S. F. A. Caulfeild and Blanche Saward. Full, precise descriptions of stitches, techniques for dozens of needlecrafts—most exhaustive reference of its kind. Over 800 figures. Total of 679pp. 8⅛ × 11. Two volumes. Vol. 1 22800-2 Pa. $11.95
Vol. 2 22801-0 Pa. $11.95

THE MARVELOUS LAND OF OZ, L. Frank Baum. Second Oz book, the Scarecrow and Tin Woodman are back with hero named Tip, Oz magic. 136 illustrations. 287pp. 5⅜ × 8½. 20692-0 Pa. $5.95

WILD FOWL DECOYS, Joel Barber. Basic book on the subject, by foremost authority and collector. Reveals history of decoy making and rigging, place in American culture, different kinds of decoys, how to make them, and how to use them. 140 plates. 156pp. 7⅞ × 10¾. 20011-6 Pa. $8.95

HISTORY OF LACE, Mrs. Bury Palliser. Definitive, profusely illustrated chronicle of lace from earliest times to late 19th century. Laces of Italy, Greece, England, France, Belgium, etc. Landmark of needlework scholarship. 266 illustrations. 672pp. 6⅛ × 9¼. 24742-2 Pa. $14.95

ILLUSTRATED GUIDE TO SHAKER FURNITURE, Robert Meader. All furniture and appurtenances, with much on unknown local styles. 235 photos. 146pp. 9 × 12. 22819-3 Pa. $7.95

WHALE SHIPS AND WHALING: A Pictorial Survey, George Francis Dow. Over 200 vintage engravings, drawings, photographs of barks, brigs, cutters, other vessels. Also harpoons, lances, whaling guns, many other artifacts. Comprehensive text by foremost authority. 207 black-and-white illustrations. 288pp. 6 × 9. 24808-9 Pa. $8.95

THE BERTRAMS, Anthony Trollope. Powerful portrayal of blind self-will and thwarted ambition includes one of Trollope's most heartrending love stories. 497pp. 5⅜ × 8½. 25119-5 Pa. $9.95

ADVENTURES WITH A HAND LENS, Richard Headstrom. Clearly written guide to observing and studying flowers and grasses, fish scales, moth and insect wings, egg cases, buds, feathers, seeds, leaf scars, moss, molds, ferns, common crystals, etc.—all with an ordinary, inexpensive magnifying glass. 209 exact line drawings aid in your discoveries. 220pp. 5⅜ × 8½. 23330-8 Pa. $4.95

RODIN ON ART AND ARTISTS, Auguste Rodin. Great sculptor's candid, wide-ranging comments on meaning of art; great artists; relation of sculpture to poetry, painting, music; philosophy of life, more. 76 superb black-and-white illustrations of Rodin's sculpture, drawings and prints. 119pp. 8⅜ × 11¼. 24487-3 Pa. $6.95

FIFTY CLASSIC FRENCH FILMS, 1912–1982: A Pictorial Record, Anthony Slide. Memorable stills from Grand Illusion, Beauty and the Beast, Hiroshima, Mon Amour, many more. Credits, plot synopses, reviews, etc. 160pp. 8¼ × 11. 25256-6 Pa. $11.95

THE PRINCIPLES OF PSYCHOLOGY, William James. Famous long course complete, unabridged. Stream of thought, time perception, memory, experimental methods; great work decades ahead of its time. 94 figures. 1,391pp. 5⅜ × 8½. 20381-6, 20382-4 Pa., Two-vol. set $23.90

BODIES IN A BOOKSHOP, R. T. Campbell. Challenging mystery of blackmail and murder with ingenious plot and superbly drawn characters. In the best tradition of British suspense fiction. 192pp. 5⅜ × 8½. 24720-1 Pa. $3.95

CALLAS: PORTRAIT OF A PRIMA DONNA, George Jellinek. Renowned commentator on the musical scene chronicles incredible career and life of the most controversial, fascinating, influential operatic personality of our time. 64 black-and-white photographs. 416pp. 5⅜ × 8¼. 25047-4 Pa. $8.95

GEOMETRY, RELATIVITY AND THE FOURTH DIMENSION, Rudolph Rucker. Exposition of fourth dimension, concepts of relativity as Flatland characters continue adventures. Popular, easily followed yet accurate, profound. 141 illustrations. 133pp. 5⅜ × 8½. 23400-2 Pa. $3.95

HOUSEHOLD STORIES BY THE BROTHERS GRIMM, with pictures by Walter Crane. 53 classic stories—Rumpelstiltskin, Rapunzel, Hansel and Gretel, the Fisherman and his Wife, Snow White, Tom Thumb, Sleeping Beauty, Cinderella, and so much more—lavishly illustrated with original 19th century drawings. 114 illustrations. x + 269pp. 5⅜ × 8½. 21080-4 Pa. $4.95

SUNDIALS, Albert Waugh. Far and away the best, most thorough coverage of ideas, mathematics concerned, types, construction, adjusting anywhere. Over 100 illustrations. 230pp. 5⅜ × 8½. 22947-5 Pa. $4.95

PICTURE HISTORY OF THE NORMANDIE: With 190 Illustrations, Frank O. Braynard. Full story of legendary French ocean liner: Art Deco interiors, design innovations, furnishings, celebrities, maiden voyage, tragic fire, much more. Extensive text. 144pp. 8⅜ × 11¾. 25257-4 Pa. $9.95

THE FIRST AMERICAN COOKBOOK: A Facsimile of "American Cookery," 1796, Amelia Simmons. Facsimile of the first American-written cookbook published in the United States contains authentic recipes for colonial favorites—pumpkin pudding, winter squash pudding, spruce beer, Indian slapjacks, and more. Introductory Essay and Glossary of colonial cooking terms. 80pp. 5⅜ × 8½. 24710-4 Pa. $3.50

101 PUZZLES IN THOUGHT AND LOGIC, C. R. Wylie, Jr. Solve murders and robberies, find out which fishermen are liars, how a blind man could possibly identify a color—purely by your own reasoning! 107pp. 5⅜ × 8½. 20367-0 Pa. $2.50

THE BOOK OF WORLD-FAMOUS MUSIC—CLASSICAL, POPULAR AND FOLK, James J. Fuld. Revised and enlarged republication of landmark work in musico-bibliography. Full information about nearly 1,000 songs and compositions including first lines of music and lyrics. New supplement. Index. 800pp. 5⅜ × 8¼. 24857-7 Pa. $14.95

ANTHROPOLOGY AND MODERN LIFE, Franz Boas. Great anthropologist's classic treatise on race and culture. Introduction by Ruth Bunzel. Only inexpensive paperback edition. 255pp. 5⅜ × 8½. 25245-0 Pa. $5.95

THE TALE OF PETER RABBIT, Beatrix Potter. The inimitable Peter's terrifying adventure in Mr. McGregor's garden, with all 27 wonderful, full-color Potter illustrations. 55pp. 4¼ × 5½. (Available in U.S. only) 22827-4 Pa. $1.75

THREE PROPHETIC SCIENCE FICTION NOVELS, H. G. Wells. *When the Sleeper Wakes, A Story of the Days to Come* and *The Time Machine* (full version). 335pp. 5⅜ × 8½. (Available in U.S. only) 20605-X Pa. $6.95

APICIUS COOKERY AND DINING IN IMPERIAL ROME, edited and translated by Joseph Dommers Vehling. Oldest known cookbook in existence offers readers a clear picture of what foods Romans ate, how they prepared them, etc. 49 illustrations. 301pp. 6⅛ × 9¼. 23563-7 Pa. $7.95

SHAKESPEARE LEXICON AND QUOTATION DICTIONARY, Alexander Schmidt. Full definitions, locations, shades of meaning of every word in plays and poems. More than 50,000 exact quotations. 1,485pp. 6½ × 9¼. 22726-X, 22727-8 Pa., Two-vol. set $29.90

THE WORLD'S GREAT SPEECHES, edited by Lewis Copeland and Lawrence W. Lamm. Vast collection of 278 speeches from Greeks to 1970. Powerful and effective models; unique look at history. 842pp. 5⅜ × 8½. 20468-5 Pa. $11.95

THE BLUE FAIRY BOOK, Andrew Lang. The first, most famous collection, with many familiar tales: Little Red Riding Hood, Aladdin and the Wonderful Lamp, Puss in Boots, Sleeping Beauty, Hansel and Gretel, Rumpelstiltskin; 37 in all. 138 illustrations. 390pp. 5⅜ × 8½.   21437-0 Pa. $6.95

THE STORY OF THE CHAMPIONS OF THE ROUND TABLE, Howard Pyle. Sir Launcelot, Sir Tristram and Sir Percival in spirited adventures of love and triumph retold in Pyle's inimitable style. 50 drawings, 31 full-page. xviii + 329pp. 6½ × 9¼.   21883-X Pa. $6.95

AUDUBON AND HIS JOURNALS, Maria Audubon. Unmatched two-volume portrait of the great artist, naturalist and author contains his journals, an excellent biography by his granddaughter, expert annotations by the noted ornithologist, Dr. Elliott Coues, and 37 superb illustrations. Total of 1,200pp. 5⅜ × 8.
Vol. I 25143-8 Pa. $8.95
Vol. II 25144-6 Pa. $8.95

GREAT DINOSAUR HUNTERS AND THEIR DISCOVERIES, Edwin H. Colbert. Fascinating, lavishly illustrated chronicle of dinosaur research, 1820's to 1960. Achievements of Cope, Marsh, Brown, Buckland, Mantell, Huxley, many others. 384pp. 5¼ × 8¼.   24701-5 Pa. $7.95

THE TASTEMAKERS, Russell Lynes. Informal, illustrated social history of American taste 1850's–1950's. First popularized categories Highbrow, Lowbrow, Middlebrow. 129 illustrations. New (1979) afterword. 384pp. 6 × 9.
23993-4 Pa. $8.95

DOUBLE CROSS PURPOSES, Ronald A. Knox. A treasure hunt in the Scottish Highlands, an old map, unidentified corpse, surprise discoveries keep reader guessing in this cleverly intricate tale of financial skullduggery. 2 black-and-white maps. 320pp. 5⅜ × 8½. (Available in U.S. only)   25032-6 Pa. $5.95

AUTHENTIC VICTORIAN DECORATION AND ORNAMENTATION IN FULL COLOR: 46 Plates from "Studies in Design," Christopher Dresser. Superb full-color lithographs reproduced from rare original portfolio of a major Victorian designer. 48pp. 9¼ × 12¼.   25083-0 Pa. $7.95

PRIMITIVE ART, Franz Boas. Remains the best text ever prepared on subject, thoroughly discussing Indian, African, Asian, Australian, and, especially, Northern American primitive art. Over 950 illustrations show ceramics, masks, totem poles, weapons, textiles, paintings, much more. 376pp. 5⅜ × 8.   20025-6 Pa. $6.95

SIDELIGHTS ON RELATIVITY, Albert Einstein. Unabridged republication of two lectures delivered by the great physicist in 1920–21. *Ether and Relativity* and *Geometry and Experience*. Elegant ideas in non-mathematical form, accessible to intelligent layman. vi + 56pp. 5⅜ × 8½.   24511-X Pa. $2.95

THE WIT AND HUMOR OF OSCAR WILDE, edited by Alvin Redman. More than 1,000 ripostes, paradoxes, wisecracks: Work is the curse of the drinking classes, I can resist everything except temptation, etc. 258pp. 5⅜ × 8½.   20602-5 Pa. $4.50

ADVENTURES WITH A MICROSCOPE, Richard Headstrom. 59 adventures with clothing fibers, protozoa, ferns and lichens, roots and leaves, much more. 142 illustrations. 232pp. 5⅜ × 8½.   23471-1 Pa. $3.95

PLANTS OF THE BIBLE, Harold N. Moldenke and Alma L. Moldenke. Standard reference to all 230 plants mentioned in Scriptures. Latin name, biblical reference, uses, modern identity, much more. Unsurpassed encyclopedic resource for scholars, botanists, nature lovers, students of Bible. Bibliography. Indexes. 123 black-and-white illustrations. 384pp. 6 × 9. 25069-5 Pa. $8.95

FAMOUS AMERICAN WOMEN: A Biographical Dictionary from Colonial Times to the Present, Robert McHenry, ed. From Pocahontas to Rosa Parks, 1,035 distinguished American women documented in separate biographical entries. Accurate, up-to-date data, numerous categories, spans 400 years. Indices. 493pp. 6½ × 9¼. 24523-3 Pa. $9.95

THE FABULOUS INTERIORS OF THE GREAT OCEAN LINERS IN HISTORIC PHOTOGRAPHS, William H. Miller, Jr. Some 200 superb photographs capture exquisite interiors of world's great "floating palaces"—1890's to 1980's: *Titanic, Ile de France, Queen Elizabeth, United States, Europa*, more. Approx. 200 black-and-white photographs. Captions. Text. Introduction. 160pp. 8⅞ × 11¾. 24756-2 Pa. $9.95

THE GREAT LUXURY LINERS, 1927–1954: A Photographic Record, William H. Miller, Jr. Nostalgic tribute to heyday of ocean liners. 186 photos of Ile de France, Normandie, Leviathan, Queen Elizabeth, United States, many others. Interior and exterior views. Introduction. Captions. 160pp. 9 × 12. 24056-8 Pa. $10.95

A NATURAL HISTORY OF THE DUCKS, John Charles Phillips. Great landmark of ornithology offers complete detailed coverage of nearly 200 species and subspecies of ducks: gadwall, sheldrake, merganser, pintail, many more. 74 full-color plates, 102 black-and-white. Bibliography. Total of 1,920pp. 8⅝ × 11¼. 25141-1, 25142-X Cloth. Two-vol. set $100.00

THE SEAWEED HANDBOOK: An Illustrated Guide to Seaweeds from North Carolina to Canada, Thomas F. Lee. Concise reference covers 78 species. Scientific and common names, habitat, distribution, more. Finding keys for easy identification. 224pp. 5⅜ × 8½. 25215-9 Pa. $5.95

THE TEN BOOKS OF ARCHITECTURE: The 1755 Leoni Edition, Leon Battista Alberti. Rare classic helped introduce the glories of ancient architecture to the Renaissance. 68 black-and-white plates. 336pp. 8⅜ × 11¼. 25239-6 Pa. $14.95

MISS MACKENZIE, Anthony Trollope. Minor masterpieces by Victorian master unmasks many truths about life in 19th-century England. First inexpensive edition in years. 392pp. 5⅜ × 8½. 25201-9 Pa. $7.95

THE RIME OF THE ANCIENT MARINER, Gustave Doré, Samuel Taylor Coleridge. Dramatic engravings considered by many to be his greatest work. The terrifying space of the open sea, the storms and whirlpools of an unknown ocean, the ice of Antarctica, more—all rendered in a powerful, chilling manner. Full text. 38 plates. 77pp. 9¼ × 12. 22305-1 Pa. $4.95

THE EXPEDITIONS OF ZEBULON MONTGOMERY PIKE, Zebulon Montgomery Pike. Fascinating first-hand accounts (1805–6) of exploration of Mississippi River, Indian wars, capture by Spanish dragoons, much more. 1,088pp. 5⅜ × 8½. 25254-X, 25255-8 Pa. Two-vol. set $23.90

A CONCISE HISTORY OF PHOTOGRAPHY: Third Revised Edition, Helmut Gernsheim. Best one-volume history—camera obscura, photochemistry, daguerreotypes, evolution of cameras, film, more. Also artistic aspects—landscape, portraits, fine art, etc. 281 black-and-white photographs. 26 in color. 176pp. 8⅜ × 11¼. 25128-4 Pa. $13.95

THE DORÉ BIBLE ILLUSTRATIONS, Gustave Doré. 241 detailed plates from the Bible: the Creation scenes, Adam and Eve, Flood, Babylon, battle sequences, life of Jesus, etc. Each plate is accompanied by the verses from the King James version of the Bible. 241pp. 9 × 12. 23004-X Pa. $8.95

HUGGER-MUGGER IN THE LOUVRE, Elliot Paul. Second Homer Evans mystery-comedy. Theft at the Louvre involves sleuth in hilarious, madcap caper. "A knockout."—Books. 336pp. 5⅜ × 8½. 25185-3 Pa. $5.95

FLATLAND, E. A. Abbott. Intriguing and enormously popular science-fiction classic explores the complexities of trying to survive as a two-dimensional being in a three-dimensional world. Amusingly illustrated by the author. 16 illustrations. 103pp. 5⅜ × 8½. 20001-9 Pa. $2.25

THE HISTORY OF THE LEWIS AND CLARK EXPEDITION, Meriwether Lewis and William Clark, edited by Elliott Coues. Classic edition of Lewis and Clark's day-by-day journals that later became the basis for U.S. claims to Oregon and the West. Accurate and invaluable geographical, botanical, biological, meteorological and anthropological material. Total of 1,508pp. 5⅜ × 8½. 21268-8, 21269-6, 21270-X Pa. Three-vol. set $26.85

LANGUAGE, TRUTH AND LOGIC, Alfred J. Ayer. Famous, clear introduction to Vienna, Cambridge schools of Logical Positivism. Role of philosophy, elimination of metaphysics, nature of analysis, etc. 160pp. 5⅜ × 8½. (Available in U.S. and Canada only) 20010-8 Pa. $2.95

MATHEMATICS FOR THE NONMATHEMATICIAN, Morris Kline. Detailed, college-level treatment of mathematics in cultural and historical context, with numerous exercises. For liberal arts students. Preface. Recommended Reading Lists. Tables. Index. Numerous black-and-white figures. xvi + 641pp. 5⅜ × 8½. 24823-2 Pa. $11.95

28 SCIENCE FICTION STORIES, H. G. Wells. Novels, *Star Begotten* and *Men Like Gods,* plus 26 short stories: "Empire of the Ants," "A Story of the Stone Age," "The Stolen Bacillus," "In the Abyss," etc. 915pp. 5⅜ × 8½. (Available in U.S. only) 20265-8 Cloth. $10.95

HANDBOOK OF PICTORIAL SYMBOLS, Rudolph Modley. 3,250 signs and symbols, many systems in full; official or heavy commercial use. Arranged by subject. Most in Pictorial Archive series. 143pp. 8⅛ × 11. 23357-X Pa. $6.95

INCIDENTS OF TRAVEL IN YUCATAN, John L. Stephens. Classic (1843) exploration of jungles of Yucatan, looking for evidences of Maya civilization. Travel adventures, Mexican and Indian culture, etc. Total of 669pp. 5⅜ × 8½. 20926-1, 20927-X Pa., Two-vol. set $9.90

DEGAS: An Intimate Portrait, Ambroise Vollard. Charming, anecdotal memoir by famous art dealer of one of the greatest 19th-century French painters. 14 black-and-white illustrations. Introduction by Harold L. Van Doren. 96pp. 5⅜ × 8½.
25131-4 Pa. $3.95

PERSONAL NARRATIVE OF A PILGRIMAGE TO ALMANDINAH AND MECCAH, Richard Burton. Great travel classic by remarkably colorful personality. Burton, disguised as a Moroccan, visited sacred shrines of Islam, narrowly escaping death. 47 illustrations. 959pp. 5⅜ × 8½.   21217-3, 21218-1 Pa., Two-vol. set $19.90

PHRASE AND WORD ORIGINS, A. H. Holt. Entertaining, reliable, modern study of more than 1,200 colorful words, phrases, origins and histories. Much unexpected information. 254pp. 5⅜ × 8½.   20758-7 Pa. $5.95

THE RED THUMB MARK, R. Austin Freeman. In this first Dr. Thorndyke case, the great scientific detective draws fascinating conclusions from the nature of a single fingerprint. Exciting story, authentic science. 320pp. 5⅜ × 8½. (Available in U.S. only)   25210-8 Pa. $5.95

AN EGYPTIAN HIEROGLYPHIC DICTIONARY, E. A. Wallis Budge. Monumental work containing about 25,000 words or terms that occur in texts ranging from 3000 B.C. to 600 A.D. Each entry consists of a transliteration of the word, the word in hieroglyphs, and the meaning in English. 1,314pp. 6⅜ × 10.
23615-3, 23616-1 Pa., Two-vol. set $31.90

THE COMPLEAT STRATEGYST: Being a Primer on the Theory of Games of Strategy, J. D. Williams. Highly entertaining classic describes, with many illustrated examples, how to select best strategies in conflict situations. Prefaces. Appendices. xvi + 268pp. 5⅜ × 8½.   25101-2 Pa. $5.95

THE ROAD TO OZ, L. Frank Baum. Dorothy meets the Shaggy Man, little Button-Bright and the Rainbow's beautiful daughter in this delightful trip to the magical Land of Oz. 272pp. 5⅜ × 8.   25208-6 Pa. $4.95

POINT AND LINE TO PLANE, Wassily Kandinsky. Seminal exposition of role of point, line, other elements in non-objective painting. Essential to understanding 20th-century art. 127 illustrations. 192pp. 6½ × 9¼.   23808-3 Pa. $4.95

LADY ANNA, Anthony Trollope. Moving chronicle of Countess Lovel's bitter struggle to win for herself and daughter Anna their rightful rank and fortune—perhaps at cost of sanity itself. 384pp. 5⅜ × 8½.   24669-8 Pa. $8.95

EGYPTIAN MAGIC, E. A. Wallis Budge. Sums up all that is known about magic in Ancient Egypt: the role of magic in controlling the gods, powerful amulets that warded off evil spirits, scarabs of immortality, use of wax images, formulas and spells, the secret name, much more. 253pp. 5⅜ × 8½.   22681-6 Pa. $4.50

THE DANCE OF SIVA, Ananda Coomaraswamy. Preeminent authority unfolds the vast metaphysic of India: the revelation of her art, conception of the universe, social organization, etc. 27 reproductions of art masterpieces. 192pp. 5⅜ × 8½.
24817-8 Pa. $5.95

CHRISTMAS CUSTOMS AND TRADITIONS, Clement A. Miles. Origin, evolution, significance of religious, secular practices. Caroling, gifts, yule logs, much more. Full, scholarly yet fascinating; non-sectarian. 400pp. 5⅜ × 8½.
23354-5 Pa. $6.50

THE HUMAN FIGURE IN MOTION, Eadweard Muybridge. More than 4,500 stopped-action photos, in action series, showing undraped men, women, children jumping, lying down, throwing, sitting, wrestling, carrying, etc. 390pp. 7⅞ × 10⅝.
20204-6 Cloth. $21.95

THE MAN WHO WAS THURSDAY, Gilbert Keith Chesterton. Witty, fast-paced novel about a club of anarchists in turn-of-the-century London. Brilliant social, religious, philosophical speculations. 128pp. 5⅜ × 8½. 25121-7 Pa. $3.95

A CEZANNE SKETCHBOOK: Figures, Portraits, Landscapes and Still Lifes, Paul Cezanne. Great artist experiments with tonal effects, light, mass, other qualities in over 100 drawings. A revealing view of developing master painter, precursor of Cubism. 102 black-and-white illustrations. 144pp. 8¾ × 6⅜. 24790-2 Pa. $5.95

AN ENCYCLOPEDIA OF BATTLES: Accounts of Over 1,560 Battles from 1479 B.C. to the Present, David Eggenberger. Presents essential details of every major battle in recorded history, from the first battle of Megiddo in 1479 B.C. to Grenada in 1984. List of Battle Maps. New Appendix covering the years 1967–1984. Index. 99 illustrations. 544pp. 6½ × 9¼. 24913-1 Pa. $14.95

AN ETYMOLOGICAL DICTIONARY OF MODERN ENGLISH, Ernest Weekley. Richest, fullest work, by foremost British lexicographer. Detailed word histories. Inexhaustible. Total of 856pp. 6½ × 9¼.
21873-2, 21874-0 Pa., Two-vol. set $17.00

WEBSTER'S AMERICAN MILITARY BIOGRAPHIES, edited by Robert McHenry. Over 1,000 figures who shaped 3 centuries of American military history. Detailed biographies of Nathan Hale, Douglas MacArthur, Mary Hallaren, others. Chronologies of engagements, more. Introduction. Addenda. 1,033 entries in alphabetical order. xi + 548pp. 6½ × 9¼. (Available in U.S. only)
24758-9 Pa. $11.95

LIFE IN ANCIENT EGYPT, Adolf Erman. Detailed older account, with much not in more recent books: domestic life, religion, magic, medicine, commerce, and whatever else needed for complete picture. Many illustrations. 597pp. 5⅜ × 8½.
22632-8 Pa. $8.95

HISTORIC COSTUME IN PICTURES, Braun & Schneider. Over 1,450 costumed figures shown, covering a wide variety of peoples: kings, emperors, nobles, priests, servants, soldiers, scholars, townsfolk, peasants, merchants, courtiers, cavaliers, and more. 256pp. 8⅜ × 11¼. 23150-X Pa. $8.95

THE NOTEBOOKS OF LEONARDO DA VINCI, edited by J. P. Richter. Extracts from manuscripts reveal great genius; on painting, sculpture, anatomy, sciences, geography, etc. Both Italian and English. 186 ms. pages reproduced, plus 500 additional drawings, including studies for *Last Supper, Sforza* monument, etc. 860pp. 7⅞ × 10¾. (Available in U.S. only) 22572-0, 22573-9 Pa., Two-vol. set $29.90

THE ART NOUVEAU STYLE BOOK OF ALPHONSE MUCHA: All 72 Plates from "Documents Decoratifs" in Original Color, Alphonse Mucha. Rare copyright-free design portfolio by high priest of Art Nouveau. Jewelry, wallpaper, stained glass, furniture, figure studies, plant and animal motifs, etc. Only complete one-volume edition. 80pp. 9⅜ × 12¼. 24044-4 Pa. $8.95

ANIMALS: 1,419 COPYRIGHT-FREE ILLUSTRATIONS OF MAMMALS, BIRDS, FISH, INSECTS, ETC., edited by Jim Harter. Clear wood engravings present, in extremely lifelike poses, over 1,000 species of animals. One of the most extensive pictorial sourcebooks of its kind. Captions. Index. 284pp. 9 × 12. 23766-4 Pa. $9.95

OBELISTS FLY HIGH, C. Daly King. Masterpiece of American detective fiction, long out of print, involves murder on a 1935 transcontinental flight—"a very thrilling story"—NY Times. Unabridged and unaltered republication of the edition published by William Collins Sons & Co. Ltd., London, 1935. 288pp. 5⅜ × 8½. (Available in U.S. only) 25036-9 Pa. $4.95

VICTORIAN AND EDWARDIAN FASHION: A Photographic Survey, Alison Gernsheim. First fashion history completely illustrated by contemporary photographs. Full text plus 235 photos, 1840–1914, in which many celebrities appear. 240pp. 6½ × 9¼. 24205-6 Pa. $6.95

THE ART OF THE FRENCH ILLUSTRATED BOOK, 1700–1914, Gordon N. Ray. Over 630 superb book illustrations by Fragonard, Delacroix, Daumier, Doré, Grandville, Manet, Mucha, Steinlen, Toulouse-Lautrec and many others. Preface. Introduction. 633 halftones. Indices of artists, authors & titles, binders and provenances. Appendices. Bibliography. 608pp. 8⅜ × 11¼. 25086-5 Pa. $24.95

THE WONDERFUL WIZARD OF OZ, L. Frank Baum. Facsimile in full color of America's finest children's classic. 143 illustrations by W. W. Denslow. 267pp. 5⅜ × 8½. 20691-2 Pa. $5.95

FRONTIERS OF MODERN PHYSICS: New Perspectives on Cosmology, Relativity, Black Holes and Extraterrestrial Intelligence, Tony Rothman, et al. For the intelligent layman. Subjects include: cosmological models of the universe; black holes; the neutrino; the search for extraterrestrial intelligence. Introduction. 46 black-and-white illustrations. 192pp. 5⅜ × 8½. 24587-X Pa. $6.95

THE FRIENDLY STARS, Martha Evans Martin & Donald Howard Menzel. Classic text marshalls the stars together in an engaging, non-technical survey, presenting them as sources of beauty in night sky. 23 illustrations. Foreword. 2 star charts. Index. 147pp. 5⅜ × 8½. 21099-5 Pa. $3.50

FADS AND FALLACIES IN THE NAME OF SCIENCE, Martin Gardner. Fair, witty appraisal of cranks, quacks, and quackeries of science and pseudoscience: hollow earth, Velikovsky, orgone energy, Dianetics, flying saucers, Bridey Murphy, food and medical fads, etc. Revised, expanded In the Name of Science. "A very able and even-tempered presentation."—The New Yorker. 363pp. 5⅜ × 8. 20394-8 Pa. $6.50

ANCIENT EGYPT: ITS CULTURE AND HISTORY, J. E Manchip White. From pre-dynastics through Ptolemies: society, history, political structure, religion, daily life, literature, cultural heritage. 48 plates. 217pp. 5⅜ × 8½. 22548-8 Pa. $5.95

SIR HARRY HOTSPUR OF HUMBLETHWAITE, Anthony Trollope. Incisive, unconventional psychological study of a conflict between a wealthy baronet, his idealistic daughter, and their scapegrace cousin. The 1870 novel in its first inexpensive edition in years. 250pp. 5⅜ × 8½. 24953-0 Pa. $5.95

LASERS AND HOLOGRAPHY, Winston E. Kock. Sound introduction to burgeoning field, expanded (1981) for second edition. Wave patterns, coherence, lasers, diffraction, zone plates, properties of holograms, recent advances. 84 illustrations. 160pp. 5⅜ × 8¼. (Except in United Kingdom) 24041-X Pa. $3.50

INTRODUCTION TO ARTIFICIAL INTELLIGENCE: SECOND, ENLARGED EDITION, Philip C. Jackson, Jr. Comprehensive survey of artificial intelligence—the study of how machines (computers) can be made to act intelligently. Includes introductory and advanced material. Extensive notes updating the main text. 132 black-and-white illustrations. 512pp. 5⅜ × 8½. 24864-X Pa. $8.95

HISTORY OF INDIAN AND INDONESIAN ART, Ananda K. Coomaraswamy. Over 400 illustrations illuminate classic study of Indian art from earliest Harappa finds to early 20th century. Provides philosophical, religious and social insights. 304pp. 6⅜ × 9⅜. 25005-9 Pa. $8.95

THE GOLEM, Gustav Meyrink. Most famous supernatural novel in modern European literature, set in Ghetto of Old Prague around 1890. Compelling story of mystical experiences, strange transformations, profound terror. 13 black-and-white illustrations. 224pp. 5⅜ × 8½. (Available in U.S. only) 25025-3 Pa. $6.95

ARMADALE, Wilkie Collins. Third great mystery novel by the author of *The Woman in White* and *The Moonstone*. Original magazine version with 40 illustrations. 597pp. 5⅜ × 8½. 23429-0 Pa. $9.95

PICTORIAL ENCYCLOPEDIA OF HISTORIC ARCHITECTURAL PLANS, DETAILS AND ELEMENTS: With 1,880 Line Drawings of Arches, Domes, Doorways, Facades, Gables, Windows, etc., John Theodore Haneman. Sourcebook of inspiration for architects, designers, others. Bibliography. Captions. 141pp. 9 × 12. 24605-1 Pa. $6.95

BENCHLEY LOST AND FOUND, Robert Benchley. Finest humor from early 30's, about pet peeves, child psychologists, post office and others. Mostly unavailable elsewhere. 73 illustrations by Peter Arno and others. 183pp. 5⅜ × 8½. 22410-4 Pa. $3.95

ERTÉ GRAPHICS, Erté. Collection of striking color graphics: *Seasons, Alphabet, Numerals, Aces* and *Precious Stones*. 50 plates, including 4 on covers. 48pp. 9⅜ × 12¼. 23580-7 Pa. $6.95

THE JOURNAL OF HENRY D. THOREAU, edited by Bradford Torrey, F. H. Allen. Complete reprinting of 14 volumes, 1837–61, over two million words; the sourcebooks for *Walden*, etc. Definitive. All original sketches, plus 75 photographs. 1,804pp. 8½ × 12¼. 20312-3, 20313-1 Cloth., Two-vol. set $80.00

CASTLES: THEIR CONSTRUCTION AND HISTORY, Sidney Toy. Traces castle development from ancient roots. Nearly 200 photographs and drawings illustrate moats, keeps, baileys, many other features. Caernarvon, Dover Castles, Hadrian's Wall, Tower of London, dozens more. 256pp. 5⅜ × 8¼. 24898-4 Pa. $5.95

CATALOG OF DOVER BOOKS

AMERICAN CLIPPER SHIPS: 1833–1858, Octavius T. Howe & Frederick C. Matthews. Fully-illustrated, encyclopedic review of 352 clipper ships from the period of America's greatest maritime supremacy. Introduction. 109 halftones. 5 black-and-white line illustrations. Index. Total of 928pp. 5⅜ × 8½.
25115-2, 25116-0 Pa., Two-vol. set $17.90

TOWARDS A NEW ARCHITECTURE, Le Corbusier. Pioneering manifesto by great architect, near legendary founder of "International School." Technical and aesthetic theories, views on industry, economics, relation of form to function, "mass-production spirit," much more. Profusely illustrated. Unabridged translation of 13th French edition. Introduction by Frederick Etchells. 320pp. 6⅛ × 9¼.
(Available in U.S. only) 25023-7 Pa. $8.95

THE BOOK OF KELLS, edited by Blanche Cirker. Inexpensive collection of 32 full-color, full-page plates from the greatest illuminated manuscript of the Middle Ages, painstakingly reproduced from rare facsimile edition. Publisher's Note. Captions. 32pp. 9⅜ × 12¼. 24345-1 Pa. $4.95

BEST SCIENCE FICTION STORIES OF H. G. WELLS, H. G. Wells. Full novel *The Invisible Man,* plus 17 short stories: "The Crystal Egg," "Aepyornis Island," "The Strange Orchid," etc. 303pp. 5⅜ × 8½. (Available in U.S. only)
21531-8 Pa. $6.95

AMERICAN SAILING SHIPS: Their Plans and History, Charles G. Davis. Photos, construction details of schooners, frigates, clippers, other sailcraft of 18th to early 20th centuries—plus entertaining discourse on design, rigging, nautical lore, much more. 137 black-and-white illustrations. 240pp. 6⅛ × 9¼.
24658-2 Pa. $6.95

ENTERTAINING MATHEMATICAL PUZZLES, Martin Gardner. Selection of author's favorite conundrums involving arithmetic, money, speed, etc., with lively commentary. Complete solutions. 112pp. 5⅜ × 8½. 25211-6 Pa. $2.95

THE WILL TO BELIEVE, HUMAN IMMORTALITY, William James. Two books bound together. Effect of irrational on logical, and arguments for human immortality. 402pp. 5⅜ × 8½. 20291-7 Pa. $7.50

THE HAUNTED MONASTERY and THE CHINESE MAZE MURDERS, Robert Van Gulik. 2 full novels by Van Gulik continue adventures of Judge Dee and his companions. An evil Taoist monastery, seemingly supernatural events; overgrown topiary maze that hides strange crimes. Set in 7th-century China. 27 illustrations. 328pp. 5⅜ × 8½. 23502-5 Pa. $5.95

CELEBRATED CASES OF JUDGE DEE (DEE GOONG AN), translated by Robert Van Gulik. Authentic 18th-century Chinese detective novel; Dee and associates solve three interlocked cases. Led to Van Gulik's own stories with same characters. Extensive introduction. 9 illustrations. 237pp. 5⅜ × 8½.
23337-5 Pa. $4.95

Prices subject to change without notice.

Available at your book dealer or write for free catalog to Dept. GI, Dover Publications, Inc., 31 East 2nd St., Mineola, N.Y. 11501. Dover publishes more than 175 books each year on science, elementary and advanced mathematics, biology, music, art, literary history, social sciences and other areas.